More than Just Jobs: Workforce Development in a Skills-Based Economy

Edited by
Sylvain Giguère

OECD

ORGANISATION FOR ECONOMIC CO-OPERATION AND DEVELOPMENT

The OECD is a unique forum where the governments of 30 democracies work together to address the economic, social and environmental challenges of globalisation. The OECD is also at the forefront of efforts to understand and to help governments respond to new developments and concerns, such as corporate governance, the information economy and the challenges of an ageing population. The Organisation provides a setting where governments can compare policy experiences, seek answers to common problems, identify good practice and work to co-ordinate domestic and international policies.

The OECD member countries are: Australia, Austria, Belgium, Canada, the Czech Republic, Denmark, Finland, France, Germany, Greece, Hungary, Iceland, Ireland, Italy, Japan, Korea, Luxembourg, Mexico, the Netherlands, New Zealand, Norway, Poland, Portugal, the Slovak Republic, Spain, Sweden, Switzerland, Turkey, the United Kingdom and the United States. The Commission of the European Communities takes part in the work of the OECD.

OECD Publishing disseminates widely the results of the Organisation's statistics gathering and research on economic, social and environmental issues, as well as the conventions, guidelines and standards agreed by its members.

This work is published on the responsibility of the Secretary-General of the OECD. The opinions expressed and arguments employed herein do not necessarily reflect the official views of the Organisation or of the governments of its member countries.

Corrigenda to OECD publications may be found on line at: *www.oecd.org/publishing/corrigenda*.

© OECD 2008

Foreword

*F*or ten years now, the OECD has been exploring the relationship between employment, skills and local governance in search of orientations and guidelines for policy makers trying to tackle critical challenges faced by our societies in a globalised economy. The LEED Directing Committee, which supervises this work, has disseminated the considerable expertise gained in this area in a series of influential reports on issues ranging from partnerships and decentralisation to skills upgrading and the integration of immigrants. Each publication has increased our understanding of how we can fill policy gaps and re-orient policies so that they are in line with how our economy works.

More than Just Jobs proposes a framework for policy and practice that builds on the lessons learnt from this work programme so far. It outlines a new vision for labour market policy that has a broader role in shaping our economies. It demonstrates that there is a great deal that government can do in relation to workforce development, in co-operation with business and civil society, that would enhance living standards even as our economies are faced with increasing competition from low-wage economies. The work demonstrates that policymakers and practitioners should not be afraid to make bold moves and assume greater responsibilities. In a network society, few important tasks can be achieved alone by one single actor. In the area of employment and skills, public sector actors should be at the core of simulating the collaborative work which is required at the local level in order to generate greater prosperity.

For the most part, the material contained in this report originates from an ongoing project on the local management of employment and training in East Asia. The project supports a dialogue on the governance of employment and skills with East Asian economies that have expressed a growing interest in decentralisation, partnerships and local employment and skills strategies. Seminars have already been held in Beijing (2007), Seoul (2005, 2008), Taipei (2007) and Tokyo (2005) as part of this project supported by the Ministry of Health, Labor and Welfare (MHLW) of Japan, the Ministry of Labor (MOL) of Korea, the Ministry of Labor and Social Security (MOLSS) of the People's Republic of China, the Council of Labor Affairs (CLA) of Chinese Taipei, the Japan Institute for Labor Policy and Training (JILPT), the Korea Labor Institute (KLI) and the International Labour Organization (ILO).

I am convinced that this publication will serve well the new agenda for labour market policy and training that is ahead of us, and that it will have considerable influence on policy and practice.

Sergio Arzeni
Head, LEED Programme
Director, Centre for Entrepreneurship,
SMEs and Local Development

Acknowledgments. Sylvain Giguère, Deputy Head of Local Economic and Employment Development (LEED) at the OECD, prepared and edited this publication. Lending invaluable assistance to the project were Francesca Froy, who advised on content; Kay Olbison, who helped prepare the manuscript and, together with Debbie Binks and Sheelagh Delf, provided administrative support to the projects feeding the analysis contained herein; Lucy Clarke, who co-ordinated the publication process; and Randy Holden, who provided assistance in editing the manuscript.

Many thanks go to the contributors: Petra Bouché, Randall Eberts, Xavier Greffe, Yoshio Higuchi, Hyo-Soo Lee, Cristina Martinez-Fernandez, Hugh Mosley, Dave Simmonds and Andy Westwood.

Table of Contents

MORE THAN JUST JOBS: WORKFORCE DEVELOPMENT IN A SKILLS-BASED ECONOMY – ISBN 978-92-64-04327-5 – © OECD 2008

ISBN 978-92-64-04327-5
More than Just Jobs:
Workforce Development in a Skills-Based Economy
© OECD 2008

Executive Summary

In a globalised economy, where both capital and labour are highly mobile and technology evolves rapidly, workforce development institutions have a key role to play in improving prosperity and living standards. An analysis of local drivers of growth shows that human resources are a fundamental source of economic development in a knowledge-based economy. Policy makers within the field of labour market policy and training have a major contribution to make, not only in providing the pool of skills that the economy needs locally, but also in fostering innovation, entrepreneurship and social cohesion. Labour market institutions may tackle a wide range of issues locally, from the attraction and retention of talent to solving skill deficiencies, integrating immigrants, incorporating the disadvantaged into training and employment, improving the quality of the workplace, and enhancing the competitiveness of local firms. They have a unique capacity to contribute in view of the scale of their programmes and services, and their presence throughout the national economy and at a number of layers within the administration.

However, the target of labour market policy has been relatively narrowly defined in the past, with most public employment service institutions limiting themselves to matching jobseekers to vacancies and providing basic training to support immediate employability; training organisations have not always been attentive to business demands and strategic orientations defined locally. In order to maximise the potential contribution of workforce development institutions to lifting prosperity, a new broader goal for workforce development must now be set: *The comprehensive management of human resources, so as to meet better the demands of a global economy at both the national and local levels, through improving economic competitiveness and social cohesion.*

In practice, attempts to achieve this goal inevitably encounter a number of obstacles. One is the difficulty of speeding up changes to local education and training systems so that they can deliver skills currently in demand. Another is tackling the fragmentation in local decision making when it comes to human resources; policies on immigration, integration and training are often developed by different people in different institutions. The situation is made worse by a separation of economic development from labour market policies, which are often delivered in "silos". A lack of willingness to look at longer-term issues is another impediment to harmonising local and national concerns in the implementation of labour market policy and training.

Workforce development institutions cannot work alone to achieve their objectives. In order to foster human resources development in a manner consistent with the workings of today's economy, it is important to improve the local *governance* of workforce development. In particular, it will be critical to generate a higher degree of policy co-ordination, better adaptation of policy to local conditions and a greater level of participation of business and civil society in the shaping of measures.

The review of the OECD experience and the contextual evidence from seven countries contained in this volume point to the need to achieve better co-ordination and a more effective balance between the efforts of policy makers at the national and local levels. While there is a need for greater differentiation and experimentation at the local level, it will also be important to maintain the efficiency and accountability of the overall policy framework. The lessons emerging from this cross-country comparative analysis can be summarised by the following guidelines:

1. *Inject flexibility into management.* It should be possible for the local level to decide on and provide strategic orientations in the implementation of public programmes and services, in addition to pursuing predetermined objectives. In a management-by-objectives framework, this means that policy targets set by central government would need to be negotiated with the local level in light of current local strategic priorities.

2. *Establish an overarching management framework that embeds local flexibility.* Workforce development policy should be managed in a way that supports greater local differentiation while still paying attention to aggregate impacts at the national level. The process of negotiation with the local level on targets should be embedded in a framework that ensures that aggregate national policy goals continue to be met.

3. *Build strategic capacity.* Enhancing local capacities becomes particularly important in this context, as strategies for human resources development must be integrated and matched to the economic reality on the ground. The staff of labour market institutions should have a strong knowledge of local business practices, local economic conditions, industry developments, and appropriate methods to identify skill gaps and deficiencies in local economic sectors. They should also develop the analytical skills necessary to use this knowledge as a basis for developing broad strategic orientations locally.

4. *Build up local data and intelligence.* Building an understanding of economic and labour market conditions demands, as a prerequisite, refined databases gathered and managed locally and expertise in a wide variety of fields. The

capacity to gather data locally and organise them in a way that enables strategic planning exercises is critical. The national level can support this process by ensuring that data are disaggregated to the local level and by making available analytical tools that can be adapted to local circumstances.

5. *Improve governance mechanisms.* Labour market institutions should collaborate effectively with business, trade unions, civil society, higher education institutions, research centres, economic development agencies and local authorities. There is no governance mechanism that fits all institutional frameworks, but partnerships have a certain value in bringing different stakeholders together to develop appropriate and realistic strategies.

6. *Improve administrative processes.* Aligning policies through institutional reform such as decentralisation is a difficult challenge. In large countries with complex distributions of power, a perfect match may always seem just beyond reach. A wide-scale review of how administrations function, co-operate and manage policies is needed to support better collaboration between different administrative layers and between different policy institutions. This is particularly important given that the new, broader goals for human resources development cut across a number of different policy areas.

PART I

Introduction and Findings

ISBN 978-92-64-04327-5
More than Just Jobs:
Workforce Development in a Skills-Based Economy
© OECD 2008

PART I

Chapter 1

A Broader Agenda for Workforce Development

by

Sylvain Giguère

There is currently a debate as to whether labour market policy would serve its economic and social goals better by concentrating on its core business or by widening its perspective. Should the goal of employment and training policy be purely the efficient functioning of the labour market, or should it serve wider economic and social purposes? In a globalised economy, labour market policy has a unique contribution to make in tackling a wide range of issues, from attracting and retaining talent to enhancing the competitiveness of local firms. Labour market institutions can have a significant impact in these areas given their unique capacity as a source of expertise, programmes and services and their presence throughout the national economy and at a number of layers within the administration. However to achieve this, a new broader goal for workforce development has to be set: *The comprehensive management of human resources, so as to meet better the demands of a global economy through improving economic competitiveness and social cohesion.*

Introduction

There is currently a debate as to whether labour market policy would better serve its economic and social goals by concentrating on its core business or by broadening its perspective. Should employment and training policy work purely towards the effective functioning of the labour market, or should it serve wider economic and social purposes?

Traditionally, the two main goals of labour market policy have been to ensure that labour markets function efficiently and to develop the employability of the most excluded. Labour market adjustment is facilitated through matching jobseekers with vacancies, promoting mobility, training the unemployed, and subsidising employment for the most disadvantaged. Policies pursuing that agenda have become important instruments in promoting full employment and fighting against exclusion, as well as helping to keep inflationary pressures low.

However, an increasing number of analysts, practitioners and policy makers believe that the responsibility of labour market institutions goes beyond this. Policy makers in the United States have so far been the most proactive advocates of a broader view of workforce development; their demands have become better articulated as the impacts of globalisation are more clearly perceived. This drive for change has now spread to Europe at a time when countries are modernising their labour market models. In Asia, discussion is under way on how to adjust labour market institutions to emerging challenges. In Korea, the need to establish a "new paradigm" for labour market policy and training has been evoked.

Today labour market institutions need to become major economic players, not just at national level but also at local level, through interacting with economic development to build competitive and sustainable communities. In a globalised economy, where both capital and labour are highly mobile and technology advances at an extremely rapid pace, human resources have an increasing impact on the capacity of business to react to changes in the economic environment and respond to new opportunities. Likewise, for individuals, the acquisition of skills is increasingly vital in maintaining living standards in a competitive labour market where the demand for qualifications changes quickly. Workforce development is no longer about developing short-term employability, but about helping people develop longer-term career pathways that feed local prosperity.

Implications of capital mobility

Capital is mobile, not only throughout the globe but also among regions in the same country. It settles where it finds a combination of conditions that suit the characteristics of production. Unit production cost is only one of these conditions. A further crucial element is the quality of labour to support the production of local goods and services. One of the responsibilities of labour market policy and training is therefore to help generate skills that are adapted to the local economy, and to be responsive to investment and economic development decisions that may have an impact on future skill needs. The ability to fuel local growth by cultivating relevant skills is the best guarantee that the business sector will thrive in a given region and, as a result, throughout the whole country. The local adaptation of policies is therefore of paramount importance – uniform policies throughout the territory do not necessarily yield this sort of outcome, and thus have less value.

The globalisation process has a number of implications for workers. One is that their skills can become obsolete rapidly. A high degree of capital mobility is accompanied by considerable shifts in employment at the local level, from one sector to another and from one skill type to another. Fewer and fewer sectors are immune to this process, as even service sector businesses become subject to delocalisation. It thus becomes all the more important that skills be recycled easily. While internal mobility of labour within the same country (and across borders) can help to mop up some of the effects of delocalisation, those responsible for skills development have an important role to play in matching local human resources with local business demand. This is particularly important for less-qualified workers, who are less prone to move to another region to pursue job opportunities and most likely to be affected by the shift of economic activities to low-wage countries.

Wages in many advanced countries have stagnated in recent years, while working conditions and employment benefits have diminished in several sectors. This is partly due to the weakened position of workers in collective bargaining processes, which is in turn a reflection of the increasing vulnerability of production to competition with emerging economies. To ensure that all segments of the labour force reap the benefits of globalisation and continue to increase their living standards, labour market policy and training institutions have a responsibility to help individuals fulfil their labour market potential, through ensuring that they achieve the best qualifications possible and acquire better-paid jobs in the area where they live. This means enabling people to continue to update their skills over their working life and to acquire new ones that are in line with the current and future local needs. It also means ensuring that education curricula are themselves better adapted to their local context, to minimise the risk that people end up with skills that are no longer in demand.

Mobility of labour: Skills mismatch

Labour market conditions are further complicated by labour's increasing mobility. As more regions and sectors lack the labour and skills they need to prosper, barriers to movement are decreasing, making it possible for people to move to another country and fill these gaps. Immigration has become an increasingly important issue for policy makers, particularly as the integration of immigrants into the labour market is not as successful now as it has been in the past (OECD, 2006). Local stakeholders in some countries also express concerns that immigration is being exploited as a "quick fix" to solve immediate skills gaps, without enough attention paid to the educational and training reforms necessary to enable the wider population to meet these needs. Local businesses frequently find it less costly to attract foreign workers from abroad than to invest in the training and support required to enable local people to fill the jobs available. This difference in cost is constituted by the sum of barriers faced by disadvantaged individuals within the domestic labour market, such as the long-term unemployed, the elderly, youth and ethnic minorities.

The education system is also slow to adapt to new demands from the business sector and changing job requirements. Universities generate qualifications in fields where employment is decreasing; not enough resources are devoted to training in study areas that would generate better-paid jobs (and require shorter studies). This partly explains why so many graduates in advanced economies are underemployed and live in precarious situations. This issue has led some to call for "less choice, more guidance" in education and training (Chapple, 2006).

While some immigrants are attracted from overseas to perform highly skilled work, others come to take up low-skilled jobs that the local labour force is not interested in carrying out. In part this situation reflects the reluctance of local jobseekers to take up certain jobs, particularly where living costs mean that low-paid employment is no longer advantageous compared with remaining on social assistance or working in the informal economy (or both). Helping disadvantaged local workers improve their skills level and find jobs is not sufficient when the economic incentives to undertake such jobs are limited. In many cases migrants step in to fill these gaps, making sacrifices in their living conditions in the first few years after arrival in a country. However, many migrants are overqualified for the jobs they are obliged to take, and such positions provide little scope for progress in employment. The higher-level skills that migrants bring to local economies are often not harnessed by employers due to various obstacles (Froy and Giguère, 2006). Some of these obstacles are relatively complex, such as the failure of local institutions and businesses to recognise qualifications gained overseas. That situation can only be overcome by greater collaboration between labour market institutions, professional unions and higher education institutions. In the meantime, as migrants take on jobs for which they are overqualified, their skills rapidly become obsolete. Immigration is certainly not an optimal solution to labour shortages when it creates such skills mismatch and skills obsolescence.

In response, labour market policy can play a useful role in improving the quality and attractiveness of local jobs. Modifying the human resources policies of enterprises is certainly a slow process, but a necessary one if commitment to training and upskilling is to be increased (Osterman, 2005). Developing career ladders to ensure progress in employment and simultaneously enhancing the flexibility of workers through skills diversification are two key avenues to explore; such actions require the establishment of effective partnerships with local employers. Responding adequately to labour shortages may also have implications for production processes. As shortages become generalised, it is not sustainable for employers to continue to address them through perpetual recruitment. The high staff turnover associated with low-quality, low-paid employment can be costly, and ultimately such shortages may be more effectively addressed by improvements in technology that would translate into higher productivity. While this may generate fewer jobs, those that remain will provide higher wages and better working conditions. In a number of OECD regions trapped in a "low-skilled equilibrium", policy makers are starting to work with higher education institutions and research centres to achieve such an aim, raising the game of local employers, improving production processes and enhancing productivity, while at the same time enhancing the competitiveness of local industry and the attractiveness of the local economy.

A new agenda for employment and training policy

In light of these issues, it seems increasingly inappropriate to view labour market policy as having just a narrow role to play in the placing, counselling and training of the unemployed, in supporting labour market reintegration, and in filling vacancies. While such actions are helpful in themselves, they do not necessarily ensure that overriding economic and labour market objectives will be achieved. As the above analysis has shown, in a globalised economy, labour market policy has a unique contribution to make in tackling a wide range of issues, from attracting and retaining talent to solving skill deficiencies, integrating immigrants, incorporating the disadvantaged not only into jobs but also into the education and training system, improving the quality of the workplace, and enhancing the competitiveness of local firms.

Labour market institutions can have a significant impact in these areas given their unique ability to contribute expertise, programmes and services throughout the national economy and at a number of layers within the administration. Thus labour market policy has the capacity to become a major instrument in advanced economies for delivering prosperity and increasing living standards. That delivery, however, calls for a new, broader goal for workforce development: *The comprehensive management of human resources, so as to meet better the demands of a global economy at both the national and local levels, through improving economic competitiveness and social cohesion.*

Pursuing such a goal has a number of implications. It first requires that the staff of labour market institutions have a strong knowledge of business practices, economic conditions and industry developments, in addition to appropriate methods for identifying skills gaps and deficiencies in the sectors concerned. Second, institutions must collaborate with business, trade unions, civil society, higher education institutions, research centres, economic development agencies and local authorities. Last but not least, local staff must be able to make decisions on the orientation and implementation of public programmes and services locally. Collaboration between all administrative layers and across a number of different policy institutions is required, as the new goal for human resources development cuts across different policy areas. Updating the goal of labour market policy will therefore involve a wide-scale review of how administrations function, co-operate and manage policies.

A governance challenge

The challenge facing workforce development institutions is clearly a difficult one. As Chapple (2005) aptly put it, "Workforce development is not a complicated policy problem. An established literature explains what works and what does not (...). Workforce development only becomes complex when linked to economic development goals, particularly regional economic growth and competitiveness".

Local and regional stakeholders already look at labour market policy and training through the prism of their wider economic development strategies, as human resources is at the core of the local drivers of growth (see Box 1.1). Accordingly, they are often prepared to play a greater role in the shaping of policy. However, the management of human resources development is often hampered by a number of deficiencies and governance problems.

One obstacle is the *rigidity of training*. Skill needs change constantly, and at a pace that places heavy demands on local vocational training institutions. Even firms settled in a locality can leave rapidly if they do not find the pool of skilled labour they need. Municipalities, regional governments and economic development agencies often mediate between enterprises and the training institutions involved. But curricula are not easy to change, and programmes take time to establish. Institutions also have a duty to take into account qualification demands from the local student population. It is not easy, therefore, to adapt vocational training to business needs.

Box 1.1. **Human resources and the local drivers of growth**

Human resources have a direct impact on the capacity of business to react to changes in the economic environment and to respond to new opportunities. To seize possibilities of enhanced economic development, localities and regions must compete to attract, retain and stimulate the creation of businesses, drawing on local assets and resources, thereby driving national prosperity. Labour market policy can make a central contribution to this process, as the local labour pool is now one of a region's most important assets – in terms of ideas, innovations, talents, skills, specialisations, culture, methods and approaches to work.

Human resources have relevance for several drivers of local growth. They directly impact on four drivers in particular: skills, innovation, entrepreneurship and social cohesion.

Skills – The most obvious linkage between human resources and local growth is the quantity and quality of skills in a local economy. To prosper, local businesses need a pool of skilled and diversified labour in their sectors, and rely on the capacity of local education systems to provide appropriately qualified graduates. To achieve this, vocational training institutions must adapt their technical curricula to the changing needs of local industry. However, in order to maximise the skills available in the local labour force, labour market and training institutions need to focus not only on youth but also on low-skilled workers and those who have been made redundant by the downsizing and closure of local enterprises. The shift from low-tech to high-tech industries requires an equivalent capacity to adapt the labour force to changing needs. It is estimated that by 2010 almost half of the net additional jobs created in the European Union will require people with tertiary-level education; just under 40% will require education beyond high school and only 15% basic schooling (Tessaring and Wannan, 2004). In such a context, older members of the population with less schooling face a sharp learning curve if they are to remain employable. In regions where demographic change is reducing the overall pool of potential workers, local policy makers may also need to think about attracting new talent through immigration to the region, from elsewhere in the country or from abroad.

Innovation – Innovation can take various forms, from new product design to new production processes. Normally innovation is itself the result of a process, consisting of three distinct phases: the generation of knowledge; the sharing and distribution of that knowledge among potential users; and the application of new knowledge to product development, whereby it translates into a new business activity or the regeneration of existing activities. These phases are controlled by different factors. The generation of knowledge depends on the research capacities of educational institutions, the R&D activities of

---

Box 1.1. **Human resources and the local drivers of growth** (cont.)

enterprises, and the level of human capital involved. Distribution and application rely on the effectiveness with which education, research, business and training organisations and networks co-function. Thus for localities and regions, fostering innovation means: i) building a knowledge base, i.e. encouraging research activities and attracting enterprises with advanced technology as well as talented researchers and students; and ii) facilitating co-operation and co-ordination among organisations responsible for research production, distribution and exploitation activities. Attracting qualified researchers and students depends on a variety of factors, such as the quality of the region's higher education institutions and regional quality of life. Local government can provide grants, scholarships, tax breaks, facilitated immigration procedures and repatriation schemes as incentives to settle in their region.

Entrepreneurship – The education system can play a significant role in fostering entrepreneurship. Local entrepreneurship programmes within elementary and secondary schools have shown a high capacity to contribute to the development of aptitudes associated with successful entrepreneurs. Higher education institutions also have a role here. Many have developed specialised education methods that include hands-on training, creativity techniques, the exploration of case studies, communication training, interpersonal skills development, team working, teaching by entrepreneurs, role-playing, practice firms and business plan development. In addition, they use a variety of strategies, mechanisms and instruments to promote knowledge transfer. Typical support measures for knowledge transfer to the local SME sector include specialist offices and brokers, science parks and incubators, the creation of new firms from university research activities (academic spin-offs), work-related training and business training (OECD, 2008 forthcoming).

Social cohesion – Social cohesion is a critical aspect of the local quality of life, which is in turn conducive to a good business climate that attracts capital and talent. Social cohesion in part relates to the capacity to integrate disadvantaged individuals and minority groups into the labour market and facilitate their participation in the local development of prosperity. The more a local economy succeeds in bringing the people most remote from the labour market into decent jobs, the more it contributes to the development of a cohesive society. Thus, both labour market policy and the vocational training system must be able to translate local labour demand into opportunities for the more disadvantaged people on the labour market. In addition, skills upgrading of the unemployed and those recently in work is a particularly important element of the vocational training system.

Another difficulty arises from the fact that employment is a relatively *fragmented policy* area, with several organisations involved in decision making. In this context there is often a lack of connection between decisions taken by local actors. The trade-offs between different policy decisions are rarely fully discussed, let alone addressed. For example, employer organisations often recruit their labour force abroad on behalf of their members, and vocational training organisations or employment services may not be aware of their actions. Decisions to attract talent and labour from abroad are not independent from the decision to integrate disadvantaged workers into the training system, or to recycle or upgrade the skills of the low-qualified. Each option has a resource cost relevant to the policy decisions being taken in other areas. When employment services, local government services and vocational training services are not co-ordinated, the wider impact of decisions can go unconsidered and discrepancies can appear between local policies and actions.

This situation is made worse by the complete *separation* frequently observed at the local level *between economic development and human resource development*. The different strategies pursued involve different actors and often contradict one another. Employment and skills are often managed in a labour supply perspective, while economic development is run from the demand point of view. For example, employment services may devote important resources to develop the immediate employability of disadvantaged workers, while more sustainable employment would be available through more specific vocational training.

Finally, in order to foster economic growth, strategies for human resource development need to take the *long view*, and also take on a certain amount of risk. To plan ahead, policy makers need to make an informed guess as to the potential growth areas at the local level that will provide employment opportunities for tomorrow's generation of school- and college-leavers. This approach is not always compatible with concerns associated with annual work plans and electors' mandates, or with the desire to conform as much as possible to the broad goals of mainstream funding programmes.

Many challenges thus lie ahead. Better co-ordination is imperative in a globalised economy, where business needs a pool of skilled labour; where skills and innovation are two sides of the same coin; and where capital follows high-quality human resources. Labour market policy and training need to have a strong demand dimension, in which information and training are geared to meet the needs of local business while balancing the needs of local people for decent jobs. There must be strong co-ordination between labour market policy and economic development activities, as well as efficient links with the local business community and with training organisations. And actions pertinent to skills and employment at the local level need to be organised around consistent strategies that accord priority to areas of local opportunity and that take a sustainable longer-term view.

How can labour market policy and training better meet those requirements? How can labour market institutions reconcile national policy goals with local concerns?

Reforming institutional structures

In answering such questions, OECD countries have some experience to draw upon. Several member countries have undertaken to change the way labour market policy and vocational training policies are managed. These experiences can be grouped in two categories: those relating to policy decentralisation, and those relating to the development of partnerships.

Decentralisation

Labour market policy is often centralised in order to ensure that national policy goals are met. Accordingly, it often does not allow a great deal of leeway for responding to local conditions and supporting local initiatives. Decentralisation is one way to tackle this problem. In the 90s, several countries undertook to decentralise labour market policy to bring it nearer to the level at which strategies for economic development are defined and social demands expressed.

Labour market policy has experimented with two forms of decentralisation: devolution to regional government; and administrative decentralisation within the public employment service (PES) (Giguère, 2003).

Devolution – A popular form of decentralisation involves the devolution to regional governments of powers to design and implement policies. The central government usually remains responsible for the broad policy framework, the main orientation of policies, and funding. Some federal countries provide examples of this form of decentralisation – Belgium, Canada and Mexico – as do unitary states, such as Italy and Spain. Canada has pioneered devolution in an asymmetric fashion, giving more powers to some regions according to their administrative capacity and willingness to take on responsibility. Devolution has also been negotiated on a case-by-case basis between the central government and the regions in Italy and Spain. Other federal states, such as Switzerland and the United States, have traditionally shared the powers more equally between different layers of government.

Administrative decentralisation – A second form of decentralisation occurs within the framework of an integrated, country-wide PES, where some degree of autonomy in implementing policies and designing programmes is granted to regional or local officers. These officers act in accordance with guidelines or within a policy framework established at national level. Often the PES is managed in a tripartite fashion, with trade unions and employer organisations protecting the interests of their members at both national and regional level. Austria and Denmark are examples of this form of decentralisation.

The impact of these reforms on the harmonisation of central and local goals is mixed. Devolution would appear to offer significant flexibility in the management of labour market policies; often however, that is not really the case. Not only does central government often remain responsible for a large share of the power (*e.g.* orientations, funding), but the recipients of the delegated powers are often very large regions, for which the local-level concerns remain equally remote. In addition, funding transferred to the regions can represent a large sum of money and there are frequently political and administrative pressures to centralise spending powers in the regions, with a view to preserving efficiency and accountability. Indeed, cases have been reported of decision-making power being removed from the local level within the context of devolution and transferred to regional headquarters (OECD, 1998). Accountability and efficiency concerns also tend to limit the scope of joint planning exercises that involve other public organisations, business and civil society.

In the second, "integrated PES" model of decentralisation, all chains of command report to one decision-making body. The main determinant of flexibility in policy management in this case lies within the performance management system, and more particularly with the targeting mechanism. It is a typical management-by-objectives framework: broad policy orientations and funding are provided at the national level, while local officers are free to vary the use of the different measures available provided that they meet the targets set for a series of outputs (*e.g.* job placements, referrals to various programmes, the number of people trained). These aspects are broken down into categories of users – the unemployed, the long-term unemployed, social assistance recipients, women, youth, ethnic minorities, etc. Performance monitoring ensures that progress is made with respect to those targets.

The actual degree of flexibility in such a decentralised framework depends largely on how and by whom the targets are fixed. Are targets set unilaterally at national level? Are they negotiated with the regional and local offices? Is there any role for other government departments, social partners or other local stakeholders in establishing them? Are cross-sector targets established with other policy areas, for example vocational training and regional development? The methods for targeting measures vary significantly across countries. In decentralised PESs, regions usually have a say regarding the annual targets although the actual bargaining power depends on a number of factors, including budget constraints at national level. Only in very rare cases does this "bargaining process" extend to the local level.

Within this type of system, the flexibility provided is often insufficient to have an impact on the degree of co-ordination and adaptation of policies. In many countries the performance of public services is managed in such a way as to maximise output-based efficiency, and civil servants are sometimes put in direct competition with private service providers; this generates "creaming" effects whereby only the easiest cases are treated, and a narrow approach is preferred to implementation over a longer-term strategic approach.

Indeed it has become fashionable to introduce market mechanisms in service delivery and to delegate responsibility to non-public actors for part or all of the services to be delivered, a model which has been particularly developed in Australia and the Netherlands. In this system, private and non-profit providers often pursue well-specified targets and report on the results obtained in a format agreed by both parties, thereby preserving the accountability chain. Financial incentives to meet targets may stimulate problem-solving and a more entrepreneurial approach. However, harmonising policy goals goes beyond the service delivery aspect: it concerns strategic dimensions as well. Delegating service delivery cannot really play a significant role in this respect.

Partnerships

Various forms of partnerships between the employment services and other stakeholders have been attempted in the last few decades in order to better harmonise national and local policy goals. Partnerships were first recognised some twenty-five years ago as a promising way of helping local communities to solve problems specific to their region. In response to growing pressures, local authorities, private companies and civil society organisations set about finding new ways to promote economic and social development at local level. Partnerships were proposed as a way of mobilising resources and achieving the biggest possible impact, and they helped to provide an answer to crisis situations such as factory closures and the problems of disadvantaged areas. Partnerships were therefore a frequent feature of local employment and economic development initiatives in the late 1970s and the 1980s.

Public authorities very soon recognised the benefits of these initiatives and incorporated partnerships in policy intervention frameworks in various ways. In Canada, the Community Future Development Programme was set up in 1986 to help local communities achieve lasting economic independence through partnership activities. In Europe, the first pilot experiments with partnerships took place in Ireland in 1991, with the government initially setting up 12 to combat long-term unemployment, later extended to 38 (in 1995) and then, following a recent policy decision, to 60 or 70 in order to cover the whole country. The European Union in the meantime has come to consider partnerships as a way of facilitating measures to combat unemployment and reducing development disparities. The partnership principle governs a large proportion of interventions within the European Structural Funds; more specifically in relation to employment, the EU has provided special financial assistance from 1997 to 1999 for a series of "territorial employment pacts". The latter are still in operation in a number of EU countries and regions, especially in Austria, Finland, France, Greece, Ireland, Italy and Spain.

Area-based partnerships mainly pursue missions of social cohesion and employment and skills development. In some instances they also work to identify endogenous development opportunities and contribute to the development of entrepreneurship. They maintain close contacts with local authorities, community representatives and civil servants, and typically cover sub-regional or local territories. OECD (2001a) has demonstrated that their principal impact is to stimulate the uptake of public programmes that can help local actors move forward on their own local agendas, assisting in furthering local development and connecting local initiatives with government programmes. Their close relationship with the local community can also allow partnerships to identify new productive activities that bring difficult target groups back into the labour market.

However, overall, partnerships have a poor track record in harmonising labour market policy goals with local concerns. National goals and targets are often not negotiable at local level, and so any partnership initiative is likely to have only a marginal effect on how labour market policy is implemented. Education and training are often also very much centralised and, as identified above, slow to adapt to emerging local concerns. Co-ordination of labour market policy with other policy areas is also a considerable challenge for partnerships. Cases of more than one government department becoming actively involved in a strategic planning process led by a partnership are rare; sometimes, parallel strategic planning processes are run at regional level by different sectoral departments.

Attempts to co-ordinate employment and social issues have met with some success in the case of Workforce Investment Boards (United States) and sub-regional employment committees (Flanders). These partnerships take the form of evolved tripartite bodies tasked with co-ordinating labour market policies. Some of these labour market councils – traditionally grouping business, trade unions and public service representatives locally or regionally – have been enlarged and strengthened to play a more significant role in policy and governance. Yet the economic development actions of these bodies have remained weak despite significant business participation. In the United States, partnerships for economic development have in many places been established in parallel to the Workforce Investment Boards. In Flanders, a new reform has merged the sub-regional employment committees with the more economic development-focused district platforms (*Streekplatformen*) to overcome such a situation, but it will be some time before any evaluation can be made of its impact.

"Regional skills alliances", mushrooming in the United Kingdom and the United States, also try to bridge the gap between economic development and labour market policy. They use skills as a focal point for joint planning, business improvement and employment services, with the aim of aligning provision and services to meet employer demands and regional and local economic needs. The greatest added value provided by such voluntary alliances is to encourage an orientation of employment and training activities more in line with the demand side of labour. However, regional skills alliances have a relatively narrow focus. Discussions taking place in these forums mainly concern the difficulties faced by business in obtaining the short-term labour and skills they need. They are not the place for longer-term planning for workforce and economic development; which makes it difficult for such partnerships to lead strategic processes for broader endogenous development activities, or to be a forum where strategic decisions are taken.

The governance of employment and skills is complex. Neither decentralisation nor partnerships appear to provide sufficient answers to the harmonisation of national and local objectives. Overall, the problems of human resource development have not been satisfactorily addressed through the transfer of powers to regions; and co-ordination of policies cannot be forced at local level. The main reason for this seems to be that the strict performance requirements associated with management of public programmes at local level by and large reflect national policy goals. Therefore, a key challenge for the future will be the provision of greater flexibility in the management of policies; that way, they can be better adapted to local circumstance and co-ordinated with other initiatives if needed, while maintaining accountability and efficiency in service delivery. Secondly, stronger strategic capacity is required at local level to link up programmes, initiatives and local stakeholders.

Case examples

As outlined in the introduction, two of the main issues emerging for workforce development in a globalised economy are the needs to upgrade the skills of the low-qualified workers and to integrate immigrants in the labour market. Both are central concerns for governments nowadays, but the latter have for the most part lacked appropriate national policies for addressing them so far. In the absence of a national approach, local initiatives have very actively been set up to fill the gaps. We can learn from these experiments on the sort of flexibility and capacity that is required locally for public policy to be able to tackle such issues.

Upgrading the skills of the low-qualified

Skills upgrading has only recently emerged as a government priority in many countries. For decades, the attention of policy makers in an industrialised world struggling with unemployment was on issues of long- and medium-term unemployment. Integration or reintegration into the labour market was of chief concern, giving rise to the development of job subsidies, training programmes for the unemployed and counselling services. Now, their attention is increasingly shifting to upgrading the skills of those already employed. There are three main reasons for this (Giguère, 2006a):

- *Skill shortages* – Unemployment has fallen in OECD countries and many countries are now experiencing skill gaps and shortages: In specific industrial sectors, employers cannot find suitably qualified workers. As economies restructure and manufacturing businesses relocate their production centres to countries with lower labour costs, there is strong pressure to upgrade the skills of low-qualified workers on the domestic market so that they can fill vacancies for more qualified jobs and fuel economic growth. A similar situation is arising in some sectors and regions within emerging economies.

- *The need to increase productivity growth* – Higher productivity improves the position of firms on the global market, attracts inward investment and sustains job creation. Differences in productivity across countries are often explained by differences in skills and educational attainment. The ageing of the population makes this dimension all the more important. The fact that most of the workers who will be applying new technologies in the future will also be long past their school days calls for more investment in training the adult labour force, not just upcoming generations (OECD, 2003).

- *Poverty among working households* – The successful reintegration of former welfare recipients into entry-level jobs has contributed to the creation of a vast category of workers in low-paid employment involving harsh working conditions and offering few social benefits. The high incidence of poverty among working households suggests that policies emphasising job placement must be supplemented by measures to improve employment retention and enhance upward mobility (OECD, 2001b).

The skills upgrading principle is embedded in the lifelong learning process. The importance of providing individuals with opportunities for lifelong learning is well recognised in OECD economies. The emphasis on a knowledge-based economy and the need to invest in human capital to increase productivity and competitiveness has significantly raised the profile of adult vocational training and learning in public policy over the past decade.

However, the rhetoric about lifelong learning seldom translates into targeted programmes for low-qualified workers. The low-skilled receive far less training than the high-skilled in the OECD area. The probability of receiving employer-sponsored training has been estimated to be on average 9 percentage points smaller for workers with less than upper secondary education than for individuals with a tertiary qualification (OECD, 2003). Both the employer and the employee invest too little, due to difficulties in internalising benefits and in linking pay scales to productivity.

To this market failure must be added a governance failure. Among the low-skilled, those who have returned to the labour market after a spell of long-term unemployment or have just entered the labour market for the first time have the most obvious needs, as their lack of work experience and credentials mean that they are at risk of not being able to maintain their employment and returning onto the unemployment register. The difficulties faced by this category of worker have unveiled a gap between the public employment service and the vocational training system. Despite the fact that few vocational training resources are currently available to support those who are in precarious employment, the PES has insufficient resources or no mandate to follow up those who obtain a job. Lack of co-ordination between these two policy areas exacerbates not only skills gap but also the unemployment problem.

Integrating immigrants

Another issue that has reached the top of government priorities recently is the integration of immigrants into the labour market. There is much consensus on the fact that immigration is healthy for advanced economies. Given the ageing of the population resulting from low birth rates, the natural growth of the population in many countries is too low to ensure the maintenance of current standards of living in the foreseeable future. A number of sectors of the economy are already lacking the labour and skills they require in order to meet demand. Labour is needed to ensure the direct delivery of services to the population; these pressures are bound to increase in line with the changing demand for workers in health services and care for the elderly, which will accompany demographic change.

However, integration has become an issue as the labour market situation of immigrants has started to deteriorate over the past decade. Immigrants are today relatively more exposed to long-term unemployment and social exclusion. Even in countries where migrants have an employment rate similar to that of the native population, immigrants are more likely to suffer from poorer working conditions and temporary employment. A lack of integration not only affects the low-skilled but also and increasingly the highly skilled, partly reflecting difficulties associated with the recognition of qualifications overseas. Moreover, integration problems that at first glance seemed to apply only to new waves of immigrants appear also to be experienced by second or third generations.

The problem of integration of migrants, their families and their descendants can be traced to two governance issues (Giguère, 2006b). The first is the mismatch between immigration and integration policies; the second is the multifaceted nature of integration.

A policy gap – There is a mismatch between immigration and integration policies in many countries, with policies to manage the former rarely accompanied by strong policies to support the latter. While most countries provide specialised support to immigrants on arrival (particularly language training), after this initial period labour market integration is generally felt to be the responsibility of mainstream labour market policies. Unfortunately, mainstream labour market programmes do not always significantly help migrants to access the labour market. This is due to specific obstacles that migrants face: lack of local references and work experience, lack of knowledge about the value of qualifications, lack of familiarity with local social networks, lack of language skills. In addition, certain migrants fail to see the qualifications obtained in their native country recognised, and find it difficult to make the right decisions to adapt their skills to local needs. Employment services, ill-equipped to assess the value of foreign qualifications or profile the capacities of the migrant, find it difficult to provide the right advice.

A collective action problem – The second governance problem relates to issues of co-ordination and collective action. Immigrants and their offspring often face multiple barriers to the labour market. Solutions require actions to be taken in areas as diverse as education, vocational training, economic development, social assistance, healthcare and security. An integrated approach is needed, involving cross-sector policy co-ordination and strategic planning. In particular, when new immigrants and their offspring become concentrated in areas of urban deprivation they may face social and economic problems that have become embedded over a long period. Only intensive and long-term co-ordinated action will be able to address these issues successfully. But this is not an easy task for public policy, which is delivered through a complex set of organisations operating at various levels and linked through various bilateral mechanisms. Responsibility for immigrant integration theoretically falls across several government departments, each often having services that have been contracted out and delegated to others; this raises a collective action problem. As the gains from successful integration are likely to benefit all who are involved, there are limited incentives for any one department to take an active role and lead the process. Some agencies may in addition be reluctant to get involved in tackling a politically sensitive issue whose very complexity means that it is difficult to highlight immediate positive results. The outcome is often a lack of public sector activity, which is obviously suboptimal for society as a whole.

Local responses

What is common to the governance problems undermining the upskilling of the low-qualified and the integration of immigrants and their families is that responses have been provided at local level, perhaps because it is here that the strategic importance of these issues has been more obvious and felt more urgently. Local initiatives have been taken to fill the gaps between access to work and training; others have targeted the multifaceted barriers to the labour market encountered by immigrants and the low-skilled.

Local initiatives are particularly noticeable in the field of labour market integration, where there are often public and charitable funding streams available through public tendering processes. Many different types of local organisation, particularly non-government organisations (NGOs), get involved in providing services to those disadvantaged in the labour market, such as migrants. However, such actions are often relatively small in scale, linked to a limited target group and delivered in a single location. In many cases there is limited co-ordination between these actions, resulting in the lack of a strategic approach, duplication, and a lack of signposting between actions. Such organisations have few resources to invest in their own training to enhance capacities, and their expertise in the local labour market and their links with the employment services are especially weak. In a number of local areas, area-based partnerships have been set up to attempt to tackle the challenges posed by fragmentation, but these partnerships do not always have considerable success if they are not accompanied by other policy measures. As noted above, the establishment of area-based partnerships is not in itself a sufficient condition for effective policy co-ordination.

And yet, local-level action can add significant value if managed correctly. In reviewing examples of initiatives in both these policy fields, it is clear that two mechanisms in particular seem to be successful in producing change: local intelligence and "entrepreneurial" intermediation.

Local intelligence – The first of these mechanisms is the gathering and analysis of information locally. It is essential to perform an analysis of the structure of labour demand and of skills shortages, and to assess the potential offered by such labour demand for disadvantaged groups of workers at local level, in order to inform the orientation of programmes and/or local initiatives. Shared diagnosis of the local situation is itself a necessary condition for a co-ordinated approach. Analytical capacities are thus imperative at the local level.

"Entrepreneurial" intermediation – Another mechanism is intermediation between workers and employers, employment services and vocational training organisations to better link demand with labour supply. Intermediaries in the labour market (*e.g.* community colleges, specialised non-profit organisations)

are best placed to design skills assessment tests and training programmes to meet the specific needs of employers, employees and potential employees, and to provide the organisational support required. Local leadership is often key in the development of such intermediation, and is the missing link or trigger that determines whether an action to integrate the disadvantaged or upgrade skills takes place or not in a locality, a community or an enterprise.

National responses

While both these approaches establish whether a local policy initiative is successful or not in delivering long-term outcomes, such actions have been used in too few places, and the means put at their disposal insufficient. The challenge for government is to find ways to support these relatively resource-intensive mechanisms and to incorporate them into broader policy initiatives. This can of course be promoted through the provision of financial support for local labour market intelligence and intermediation. But there are other forms that supportive national action can take.

Providing analytical tools. "Job profiles" are an important tool that can enable stakeholders – employers, employment services, consultants, community colleges and the target groups themselves – to make the right decisions. These profiles help to make the labour market more transparent by providing concrete information on the various skills required for particular jobs, and approximating the level of qualifications for each of them. Employees can thus decide on appropriate progression routes within a company. If this information is made more broadly accessible, it can also help migrants to nurture the right expectations when deciding to emigrate, and to make appropriate qualifications decisions.

The information can in turn provide the basis for *skill assessment tests*, a critical instrument for ensuring effective training provision. Performing tests on a case-by-case basis enables identification of what the worker's needs are in line with the job's requirement and hence the employer's interest. By generating tailor-made training programmes, this approach encourages investment from both the employer and the employee. Such information is also helpful in identifying whether immigrants who have not participated in the local education system are nevertheless suited to a job. This is particularly useful where migrants do not have local references and their previous qualifications are not recognised.

Increasing the flexibility and coherence of mainstream policies. Improving local coordination and providing appropriate instruments and tools for action are obviously important; however, it is clear that in tackling both integration and upskilling, ultimately it will be more effective to make national policies more adaptable and flexible so that the proliferation of local initiatives is no longer necessary. There are a number of policy areas where improved flexibility could have a dramatic impact on the ability of local actors within existing institutions (employment services, colleges, economic development agencies) to address these complex areas for policy:

- *Social policy* – Social policy needs to adjust to the new labour market situation of working households. Government should recognise that promoting access to employment is not sufficient to fighting poverty and social exclusion. To make outcomes sustainable, support in attaining a job needs to be accompanied by a career planning and skills-upgrading dimension. For example, the recent federal policy in the United States to promote "career clusters" provides an effective way for individuals to plan their route through a series of lower-skilled jobs while obtaining relevant training towards a longer-term occupational goal in a related profession.

- *Education and training* – Tackling both integration and the skills upgrading issue requires changes in the education system. There is often a mismatch between the skills taught in schools and colleges and those demanded by firms. Many education and training institutions also operate to annual calendars and provide longer-term courses that are ill-adapted to businesses, where new skills are needed quickly and in a time-efficient way to minimise negative impacts on productivity. Modular "custom-designed" training courses are especially valuable here (Froy, 2006).

- *Labour market policy* – Flexibility is required to allow local officers to link employment services with their local business needs. It is important that these officers also have the analytical tools to articulate labour demand, to analyse the strengths and weaknesses of sectors and develop labour market and training actions accordingly. The business community should be involved as well as economic development agencies. This typically requires the introduction of a longer term perspective in the performance management framework for labour market policy and the possibility to revise the targets set by the central level in lights of the local circumstances.

Conclusion

These case examples suggest that a mix of local and national actions and reforms are needed for labour market policy and training to play a significant role at local level and contribute to enhance living standards. They confirm that gearing the management of national policies some way toward meeting local concerns is also in the interest of central governments. Flexible labour market policy and vocational training will ultimately contribute more to the fulfilment of local economic and employment development strategies than any successful local initiative.

The demand for more flexibility in the management of policy is illustrated by the fact that policy now needs to recognise: the difficulty that low-paid workers experience in upgrading their skills; the necessity for education and training to be better geared to market needs; and the importance that labour market policy understands the long-term challenges faced by local industry.

At the same time, there are significant variations at local level in terms of how opportunities can be used and initiatives created. The same policy needs and implementation can yield very different outcomes in different locations. Conversely, similar achievements can be observed in different policy environments. This highlights the key role that local actors can play in activating the various tools available to achieve optimal outcomes at given local levels. A strong capacity building component for local actors is thus a necessary complement to sound local government action and initiatives. Local capacity particularly needs to be boosted in analysis of labour market information; facilitation of a shared diagnosis of the local situation by the main stakeholders; provision of intermediation between the private sector and local key stakeholders; and the efficient use of labour market and educational tools and instruments. The capacity to gather data locally and organise it in a way that can support strategic planning exercises is critical (Chapple, 2006). The national level can support this process by ensuring that disaggregated data is assembled locally and by making available analytical tools that can be adapted to local circumstances.

These challenges amount to making national policy goals compatible with greater differentiation at the local level. Greater capacity and flexibility in policy making should enable greater experimentation, which is seen by many as a critical factor of success for policy in meeting local needs (see for example Osterman, 2005).

As this chapter has shown, government has a clear role to play in supporting these actions. Labour market and training policies can shape the future of our local economies in a fast-changing environment. Their local impact is a complement to their national impact on labour productivity and economic growth through more efficient markets. However, local growth and cohesion cannot be achieved by promoting employability and mobility alone. At local level, labour market policy must play a number of different roles, all critical to spurring growth and prosperity. Achieving this breadth of involvement and influence is not an easy process. It is the goal of this publication to help tackle this challenge, by informing the debate on the role of workforce development in a globalised economy, and providing evidence for the need to broaden its associated policy goals. A fresh approach to the governance of employment and skills development should lead to a greater harmonisation of local and national goals in a more prosperous economy.

Bibliography

Chapple, Karen (2005), "Building Institutions from the Region Up: Regional Workforce Development Collaboratives in California", University of California, Berkeley, CA.

Chapple, K. (2006), "Moving Beyond the Divide: Workforce Development and Upward Mobility in Information Technology – A Policy Brief", PolicyLink, Oakland, CA.

Froy, Francesca (2006), "From Immigration to Integration: Comparing Local Practices", F. Froy and S. Giguère (eds.), *From Immigration to Integration: Local Solutions to a Global Challenge*, OECD, Paris.

Froy, F. and S. Giguère (eds.) (2006), *From Immigration to Integration: Local Solutions to a Global Challenge*, OECD, Paris.

Giguère, Sylvain (2003), "Managing Decentralisation and New Forms of Governance", OECD, *Managing Decentralisation: A New Role for Labour Market Policy*, OECD, Paris.

Giguère, S. (2006a), "An Introduction to Skills Upgrading: Why a Shift in Policy is Needed", *Skills Upgrading: New Policy Perspectives*, OECD, Paris.

Giguère, S. (2006b), "Integrating Immigrants: Finding the Right Policy Mix to Tackle a Governance Problem", F. Froy and S. Giguère (eds.), *From Immigration to Integration: Local Solutions to a Global Challenge*, OECD, Paris.

OECD (1998), *Local Management for More Effective Employment Policies*, OECD, Paris.

OECD (2001a), *Local Partnerships for Better Governance*, OECD, Paris.

OECD (2001b), *Employment Outlook*, Editorial, OECD, Paris.

OECD (2003), "Upgrading Workers' Skills and Competencies", *Employment Outlook* (Chapter 5), OECD, Paris.

OECD (2006), *Skills Upgrading: New Policy Perspectives*, OECD, Paris.

OECD (2008, forthcoming), *The Role of Higher Education in Fostering Entrepreneurship*, OECD, Paris.

Osterman, Paul (2005), "Employment and Training Policies: New Directions for Less Skilled Adults", Paper prepared for Urban Institute Conference "Workforce Policies for the Next Decade and Beyond", October, MIT Sloan School, Boston.

Tessaring, M. and J. Wannan (2004), *Vocational Education and Training: Key to the Future*, CEDEFOP, Luxembourg.

ISBN 978-92-64-04327-5
More than Just Jobs:
Workforce Development in a Skills-Based Economy
© OECD 2008

PART I

Chapter 2

The Governance of Workforce Development: Lessons Learned from the OECD Experience

by

Sylvain Giguère

The experience of seven OECD countries illustrates the issues that emerge when a narrow implementation approach is taken that is not adapted to local strategic needs. It shows that there is now a more accurate appraisal of the difference in impact between short-term top-down employment measures and more flexible policies supporting economic and social development in a longer time frame. The lessons from this experience suggest that a balance of efforts is necessary at both the national and local levels in order to maintain the efficiency and accountability of the policy framework. The implementation of programmes should be allowed to receive strategic orientations locally, in a process that ensures greater local differentiation while at the same time ensuring that aggregate national policy goals continue to be met.

Introduction

Chapter 1 provided a theoretical basis for the need to harmonise national and local concerns in a perspective that encompasses economic competitiveness and social cohesion objectives. The analysis of local drivers of growth shows that human resources are a fundamental source of economic development in a knowledge-based economy. Not only does human resources development seek to provide the pool of skills that the economy needs locally; it is also a central element in efforts to foster innovation, entrepreneurship and social inclusion.

However, attempts to translate this into reality inevitably encounter a number of obstacles. One is the difficulty of speeding up changes to local education and training systems so that they can deliver skills currently in demand. Another is tackling the fragmentation in local decision making when it comes to human resources: policies on immigration, integration and training are often developed by different people in different institutions. The situation is made worse by a separation of economic development from labour market policies, which are often delivered in "silos". A lack of willingness to look at longer-term issues is another impediment to harmonising local and national concerns in the implementation of labour market policy and training.

In order to foster human resources development in a manner consistent with the workings of today's economy, it is important to invest more in governance issues. In particular, it will be critical to generate a higher degree of policy co-ordination, better adaptation of policy to local conditions and a greater level of participation of business and civil society in the shaping of measures. A review of OECD experience in trying to meet those challenges through decentralisation and partnership at local level reveals mixed results. The evaluation points to two key recommendations for governments: 1) inject greater flexibility into policy management and 2) build capacity at the local level, in terms of data and analysis on the one hand and intermediation on the other.

How can these challenges be tackled in practice? The rest of this volume will present analysis from seven OECD countries that have attempted, or should attempt, to broaden the scope of workforce development.

United States: Building partnerships to overcome policy gaps

The labour market situation in the United States can be characterised as highly fragmented. Labour market policy is decentralised, with a significant share of programmes and budgets coming from the states. The federal level is responsible for some key policy areas – notably training for the unemployed – and provides financing for others, such as welfare assistance and its various programmes. In economic development, municipal and state governments play the most important role, in collaboration with business organisations. A tradition of minimal government has stimulated a contractual attitude that translates into the involvement of a great number of organisations from the private and non-profit sectors in the management of activities and services in the spheres of employment, training and education and economic development.

In this context there is a general understanding that better co-ordination and a realignment of policies and programmes with local needs and conditions can be achieved through the establishment of partnerships. The experience of the United States is rich with partnership initiatives. What does this tell us about the ability of partnerships to make human resources development more coherent with the needs of localities in terms of economic competitiveness and social cohesion?

In Chapter 3, Eberts offers evidence of the added value of several different partnerships in bringing workforce development closer to business needs while providing opportunities for those disadvantaged within the labour market. A good example of this is the partnership established between Missouri's Division of Workforce Development and the private sector. The partnership works to better identify and meet skills gaps in sectors such as biotech, healthcare and information technology (IT), while developing career ladders for workers.

However, such outcomes, when they are measured, may appear insignificant compared with the mass of participants in national public programmes or the amount of funding devoted to those programmes. This raises the problem of providing evaluation results that can translate into meaningful guidance for governments and justify wider reform. Several reviews have been made of the outputs and outcomes of collaborative regional agreements, intermediaries, partnerships, networks and other area-based projects that seek to bridge workforce and economic development locally and overcome the weaknesses of the employment and training system (OECD, 2001, 2004; Giguère, 2002, 2003; Giloth, 2004; Chapple, 2005; Osterman, 2005). They generally show that such experiments succeed in making programmes more effective, because the latter become better informed, targeted and steered, and are often successfully combined with other policy initiatives for maximum effect. Many are creative and innovative in nature, and have a genuine effect on people's lives.

However, the work underlying these initiatives is typically labour-intensive, and requires building networks and trust relationships using limited financial and human resources. As a result, most initiatives work with a relatively small number of participants – enterprises and individuals. Their effect can appear very small compared with the overall impact of broad national programmes run without local intervention. Unsurprisingly, evaluations are not able to prove beyond doubt that such local experimentation can solve the complex problem of linking economic and workforce development.

To evaluate the effectiveness of partnerships, Eberts employs an assessment tool widely used in the United States – the Baldrige criteria – and applies it to generic partnerships involved in either workforce or/and economic development. This analysis leads to several important lessons on the themes of leadership, shared vision, strategic planning processes and capacity, discussed in Chapter 1. One lesson that Eberts has identified in common with other contributors to this book is the importance of information. A partnership must be able to use a shared pool of data that can support its strategic planning processes. Such data must help the partnership form its own intelligence, which will in turn help the partners take a more objective viewpoint, leaving aside their own specific institutional concerns and objectives.

France: Doing what is possible given the limits of decentralisation

Aligning labour market policy and economic development through institutional reform such as decentralisation is a difficult mission. In large countries with complex distributions of power and a large degree of differentiation in local conditions, a perfect match may always seem just beyond reach. In this context, multi-level partnership mechanisms appear as a valuable "second-best solution".

In France, most responsibilities for economic and regional development lie with the regions, the result of various institutional innovations such as long-term contracts between the state and the regions, and a "poles of competitiveness" cluster-oriented initiative. Responsibility for labour market policy remains with central government, though specific duties are increasingly being transferred to local governments, especially with regard to the integration of the disadvantaged in the labour market. It is also at the local level that various partnerships are set up to address the multifaceted problems associated with unemployment and social exclusion.

In Chapter 4, Greffe shows that training can act as a bridge between employment issues and regional development. In France, responsibility for vocational training lies with the regions; this allows them to make strategic training decisions in line with the economic priorities that are also identified at this level. It could be argued that managing training at a different level to that of labour market policy could provide obstacles to the effective upgrading of the skills of the low-qualified and integration of the disadvantaged into the workforce development system. However, Greffe sees an advantage to regional management of training: the perspective of training provision is widened, which supports workers' adaptation to new skills requirements and encourages their mobility.

The centralisation of decision making in relation to the major orientations of labour market policy remains an obstacle, however. One particular challenge is how to set objectives for the implementation of labour market policy in a way that reflects local conditions. Devolution of certain categories of service may make the system even more difficult to manage, as it increases the complexity of the target setting process. The multiplicity of accountability streams has also been identified as an obstacle to the strategic approach taken by the Workforce Investment Boards (WIBs) in the United States (Eberts and Erikcek, 2001; OECD, 2001; Straits, 2003), which are obliged to co-ordinate and implement federal and state policies locally. In France, as in the United States, one important mechanism for progress is a change in behaviour by stakeholders: civil servants are able to play the role of "civic entrepreneurs". That is to say, they can establish operational collaborative relationships where needed and work towards developing a collective outcome-based strategic framework that provides orientations to all administrative authorities involved (central, regional and local government).

Germany: Making employment services more effective

The case of Germany effectively illustrates the trade-off that exists between broadening the perspective of labour market policy and making it more effective. The country has long awaited reform of the public employment service and labour market policy. Unemployment is relatively high and labour market programmes have been used to absorb a surplus of workers, many of whom have a high level of qualification. At the same time, the employment and training system has been characterised as bureaucratic, centralised and fragmented.

The recent reform of the employment service (Hartz IV) has not solved all these problems, as Mosley and Bouché demonstrate in Chapter 5. Fragmentation is an important issue, as different agencies address different target groups depending on the type of benefits they receive. However, the system is now more uniform for the long-term unemployed and those individuals excluded from the labour market. These groups are now served by new local Job

Centres, which combine the services of the labour offices with those of municipalities. Their offices now have a greater level of flexibility than before in assigning unemployed people to labour market programmes (OECD, 2007). However, the new system can mean less responsibility and involvement for municipalities in the new merged offices, which has led 69 municipalities to opt out and run their own integrated local services.

One of the most important obstacles to defining a new role for labour market policy as a local driver for competitiveness is the perpetuation of a solely "supply driven" agenda within labour market institutions. The local public employment service offices in Germany have limited mechanisms for providing orientations to workforce development inspired by the local economic development context. This problem persists in spite of the Hartz recommendation to create a "competence centre" in each state to integrate labour market policy and economic development.

It is in this context that the role of intermediary organisations at state level can better be appreciated. These agencies monitor and co-ordinate implementation of employment programmes funded by the state and, increasingly, the European Union. As they are also involved in regional economic development, it is common sense for them to support co-ordination between the two streams of policy. This way they can ensure that skills are adapted to the innovation process and fuel local growth. They have a sufficiently high critical mass to leverage good collaboration in the state among the various partners of the public and private sector, and can develop their own expertise based on the data they assemble. The example of North Rhine-Westphalia is exemplary of what can be achieved by this type of agency in terms of improving the relevance of public policy locally.

United Kingdom: Empowering the cities

Urban agglomerations represent a special case for human resource development, as it is in these geographical areas that the need to harmonise national policy goals and local concerns is perhaps most obvious and urgent. Cities are where most people in a country live and work. The concentration of living and working activities into certain agglomerations is a phenomenon that has shaped local economies and societies, generating wealth and high living standards at the same time as causing concerns regarding social cohesion and quality of life. In a globalised economy where local assets matter to economic and social development, competition has increased between urban agglomerations – within the same country and across countries – making human resource development a highly strategic issue. Today, in Boston, Moscow and Singapore, more than ever the priority is to attract and retain talent and upgrade the skills of the existing workforce. To cope with these challenges, large cities have set up their own workforce development programmes. Underlying their approach is a conviction that national policies should be better tailored to local contexts, or else responsibility should be devolved to cities themselves.

That cities could be engines of growth in a knowledge-based economy has recently been acknowledged by policy makers in the United Kingdom, as Simmonds and Westwood explain in Chapter 6. Devolution of powers has so far concerned Scotland, Wales and Northern Ireland unevenly, while regional development agencies have been set up to play a strategic planning role in the regions of England. Apart from London, which has seen its decision-making responsibility enhanced in a number of policy areas under the Labour government, local governments have had very little to say in the implementation of any policies, labour market or otherwise. Central government is responsible for setting the targets for policies to be implemented by local agencies. While various sorts of partnerships have been set up to stimulate local co-ordination, these partnerships have had little influence on targets and programmes.

The situation in the cities is today one of many contrasts. If cities present the competitive face of the United Kingdom, at the same time they host populations whose skill levels are relatively low, and who often exhibit high levels of inactivity, insecurity and poverty. This situation highlights the limits of achieving national outcomes, in terms of employment rates and educational attainments. Local situations can evolve in different directions, generating their own problems, which makes them harder to solve. In the United Kingdom for example, the local offices of the PES have been performing less efficiently in large cities overall, and the qualification levels of young people tend to be poorer in areas where skills are poorer. In this context it becomes all the more difficult to embark on the joined-up solutions that would be required by complex local situations.

Dealing with the problems of cities requires a particularly strong ability to co-ordinate human resource development activities while reinforcing the capacities of the various actors involved. Workforce development initiatives must be linked up with economic development strategies. That leaves a key role to local government, which must have the means to implement consistent strategies to make their area competitive and their community sustainable in the world economy. The pressure on labour market institutions to adapt policies to local conditions is often more strongly felt in urban centres, which at the same time have greater capacity (than smaller centres or rural areas) to make use of potential gains in flexibility. This suggests a case for modulating administrative flexibility in terms of the capacity of local administrations and the critical mass of regions.

Australia: Localised responses to regional diversity

Other countries present an even greater degree of discrepancy in local conditions. The situation of Australia illustrates well the differentiation required in the approach to human resources development to face a variety of local conditions. Like the United Kingdom, Australia is highly urbanised, with 85% of the population living in urban centres. Yet other regional centres and urban areas present situations that are very different, including both boom and decline. National policy instruments are only partly adapted to the diversity of challenges that are arising. The current national policy priority to solve skills shortages does address many concerns locally but the apprenticeship system has experienced difficulties in filling vacancies in trades (metal, engineering, electrical and construction), with possible negative impacts for the innovative capacity of several sectors such as manufacturing, mining and transport.

The provision of workforce development in Australia will need to continue to adapt to the extended degree of diversification in local economic situations. To learn from local innovations, Martinez-Fernandez examines three scenarios in Chapter 7: an urban agglomeration, a booming local economy, and a shrinking city. Comparison of the different responses in each of the three areas reveals a common change of attitude among industry and local government with respect to the labour market. For local government, the long-term perspective and the sustainability and quality of the jobs created locally arise as important issues that are no longer subsumed to the priorities of attracting investment and expanding the commercial base. Skills development is also becoming a strategic objective of industry networks, which increasingly understand the limits of short-term approaches to filling labour shortages.

These new developments allow a broadening of the scope of labour market issues to incorporate some more sophisticated aspects, associated with developing a skills base adapted to the local economic context and likely future trends. However, industry and local government are still reluctant to incorporate other important issues locally, such as that of integrating disadvantaged workers into workforce development initiatives. Yet, tackling the issues of housing, traffic congestion and childcare that hamper the integration of the more marginalised is complex, and requires a particularly joined up approach in which industry, for one, could play a major role. In turn, tapping into these categories of workers and helping them fulfil their potential within the labour market could also provide a boost to local economic growth. But this outcome can only be achieved if these individuals are reintegrated not only into jobs, but also into the training and workforce development system.

Japan: Building local capacity

The need to tailor labour market policy to localities and regions is also emerging in Japan. Regional disparities are increasing due to the impact of globalisation, the ageing of the population and reduced expenditures in public works.

As Higuchi demonstrates in Chapter 8, increases in both investment abroad by Japanese firms and foreign direct investment in Japan have modified the structure and distribution of employment within the country, shifting it from rural areas to urban centres. This change has not been matched by an increased mobility of workers. On the contrary, Higuchi observes a decrease in mobility, attributed to sociological factors associated with the phenomenon of single-child families. The reduction in subsidised public employment has made the situation even worse. Public works have created a dependency effect in relation to job creation in rural areas, which have consequently been particularly harmed by the reduction in public expenditures that occurred since the burst of the Japan's economic bubble in the 1990s.

Japan, its prefectures and its localities are now at a turning point. The current period of fiscal consolidation limits the room for manoeuvre of governments, and forces them to look at alternative ways to stimulate job creation in rural areas and to tackle regional disparities. The chapter advocates greater decentralisation over labour market policy associated with increased efforts to train local and regional authorities. Employment strategies should be devised at the local or regional level to encourage co-ordination of actions and avoid conflicting measures.

Wider research has confirmed that there is a need in Japan for both greater flexibility in the policy management framework and stronger capacity at local level to exercise such flexibility. While devolution to prefectures in certain policy areas may provide a stimulus to innovative area-based strategies, it is not certain that such reform will translate into greater flexibility and better governance that can be used in designing and implementing integrated development strategies. Greater flexibility can instead be achieved by scaling down parts of decision making to lower levels within the central administration, and giving incentives to civil servant to participate in joined-up strategic planning. As with any country with a tradition of centralisation, time and effort is needed to build the necessary skills and capacity to take a strategic and integrated approach to policy development on the ground (Giguère and Higuchi, 2005).

Korea: Proposal for a new paradigm

The situation of Korea is similar to that of Japan. Employment and human resource development have traditionally been led by central government, while local governments and local public service offices are involved only with delivery. As Lee indicates in Chapter 9, this centralised top-down system is no longer adequate for securing regional innovation and competitiveness. It must be complemented by local governance initiatives fostering human resource development that are adapted to local conditions and implemented in partnership with other departments of the central government.

The chapter illustrates the need for implementing a new paradigm for human resource management in Korea by proposing concrete steps. One of them is the establishment of a strategic body that would establish broad orientations for economic, social and employment policies and initiatives delivered locally. This partnership would also be responsible for co-ordinating the work of all institutions involved in human resource development – as in many other countries, a fragmented policy area involving several stakeholders – and connecting them with industry needs and the local innovation system. That structure would also provide for the amalgamation of service delivery, in order to link up supply- and demand-driven labour market services.

This model is ambitious. It aims to develop synergies between two policy issues that are relatively remote from one another: lifelong learning, which often has poor connection with industry, and the innovation process, in which labour market institutions themselves typically have little involvement. Moreover, the co-ordination between economic development and labour market policy that it encourages aims not only to meet business needs but also to ensure that disadvantaged and marginalised individuals also benefit from the opportunities provided by thriving industry sectors. It therefore responds to an important concern identified in the Australian context by Martinez-Fernandez (Chapter 7).

Lee's model is currently being implemented in the province of Daegu-Gyongbuk, following an agreement signed in October 2007 by the main authorities and public services of the province. This will complete for the province some of the ambitious reforms recently undertaken by the Ministry of Labor. Since 2006, local offices have had more power to set their own performance objectives and define target groups. Legislation is also in place for local employment councils to be developed at the shin, gun, gu (sub-regional) level, which will allow local actors to have greater responsibility in co-ordinating programmes and developing tenders for local projects. However it is still early days in the implementation process, and these councils are as yet only operating at the provincial level (administrative regions) (OECD, 2007).

Driving change: Recommendations

As highlighted above, one major difficulty in broadening the perspective of workforce development is the lack of statistical evidence as to the potential outcome of such an approach. This is mainly due to the fact that desired outcomes are likely to be difficult to measure: more competitive firms, more efficient innovation systems, sustained integration and progression into employment, skills upgrading for low-qualified workers, a higher degree of mobility for workers, higher living standards.

Furthermore, desired outcomes foreseen within a longer, broader perspective may conflict with the goals contained within the standard labour market policy framework. For example, in order to move a locality out of a "low-skills equilibrium", it may be more logical to promote the further education of low-skilled workers rather than refer them to low-skilled vacancies. Technically however, such a solution will lessen the efficiency of labour markets as vacancies are not filled. More spending on vocational training is thus difficult to justify. Data on the impact of a broader strategic policy framework are what is needed to overcome such a governance failure.

In the absence of such statistics, contextual evidence can help support change. The chapters of this volume provide the next best thing to statistical evidence, as they identify, define and describe the issues that emerge when a narrow implementation approach is taken that is not adapted to local strategic needs. They show that there is now more accurate appraisal of the difference in impact between short-term top-down employment measures and more flexible policies supporting economic and social development in a longer time frame. Though they do not replace the scientific value of quantitative estimations, the survey generates a number of helpful lessons for policy and practice.

The lessons suggest that a balance of efforts is necessary at both the national and local levels in order to maintain the efficiency and accountability of the policy framework. The implementation of programmes should be allowed to receive strategic orientations locally, in a process that ensures greater local differentiation while at the same time continuing to meet aggregate national policy goals. Enhancing capacities becomes particularly important in this context, as strategies for human resource development must be integrated and coupled with the economic reality on the ground. There is no governance mechanism that fits all institutional frameworks, but governance and partnerships have a certain value in developing appropriate and realistic strategies. See in Box 2.1 recommendations for enhancing the governance of workforce development.

The cross-cutting issues generated by today's economy require a bridging between different policy fields in order to be effectively tackled. "Workforce

Box 2.1. **Recommendations for enhancing the governance of workforce development**

The review of the OECD experience and the contextual evidence from seven countries contained in this volume point to the need to achieve better co-ordination and a more effective balance between the efforts of policy makers at the national and local levels. While there is a need for greater differentiation and experimentation at the local level, it will also be important to maintain the efficiency and accountability of the overall policy framework. The lessons emerging from this cross-country comparative analysis can be summarised by the following guidelines:

1. *Inject flexibility into management.* It should be possible for the local level to decide on and provide strategic orientations in the implementation of public programmes and services, in addition to pursuing predetermined objectives. In a management-by-objectives framework, this means that policy targets set by central government would need to be negotiated with the local level in light of current local strategic priorities.

2. *Establish an overarching management framework that embeds local flexibility.* Workforce development policy should be managed in a way that supports greater local differentiation while still paying attention to aggregate impacts at the national level. The process of negotiation with the local level on targets should be embedded in a framework that ensures that aggregate national policy goals continue to be met.

3. *Build strategic capacity.* Enhancing local capacities becomes particularly important in this context, as strategies for human resources development must be integrated and matched to the economic reality on the ground. The staff of labour market institutions should have a strong knowledge of local business practices, local economic conditions, industry developments, and appropriate methods to identify skill gaps and deficiencies in local economic sectors. They should also develop the analytical skills necessary to use this knowledge as a basis for developing broad strategic orientations locally.

4. *Build up local data and intelligence.* Building an understanding of economic and labour market conditions demands, as a prerequisite, refined databases gathered and managed locally and expertise in a wide variety of fields. The capacity to gather data locally and organise them in a way that enables strategic planning exercises is critical. The national level can support this process by ensuring that data are disaggregated to the local level and by making available analytical tools that can be adapted to local circumstances.

> Box 2.1. **Recommendations for enhancing the governance of workforce development** (*cont.*)
>
> 5. *Improve governance mechanisms.* Labour market institutions should collaborate effectively with business, trade unions, civil society, higher education institutions, research centres, economic development agencies and local authorities. There is no governance mechanism that fits all institutional frameworks, but partnerships have a certain value in bringing different stakeholders together to develop appropriate and realistic strategies.
>
> 6. *Improve administrative processes.* Aligning policies through institutional reform such as decentralisation is a difficult challenge. In large countries with complex distributions of power, a perfect match may always seem just beyond reach. A wide-scale review of how administrations function, co-operate and manage policies is needed to support better collaboration between different administrative layers and between different policy institutions. This is particularly important given that the new, broader goals for human resources development cut across a number of different policy areas.

development is a programmatic response to societal need and thus should not be limited in scope to a specific organisation or designed to benefit one set of individuals only" (Jacobs and Hawley, 2003). It is indeed the responsibility of all actors involved, policy makers and local practitioners, to bring forward the changes required. Part II of this volume will detail examples of how this can be done.

Bibliography

Chapple, Karen (2005), "Building Institutions from the Region Up: Regional Workforce Development Collaboratives in California", University of California, Berkeley, CA.

Eberts, Randall W. and George Erikcek (2001), "The Role of Partnerships in Economic Development and the Labour Market in the United States", in OECD, *Local Partnerships for Better Governance*, Paris, OECD Publications.

Giguère, Sylvain (2002), "Enhancing Governance through Partnerships", in T. Bovaird, E. Löffler and S. Parrado-Díez (eds.), *Developing Local Governance Networks in Europe*, Nomos, Baden-Baden.

Giguère, S. (2003), "Managing Decentralisation and New Forms of Governance", *Managing Decentralisation: A New Role for Labour Market Policy*, OECD, Paris.

Giguère, S. and Y. Higuchi (2005), *Local Governance for Promoting Employment: Comparing the Performance of Japan and Seven Countries*, Nikkei and Japan Institute for Labour Policy and Training, Tokyo.

Giloth, Robert P. (2004), *Workforce Development Politics: Civic Capacity and Performance*, Temple University Press, Phildelphia.

Jacobs, Ronald and Joshua Hawley (2003), "Emergence of Workforce Development: Definition, Conceptual Boundaries, and Implications", R. MacLean and D. Wilson (eds.), *International Handbook of Technical and Vocational Education and Training*, Kluwer, Amsterdam.

OECD (2001), *Local Partnerships for Better Governance*, OECD, Paris.

OECD (2004), *New Forms of Governance for Economic Development*, OECD, Paris.

OECD (2007), "Decentralisation and Co-ordination: The Twin Challenges of Labour Market Policy", Document for Official Use, CFE/LEED(2007)14.

Osterman, Paul (2005), "Employment and Training Policies: New Directions for Less Skilled Adults", Paper prepared for Urban Institute Conference "Workforce Policies for the Next Decade and Beyond", October, MIT Sloan School, Boston.

Straits, Robert (2003), "The US: Decentralisation from the Bottom Up", OECD, *Managing Decentralisation: A New Role for Labour Market Policy*, OECD, Paris.

PART II

Country Studies

ISBN 978-92-64-04327-5
More than Just Jobs:
Workforce Development in a Skills-Based Economy
© OECD 2008

PART II

Chapter 3

The United States: How Partnerships Can Overcome Policy Gaps

by

Randall W. Eberts

Partnerships are constantly evolving as they try to position themselves to meet the changing needs of businesses and workers in order to generate or retain jobs for their constituents. They can be powerful catalysts for improving workforce development and economic development programmes. In the United States, partnerships are formed vertically among the various levels of government and horizontally among government agencies and non-government entities. As a result, they devolve more responsibility for the design and provision of workforce services from central governments to local organisations, which can lead to service delivery systems that are more responsive. This chapter identifies key criteria for developing successful partnerships, and offers several examples in the United States that highlight the lessons learned and the challenges encountered.

Introduction

As competition in the global economy intensifies, countries – including the United States – increasingly realise that their future economic success rests with building a flexible and knowledgeable workforce. For 75 years the United States has provided labour exchange and job training services to targeted groups of the nation's workers. Most of these services have been funded and administered under separate programmes. At the same time, local economic development activities have been carried out mostly by local entities that are not affiliated with the workforce development organisations. During the past two decades, the deficiencies resulting from fragmented and overlapping programmes and the gap between these programmes and the needs of businesses have become increasingly evident. In response, all levels of government have placed greater emphasis on integrating workforce development with education and economic development policies and operations that provide a continuum of lifelong learning opportunities and work support. Since education and economic development activities are provided locally, much of the integration and co-ordination efforts take place among local partnership arrangements.

With workforce development seen by many to be synonymous with local economic development, the purpose of this chapter is to identify key drivers and challenges associated with developing successful partnerships that will enhance the development of workforce skills and the creation of employment. The experience of the United States is offered to highlight the lessons learned in that country. It is widely accepted that by devolving more responsibility for the design and provision of services from central governments to local organisations, service delivery can be more responsive to the needs of individuals, can better meet the demands of local businesses, can leverage community resources, and can take into account local economic conditions. In addition, well-functioning networks of local organisations can increase the capacity to meet the needs of local communities, not only with respect to employment services but also with respect to broader social and economic needs of local areas, thus improving the prospects for economic growth.

US experience has shown that the relationships needed to bring about effective partnerships involve both vertical hierarchies within the federal system of government and horizontal relationships across organisations at local levels and across state agencies. These relationships range from formal contractual arrangements to less formal memoranda of understanding, to informal agreements. However, putting into practice effective partnerships entails many challenges. Issues regarding delegated authority, communication, performance monitoring, accountability and trust arise periodically among federal, state and local agencies. Issues regarding co-ordination, accountability and sustainability plague the ability to forge strong bonds and collaboration among local non-government entities.

While there is no universally accepted checklist of criteria that must be in place for successful partnerships and effective governmental relationships, organisations that are attempting to establish and improve such relationships are increasingly turning to the principles of good business management for guidelines. For this discussion, the author adopts a framework developed by the US Department of Commerce for determining successful organisational performance, one that has been increasingly used by private and public entities to promote performance excellence. That framework, which was designed for individual organisations, is here extended to partnerships of organisations; and examples are offered of local partnerships that have recognised and successfully addressed the challenges.

Local economic development

The United States has a strong tradition of local, decentralised initiatives that promote local economic development. Responsibility for planning and implementing local responses to economic development needs is shared by government and non-government entities. In some instances, municipalities and other local government entities, such as counties and states, assume the responsibility for administering certain programmes. In other cases, local non-profit organisations, such as chambers of commerce and economic development organisations, take on that role. These entities typically are not branches of state and federal agencies; rather, they partner with state and federal agencies to receive funding and to implement federal and state programmes, with varying degree of local discretion. In fact, many of these programmes encourage, if not require, operation through local partnerships.

One reason for the move toward decentralised, area-based approaches to economic development policies and the formation of partnerships is to bring decision making and implementation closer to those who are being served. Another is the anticipation that forming partnerships between the public sector and the private sector will help the public sector leverage its limited resources. A third reason is the reaction to the poor results attained by policies and programmes that did not have strong linkages to local stakeholders.

Considerable effort in recent years has been devoted to bringing together workforce development and economic development activities. One result has been the creation of Workforce Investment Boards (WIBs), under the Workforce Investment Act of 1998. While these were extensions of local administrative entities under a previous federal workforce programme, they have been given more local discretion and have been encouraged to form partnerships at the local level. Charged with preparing individuals for work and matching workers with businesses, WIBs create and oversee a network of providers and customers. The 600 or so WIBs administer local workforce programmes and have the capacity to work closely with other organisations, including economic development organisations and educational institutions, at the local level.

Another development has been the emergence of workforce intermediaries. Usually non-profit organisations, they too aim to match workers with employers but are typically more focused than WIBs in that they target specific industries or population subgroups. To facilitate these matches, workforce intermediaries emphasise networking, integration of services, attention to the needs of business, active involvement of the business community, worker training that fits the labour needs of existing businesses, and identification of their region's strengths and then building on them. They also address the barriers facing their region's key and emerging industries, working collectively, not individually, with customers to solve the problems (NGA, 2004).

In most locales, WIBs and workforce intermediaries are seen as partners, not as competitors. In fact, many WIBs contract with workforce intermediaries to provide services, and many workforce intermediaries network with WIBs to gain access to publicly funded services for the specific businesses and workers they target. By forming partnerships, the two have the potential to deliver services in innovative and effective ways, which in many instances can better meet the needs of businesses and jobseekers.

The US workforce system

The Workforce Investment Act of 1998 (WIA) is the most recent of a long line of federal workforce programmes dating back to the early 1960s. The first programmes were centrally administered by the federal government, with little discretion given to states and local governments in providing services. As new programmes replaced older ones, they evolved toward a more decentralised approach, giving states and local governing boards more power. The WIA was designed to address deficiencies in its predecessor, the Job Training Partnership Act (JTPA). These included poor representation of business in local decision making, overlapping and redundant programmes, limited access to services, unnecessary use of expensive training programmes, and training programmes not targeted to the needs of businesses or workers. In response to these deficiencies, WIA incorporated the following guiding principles:

1. Universal access to services.

2. System integration and service co-ordination.

3. Customer focus and empowerment.

4. Increased accountability and efficiency through performance monitoring.

5. Strengthened local decision making through WIBs.

6. Enhanced state and local flexibility.

The attempts through WIA legislation to address these six areas are described briefly.

Universal access

Universal access is accommodated through establishing a hierarchy of services: Core, intensive, and training. Core services entail little, if any, staff assistance and include job-search assistance and preliminary employment counselling and assessment. These services are available to all adults, and WIA imposes no eligibility requirements on anyone using these core services. Intensive services are staff-assisted and are provided to individuals who experience difficulty finding a job that pays enough for them to be self-sufficient. These services include case management and assistance in developing an individual employment plan. Training, the final level, is reserved for those who lack marketable skills in demand in the local area, and who fail to get a job after receiving core and intensive services. Initially, WIA was quite strict on following the sequence of services from core to training, without allowing participants to jump directly to a more intensive, staff-assisted service. As the programme evolved, its sequential requirement was relaxed and individuals who obviously needed job training in order to quality for decent employment were referred directly to job training services. Yet there are not enough funds to provide job training to all who could use it.

Training programmes under WIA are not targeted specifically and exclusively to low-wage workers, since they do not have an income requirement. However, WIA regulations stipulate that in the event funds allocated to a region for adult employment and training services are limited, priority for training services must be given to recipients of public assistance and other low-income persons. In addition, state and local programmes have targeted low-wage workers to help them overcome some of the barriers to receiving training services. Their activities include offering English as a second language in the workplace, helping to meet transportation and childcare needs, accommodating scheduling conflicts and financial constraints, and helping to overcome limited work maturity skills.

System integration and service co-ordination

WIA addresses system integration and service co-ordination primarily through the establishment of one-stop career centres. The programme requires that all states and localities offer most training services through the one-stop system. The one-stop career centre is a physical location housing all the workforce programmes. In many cases, the centre encompasses up to 17 different employment programmes, offering a comprehensive array of services to meet the individual needs of jobseekers. Training and other services may actually be provided in other locations, such as technical centres, public schools or community colleges. It was anticipated that the co-location of staff from the various programmes to one physical location would encourage collaboration and integration of services. However, other factors that affect true integration and co-ordination were not addressed. The funding streams of the various programmes were still separate, and little money was provided to provide the "infrastructure" needed to bring them together, such as sharing common management information systems and coming up with common intake procedures.

Customer focus and empowerment

WIA has taken steps to focus more on the needs of customers and to empower them to take a more active role in determining the appropriate course to finding employment. These steps include customising programmes, introducing market mechanisms and bringing decision making closer to the customers. Customers that are eligible for intensive services develop a customised, individual employment plan that lays out the various services and activities that they have chosen to pursue in consultation with a counsellor. Individual training accounts (ITAs) offer flexibility so that customers can choose the courses they believe will give them the skills necessary to qualify for current vacancies and to advance in their careers. Choice is also achieved through the subcontracting of services to outside vendors instead of providing these in-house. It was anticipated that the arm's-length relationship with providers would introduce market pressures, since WIBs could change providers if the latter were not responsive to customer and local business needs. To provide customers with the information needed to make informed decisions about training and other services, WIA offers them assessment tools and labour market information. In addition, the states are required to compile a list of eligible training providers, with sufficient information about course offerings and placement rates.

Performance measurement and accountability

System accountability is addressed by extending, with modifications, the performance measures created under the predecessor programme to WIA. After a few iterations of changes, the US Department of Labor (USDOL) settled on three measures for adult programmes and three measures for youth programmes. For adults and dislocated workers, these measures are: 1) entered employment rate, 2) retention rate after six months of entering employment, and 3) average earnings after exiting the programme. For youth (ages 14-21), the measures include: 1) attainment of a degree or certificate, 2) literacy and numeracy gains, 3) and placement in employment or education.

Performance goals are negotiated between USDOL (through its regional administrators) and the states, and states in turn negotiate with the local WIBs. These goals were expected to hold states and WIBs accountable for their performance and to set high standards for the delivery of services.

Strengthening local decision making

Under WIA, the decentralisation of responsibilities and increase in local control are further advanced with the creation of WIBs. The extent to which WIA in fact achieves its objectives of greater system integration, customer empowerment and efficiency depends upon how the 600 local workforce areas implement these policies. The local WIB is comprised primarily of local business leaders so that it is responsive to the needs of businesses. The system is built on market mechanisms and is not a command and control system. The WIBs design programmes and implement them through contractual agreements with independent vendors.

Enhanced state and local flexibility

In addition to the greater role given to local workforce boards under WIA, states are also given more discretion. State-level workforce boards develop strategies and policies that govern the administration of workforce programmes within their states. Governors are given discretion to spend a small portion of the WIA dollars that flow through their states to the WIBs. These funds are used for a variety of workforce programmes, but many states earmark them for customised training requested by businesses. The flexibility afforded states also allows them to form partnerships across state-level agencies responsible for economic development and educational operations. Some states have forged partnerships with non-profit organisations, such as charitable foundations, to help finance special programmes.

How well these reforms have been implemented and have improved the areas of concern will be addressed in a later section, which looks at the results of a recent evaluation.

Partnerships

The workforce development system in the United States is characterised by two dimensions of partnerships. The first is a vertical dimension linking the different levels of government, from federal to state to local workforce investment boards. The federal government provides a large share of the workforce programme funds and federal programmes provide the overarching structure for delivering employment services to workers. The federal government delivers these services through partnerships with state government agencies and local entities, specifically Workforce Investment Boards that have discretion (although with limits) on how the money is spent. The second dimension comprises the horizontal partnerships primarily at the local level, in which local workforce investment boards partner with local social service agencies, non-profit organisations within their local jurisdiction, and workforce intermediaries. Discussion of these two dimensions of partnerships will be included in descriptions of the key entities that comprise and catalyse these partnerships, and critical elements that bond them together.

Workforce Investment Boards

As mentioned above, WIBs are responsible for providing labour exchange and workforce training services to workers and businesses within their local areas. Increasingly, the local WIBs have become more closely integrated with the economic development efforts within their jurisdictions, as businesses find it more difficult to find qualified workers to fill their vacancies. To do so, they subcontract with local providers, including government entities, non-profit organisations, and for-profit businesses. Each WIB is governed by a local board, the majority of whose members are representatives of local businesses. In many areas, the WIBs act as facilitators to bring together the various entities – businesses, social agencies, educational institutions, labour groups – to help address workforce issues in their areas. The extent to which the local WIBs are proactive in assuming this role varies. Nevertheless, they have emerged as significant catalysts for integrating workforce and economic development activities in various areas.

Figure 3.1 shows the web of relationships between WIBs and both government and non-government entities. The left side of the figure depicts relationships among the various levels of government, along with the lines of accountability and the flows of funding. Most funds come from the federal government through the state to local governments. Each WIB has a master contract with the sponsoring local government entity (in this case a county government) to administer the programmes. Local governments may form partnerships through inter-local agreements to have one WIB serve an area covered by several government entities.

The right side of the figure shows the subcontracting of services by the WIB to local agencies and organisations. The federal regulation that WIBs cannot provide direct services to customers opens up the field to a host of potential providers, including local government agencies – such as county government agencies or educational institutions – and private organisations, non-profit or in some cases even for-profit. The WIB contracts with those

Figure 3.1. **Schematic of partnership relationship with Workforce Investment Boards**

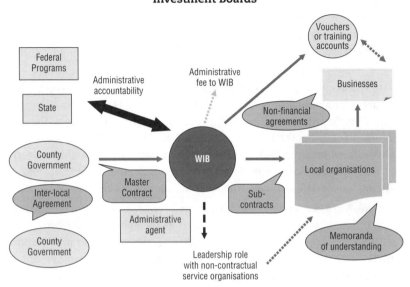

organisations to provide employment-related services to customers. In addition, WIBs serve as the conveners and facilitators of informal relationships among organisations within their jurisdictions (often through memoranda of understanding), which may include economic development organisations, educational institutions, and social service organisations.

Workforce intermediaries

Workforce intermediaries are also catalysts for forming partnerships. These are typically non-government entities and are quite diverse in their attempt to respond to the specific needs of businesses and workers within local communities. Because of this diverse and entrepreneurial nature, they are difficult to explain precisely. According to a leading authority on the topic, "they are fundamentally brokers, integrators, and learners who entrepreneurially enact workforce development rather than simply 'meeting the market' or conforming to a publicly mandated set of roles and responsibilities" (Giloth, 2004, p. 7). They have grown out of a wide variety of organisations, including community organisations, employee unions, business associations, publicly supported community colleges and human service providers. They include WIBs in their network of partners, but try to avoid the restrictions placed upon WIBs by federal and state statutes. They seek to leverage funds from a variety of sources while focusing on the needs of employers and workers in their specific location. Workforce intermediaries pursue results for specific groups via on-the-ground partnerships with WIBs, but constantly need to find sufficient funding sources to pursue their goals. Therefore, workforce intermediaries, represented in Figure 3.1 as local organisations, work with WIBs to bring together businesses, educational institutions, workforce development agencies, and economic development agencies to advocate the needs of certain subgroups of businesses and workers.

Many workforce intermediaries are formed around business sectors, such as metalworking or healthcare. According to a National Governors Association study, "The defining elements of sector initiatives include a focus on customised solutions for a specific industry at a regional level, a central role for a workforce intermediary in bringing the industry partnerships together, and the dual goals of promoting the competitiveness of industries and advancing partnerships of low- and middle-income workers" (NGA, 2006).

Some have expanded the definition of workforce intermediaries to include public and private organisations that receive funding from WIBs to serve WIA customers or perform WIA-related functions (Javar and Wandner, 2004). They operate one-stop career centres and provide employment and training programmes. Referring to Figure 3.1, workforce intermediaries are the entities that WIAs contract with to provide services.

Regardless of the inclusiveness of the definition, workforce intermediaries should be seen as partners, not competitors. Furthermore, according to Giloth (2004, p. 8), they have to be entrepreneurial, results oriented, and adaptive learners to be successful. These traits help to drive a focused approach to workforce and economic development at the local level.

The responsive and entrepreneurial nature of workforce intermediaries makes it difficult if not impossible to identify and quantify the number in operation. The National Network of Sector Partners (NNSP), a national support centre for sectoral workforce development initiatives, used four criteria to identify organisations to survey. They: 1) operate programmes with a focus on two primary customers – those whose skills are being built and the employers/ industries in which the workers work or will work; 2) expressly work with low-income individuals and low-wage workers; 3) provide a menu of services; and 4) invest in longer-term career advancement (Marano and Tarr, 2004). The second criterion of working with low-income individuals may be too restrictive for defining the workforce intermediaries that focus on broader local economic development issues.

Nonetheless, the survey provides some perspective on the nature and size of these organisations. It found 243 organisations across the United States that met the criteria listed above. Nearly three-quarters were located in non-profit organisations, with 22% in community-based organisations, 23% in WIBs, 15% in educational institutions, 10% in economic development organisations, and 4% in business organisations (Marano and Tarr, 2004). They provided a multiple of services, including job-readiness services, occupational skills training; career counselling and job placement, with percentages ranging from 81% to 79%. Sixty-eight per cent of the organisations reported providing incumbent worker training. Seventy-five per cent of the respondents reported providing services directly to employers, such as technical assistance and supervisor training and human resource services. Over half of the intermediaries responded that they target specific industries for their services (Marano and Tarr, 2004). The majority of financial support came from government programmes, with WIA and welfare funds at the top of the list. Two-thirds of the organisations received WIA funds and nearly half received welfare funds. Next on the list were foundation funds and fees for service, with 43% and 29%, respectively.

Partnerships with state and federal agencies

In addition to their relationship with WIBs, state and federal workforce agencies have initiated other partnerships. Most of those initiatives involve both WIBs and non-profit workforce intermediaries. Their purpose is to provide resources and technical assistance to help local areas forge partnerships with workforce development, education and economic development organisations. Their goal is to provide a workforce that meets the needs of local businesses and creates jobs and careers for local workers. Many of these initiatives are more targeted than the WIA programme. Instead of trying to provide employment services and training to anyone who needs it, they target specific sectors and subgroups of workers. Because of their ability to be more exclusive, the more targeted initiatives deal directly with workforce intermediaries, which in turn partner with WIBs for access to public dollars for worker training and other services. The chapter will highlight a few examples of such partnerships in order to provide more details on how they work.

Criteria for successful partnerships

Before offering examples of various partnerships that bring together workforce development and economic development interests and activities, it is important to establish criteria for successful partnerships. To evaluate the success of specific programmes or interventions, one would typically turn to net impact analysis. However, the effects of partnerships on worker and business outcomes are much more subtle than the effects of the services they provide – such as training and employment services – which confounds the use of such methodologies. Therefore, it is necessary to look to other approaches.

One that has been widely used to identify "best practice" among organisations is a set of criteria established by the US Department of Commerce to aid businesses, government organisations, and non-profit organisations in improving their performance. Since its inception in 1988, the Malcolm Baldrige National Quality Award has been a tool used by thousands of US organisations to stay current with ever increasing competition and to improve performance. Each year the Department of Commerce confers the highly coveted award on a handful of businesses and organisations, each of which has gone through a gruelling process of self-evaluation and external evaluation of their management and workforce practices. While it was designed for single organisations, it is easily extended to networks or partnerships of organisations.

While not explicitly citing the Baldrige criteria as their framework, several studies of best practice among partnerships espouse similar principles. The International Economic Development Council, for example, has adopted similar criteria to gauge the performance of local economic development agencies and help them improve their organisations. The National Governors Association has also endorsed criteria similar to Baldrige that workforce intermediaries should follow to be most effective. In many ways, the areas of reform addressed by WIA are also consistent with the Baldrige criteria.

Lessons learned from evaluations of various partnerships are also consistent with the principles laid out in the Baldrige Award criteria. While most of these evaluations are primarily process evaluations as opposed to net impact analysis with proper comparison groups, it is still instructive to note the consistency in conclusions across the various studies. Some of these studies will be mentioned in the section that gives examples of selective partnerships. Therefore, Baldrige offers a convenient framework to summarise effective practice.

The Baldrige criteria can be used as a self-assessment tool to help: 1) improve organisational improvement practices, capabilities and results, 2) facilitate communication and sharing of best practices information among organisations of all types, and 3) serve as a working tool for understanding and managing performance and for guiding planning and opportunities. For those organisations pursuing the award itself, the criteria become the basis for an independent Board of Examiners to evaluate an applicant's written response to these questions. The Baldrige Award is sponsored by the US Department of Commerce and administered by the National Institute of Standards and Technology. Since 1988, only 71 recipients have been named as Baldrige recipients among the thousands that have started the process.

Boxes 3.1 and 3.2 list the core values and criteria. The values espoused by the Baldrige Award focus on customer-driven excellence, which places the customer at the centre of strategic planning and decision making. The pursuit of excellence depends on an organisation's top leaders creating a customer focus, setting direction, and championing values and expectations that balance the needs of customers with those of other identified stakeholders, including employees and partners. Other attributes, as listed in Box 3.1, emphasise

Box 3.1. **Malcolm Baldrige National Quality Award**

Core values:

Visionary leadership

- Organisation's leadership should set directions and create a customer focus, clear and visible values, and high expectations.

- Leaders should ensure the creation of strategies, systems, and methods of achieving excellence, stimulating innovation, and building knowledge and capabilities.

- Leaders should inspire and motivate the entire workforce (and network) and should encourage all employees to contribute, to develop and learn, and to be innovative and creative.

Customer-driven excellence

- Organisation's customers judge the organisation's quality and performance.

- Customer-driven excellence is a strategic concept. It demands constant sensitivity to changing and emerging customer and market requirements and to the factors that drive customer satisfaction and retention. It also has both current and future components: understanding today's customer desires, and anticipating future customer needs.

Valuing employees and partners

- Organisations need to ensure their employees' satisfaction, development, and wellbeing.

- External partnerships are critical to better accomplish goals. Partnerships encourage the blending of an organisation's core competences or leadership capabilities with the complementary strengths and capabilities of partners.

Agility

- A capacity for rapid change and flexibility.

Managing for innovation

- Innovation means meaningful change to improve an organisation's services and processes and to create new value for the organisation's stakeholders.

Management-by-fact

- Organisations should be driven by facts, and that depends on measurement and analysis of performance. Such measurements should derive from business needs and strategy and they should provide critical data and information about key processes, outputs and results.

- Measures and indicators should best represent the factors that lead to improved customer, operational and financial performance.

Box 3.1. **Malcolm Baldrige National Quality Award** (*cont.*)

Focus on results and creating value

● An organisation's performance measurements should focus on key results. Results should be used to create and balance value for key stakeholders – customers, employees, partners, the public and the community.

Systems perspective

● The organisation should be managed from a systems perspective, and the Baldrige criteria should provide the building blocks and the integrating mechanism for that system.

---

innovation, agility, and managing-by-fact based on well-established performance measures.

Baldrige criteria promote a systems approach to organisational excellence. By extending the notion of "system" to include a network of organisations within a partnership arrangement, it is easy to see how the Baldrige criteria are pertinent to assessing the effectiveness of partnerships. The criteria are summarised in Figure 3.2. The first three criteria listed in Box 3.2 – leadership, strategic planning, and customer and market focus – represent the leadership triad. According to the Baldrige manual, these categories are placed together to drive home the importance of leadership in focusing on customers and shaping strategy. The second triad of categories represents the emphasis on results and the importance of employees and key processes in producing those results. The horizontal arrow in the middle of the figure links leadership to results and the vertical arrow toward the bottom

Figure 3.2. **Baldrige criteria: A systems approach**

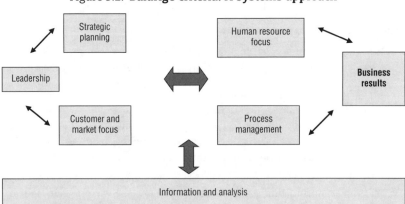

Source: Baldridge, 2001.

Box 3.2. **Baldrige's seven criteria for a successful organisation**

Leadership

- Addresses how the organisation's or network's leaders address values, directions, performance expectations while focusing on customers and other stakeholders, empowerment, innovation and learning.

Strategic planning

- Addresses how the organisation develops strategic objectives and action plans. It also asks the organisation to examine how it chooses strategic objectives and how action plans are deployed and how progress is measured.

Customer and market focus

- Describes how the organisation builds relationships to acquire, satisfy and retain customers and to develop new opportunities. Describes how the organisation determines customer satisfaction.

Information and analysis

- Examines the organisation's information management and performance measurement systems and how the organisation analyses performance data and information.
- Performance measurement is used in fact-based decision making for setting and aligning organisational directions and resource use at the work unit, key process, departmental, and whole organisation levels.
- Benchmarking refers to identifying processes and results that represent best practices and performance for similar activities, inside or outside the organisation's industry.
- This information should feed back to the leadership's organisational leadership review and strategic planning.

Human resource focus

- Examines how organisation motivates and enables employees to develop and utilise their full potential in alignment with the organisation's overall objectives and action plans. Also examines efforts to build and maintain a work environment and an employee support climate conducive to performance excellence and to personal and organisational growth.

Process management

- Examines the key aspects of the organisation's process management, including customer-focused design, product and service delivery, key business and support processes. This category encompasses all key processes and partnering organisations.

> Box 3.2. **Baldrige's seven criteria for a successful organisation**
> (cont.)
>
> **Business results**
>
> ● Examines the organisation's performance and improvement in key business areas – customer satisfaction, product and service performance, financial and marketplace performance, human resource results, and operational performance. Also examined are performance levels relative to other similar organisations.

indicates the importance of information feedback in an effective performance management system (Baldrige, 2001).

One can easily see how these criteria for a single organisation can be extended to a partnership of organisations. This will be discussed in a later section on the requisites for effective leadership.

Examples of partnerships

Vertical partnerships among governmental entities within the WIA system

The federal-state-local partnership within the WIA system has already been described in an earlier section. WIBs are, as previously mentioned, the centrepiece of this system, in which federal and state resources and overall programme goals are administered at the local level. Assessment of the effectiveness of the partnering arrangements of the WIA system requires an examination of both the vertical government relations and the horizontal public-private partnerships. The vertical relationships will be examined first.

A few years after WIA was put into operation, the US Department of Labor sponsored a process evaluation of WIA to determine how well the new features of the system were working. The process evaluation was conducted by observing the operations of 30 one-stop career centres in 16 local areas in eight states (Barnow and King, 2005).

The evaluation identified a number of challenges; at the time it was conducted these were still unresolved and for the most part they are still ongoing concerns. They involve leadership, accountability, performance monitoring, flexibility, co-operation and partner engagement. The study came to the following conclusions.

1. Balancing accountability and flexibility under a broad-based federal grant-in-aid programme such as WIA is critical for success. The challenge is finding the right mix of flexibility and accountability so that an accountability system

tailored to achieve federal goals does not thwart state and local government efforts to address what they see as their own needs. Unless the states and local WIBs are free to innovate, the system will not respond effectively to the needs of workers and businesses or promote improvements in the system.

2. Co-operation among federal, state and local government relationships must be maintained on an ongoing basis. Under WIA, most funds flow from the federal government to the states to the local workforce boards. The challenge is to achieve the appropriate mix of authority so that each level of government has an appropriate voice, federal and state requirements are harmonised, and local entities have sufficient autonomy in the design and delivery of services.

3. Reporting and performance requirements should not adversely affect customer selection, the provision of services or outcomes. However, under pressure to meet increasingly higher goals, there is a tendency for local WIBs to enrol those whom they believe are more likely to succeed, leaving the harder-to-serve without needed services. Revamping the performance measurement system to take into account the employability of participants could reduce this tendency.

4. Strong leadership at the local and state levels is necessary to provide a proper balance within this hierarchical system, and to ensure that business plays an active role.

5. Determining how to engage business entities in workforce programmes and how to sustain their participation is critical, but is still a major issue for many WIBs.

WIBs and workforce intermediaries

Workforce Investment Boards and workforce intermediaries are instrumental in forming partnerships. They partner together, through contractual arrangements, to provide training and other employment-related services. They also, together or separately, form networks with other organisations, including local economic development entities, educational institutions, businesses and social service organisations.

With respect to WIBs, the 600 or so that administer workforce services across the United States vary considerably in their effectiveness in forging partnerships with workforce intermediaries. The more exemplary partnerships strive to follow many of the Baldrige criteria, without necessarily pursuing Baldrige principles explicitly. This section presents a description of the workforce system in the City of Chicago as an example of a WIB that works with a large network of providers and community-based organisations. While other WIBs may be more exemplary in achieving their goals, Chicago provides an instructive case study of a WIB that has formed an extensive network of partners and has addressed many of the key issues necessary to achieve best practice.[1]

There are many workforce intermediaries operating in the US, and any number could be used as examples of partnerships. To illustrate the relationship of a workforce intermediary with manufacturing, a state economic development organisation, and educational institutions, the "Make It Happen" project in Minneapolis is briefly described.

The City of Chicago's Mayor's Office of Workforce Development

The Chicago Mayor's Office of Workforce Development (MOWD) partners with private business, community organisations and other government bodies to provide re-employment services to people in Chicago. MOWD focuses equally on business and individual needs to provide job placement services that benefit the city. These services are beneficial in that they reduce the incidence and associated costs of unemployment, and offer savings to the businesses of Chicago by providing qualified, pre-screened candidates who can fill their immediate openings. MOWD contracts with providers to offer services mandated by WIA through one-stop career centres. The centres provide job training for displaced workers and employment services for jobseekers in conjunction with the Illinois Employment Training Center. MOWD also offers the Quantum Opportunities programme, which provides basic vocational skills training and job/college placement services to 16- to 24-year-olds from disadvantaged areas in an attempt to improve the employability of participating members.

MOWD works through WorkNet Chicago, a network of over 130 community-based, citywide organisations that helps businesses find qualified workers and assists workers in obtaining the skills and receiving appropriate re-employment services. Included among these organisations are five WIA-funded Chicago Workforce Centers and 33 community-based affiliates. At the centres and affiliate agencies, customers attend service orientations, visit resource rooms to search the Internet for job openings, use the fax machines and printers to send resumes to employers, and receive assistance from front-line staff. In addition to these core services, local jobseekers – approximately 11 000 in 2003 – participated in intensive services, such as workshops covering job-readiness skills, job-search techniques, resume writing, English as a second language and basic skills. Nearly 2 600 received vocational training vouchers to upgrade their skills, choosing from nearly 600 training classes offered through 135 state-certified training organisations. These services helped more than 6 400 local residents get full-time jobs.[2]

The MOWD staff supports a network of partnerships. Part of their motivation stems from the lack of adequate funding to accomplish the goals set out by the local workforce system. Staff members contend that partnerships offer an opportunity to leverage their public funds. Another reason to form partnerships is that the WIA legislation, which most of MOWD's programmes come under, requires staff to spend more time forging partnerships among organisations and working with those organisations in their role as customers. One staff member offered that "partnerships are crucial to making things work for everyone; we need to have everyone moving in the same direction and need to work on partnerships in which each party will bring something to the table, particularly when funds are decreasing". Under the umbrella of programmes administered by the workforce board, staff co-ordinates services with regular meetings with caseworkers from several departments and agencies.

Partnerships are also crucial for gathering information about the needs of employers. Market-driven or demand-driven services are the current focus of state- and federally funded workforce systems. Assessing the needs of businesses starts with the composition of the local workforce boards. WIA legislation requires that local boards include a majority representation of local area employers, so that broader input can be brought to the decisions on what type of training to provide. Many local boards also focus on sectoral issues, providing services to companies and workers within designated sectors, many of which are high-tech or health industries where severe worker shortages exist. This approach follows the federal lead, in which the US Department of Labor has targeted a handful of sectors for special attention. Even with the federal government taking the lead in this initiative, the funds available for training are relatively small.

MOWD appears to have achieved several of the Baldrige criteria and recognises deficiencies in others. On the positive side, their leadership and staff focus on their customers, develop strategic objectives and action plans, and support the development of partnerships. Identified deficiencies and challenges relate to information and the use of performance monitoring and standards, and to the sharing of common values among partners. Staff acknowledged that one of the barriers to more effective integration of services is the lack of a single management information system that can track common outcomes across agencies; each has its own system. They have implemented an innovative system using "swipe cards" to record who uses core services, but this falls short of being able to share information across departments. Another difficulty is the inherent problem of aligning goals and standards among the various partners. While they may buy into a common goal, turf issues still remain and can get in the way of effective collaborations. A complicating factor is that under WIA legislation, workforce investment boards must subcontract with third-party providers to offer services. Even though these relationships are governed by contracts that specifically state performance standards, they are still arm's-length arrangements and it is not always possible to monitor the approach that subcontractors take in dealing with customers or in offering the necessary level of customer service and satisfaction.

Another issue is that partners may not share the same values. For instance, some educational institutions see a conflict between their mission of providing educational services and WIA's narrower mission of assisting jobseekers in finding employment. To offer an illustration, many training programmes are provided by community colleges, which often fit them into their regular schedules and in a format designed for regular students – not for students who are trying to balance work and home responsibilities with their educational pursuits. Even though the workforce board understands that this approach may not be what employers and employees prefer, they find it difficult to change the culture of community colleges to provide a more customised service.

According to MOWD staff, another barrier facing local workforce boards is that federally mandated performance standards may be unnecessarily rigorous and restrictive relative to their mission. Each WIB must meet performance standards imposed by federal regulations under WIA. The state can waive some requirements, such as the money that flows through the state's economic development agency for customised training to retain or attract companies. But for the regular WIA programmes, participants must satisfy specific eligibility requirements and providers must meet performance standards. As one staff person put it, "If we miss one performance standard, we could lose financially".

Staff also point out that their public status may diffuse their mission. One problem MOWD faces, along with other workforce investment boards, is that as a public agency it is in the position of trying to satisfy everyone, whereas non-government organisations can target whom they serve. Consequently, even with the focus on partnerships and strong business representation on local boards, companies still express concern that their needs are not met.

Minneapolis's Make It Happen Project

The Precision Metalforming Association, with initial funding from the National Manufacturing Association and private foundations, has brought together 37 precision manufacturing employers and a number of community organisations. The idea behind this sector initiative is to help manufacturers in the industry find the workers they need to meet production goals and expand their businesses. The initiative focuses on training employees, and has brought together several educational institutions within the Minnesota state colleges and university system to provide the training. A local non-profit organisation also offers customised training and counselling to workers from all backgrounds and experience. In addition, the partnership includes the state economic development organisation and the local WIB. At first it focused only on workers only in the precision metalforming industry. In a short time training was expanded to workers in other sectors. The state department for employment and economic development stepped in to create and fund a new "academy" to train state employees on how to better serve the industry. The success of the partnership rested on the leadership of key businesses in the local economy, the ability to identify the need, share a common vision, develop a workable strategy, and monitor performance. The result has been an increase in the number of qualified workers entering the precision metalforming industry and other key manufacturing sectors within the Minneapolis economy.

State and regional skill alliances

Several states have implemented programmes to provide technical assistance and financial incentives to help WIBs do a better job of bringing together into effective partnerships business, education, and workforce development. This section examines efforts by states and the federal government to encourage and nurture partnerships among state-level departments, WIBs and non-governmental entities, including economic development organisations. Highlighted in this section are an effort by the State of California to catalyse regional collaboration, a multi-state consortium spearheaded by the National Governors Association to assist states with partnerships, and a federal programme that provides funding for partnerships with specific regions.

Regional Workforce Preparation and Economic Development Act of California

One of the earliest state programmes to attempt regional collaboration of this sort was initiated by the State of California. Faced with a growing concern that the workforce development system was not responding to emerging workforce education and training needs, the state legislature passed the Regional Workforce Preparation and Economic Development Act (RWPEDA) in 1998. It was a unique effort designed to bring education, workforce preparation, and economic development partners together at the state and regional levels. The goal was to create an integrated, effective and responsive workforce development system that would better meet the needs of employers and jobseekers and improved the quality of life for all Californians.

In its attempt to integrate education, workforce development and economic development programmes and activities, RWPEDA formed partnerships at both the state and local levels. The act had three components.

1. The Act directed the four state agencies with responsibilities for public K-12 education, community colleges, workforce development and economic

development to enter into a memorandum of understanding (MOU) and develop a unified workforce development strategy for the state. To ensure effective implementation of RWPEDA and the MOU a Joint Management Team (JMT) was formed, consisting of executive staff from each of the four agencies.

2. The Act instructed the four state-level partner agencies to select and fund at least five regional collaboratives to participate in economic development strategies, and to deliver services to clients in a more responsive, integrated and effective manner. The JMT, operating under the MOU, funded a total of six pilot regional collaboratives. Each pilot developed its own unique strategy for addressing the needs within its region and for implementing regional economic development strategies.

3. The Act required the partner agencies to create an integrated state workforce development plan. This plan was to guide the development of an integrated workforcedevelopment system at the state and local levels. The JMT developed a policy framework document by soliciting input from a 37-member advisory group.

Regional collaborations – The RWPEDA legislation supported the creation of locally initiated regional collaboratives in order to bring together workforce development partners to test strategies for integrating and improving both service delivery and workforce development systems at the regional level. Six regional collaboratives were awarded funding. They represented a diverse range of geographic, economic, and proposed programme characteristics, including single and multiple county regions, rural and urban areas, industrial and agricultural economies, and direct service and system-based activities.

The Los Angeles County Workforce Preparation and Economic Development Collaborative is an example of one of the more diverse but successful collaboratives. It encompasses Los Angeles County, which is home to 10 million people and stretches across a large geographic area. It is served by multiple community college districts, K-12 public school districts and workforce development entities – including eight separate Workforce Investment Boards – and also includes enormous county agencies that manage the CalWORKs and employment programmes. Despite being a large county with multiple stakeholders and wide-ranging needs and interests, the collaborating partners succeeded in developing countywide projects to support employers and jobseekers, according to the evaluation. Some of the activities initiated by RWPEDA have been sustained beyond the project period; this was made possible by securing additional funding as well as also securing the continuing interest and support of the partners (BPA, 2002).

State-level collaborations – These mirrored the regional collaborative by bringing together the state agencies responsible for education (both K-12 and community colleges), workforce preparation, and economic development for

California. Historically, the disconnect between these partners has stemmed from differences in missions, priorities and cultures as well as real and perceived turf battles and competition for funds (BPA, 2002). However, in the 1990s policy makers began to encourage these agencies to work together through initiatives such as the federal School-to-Work Opportunities Act and the One-Stop Career Centers Initiative. The goal of RWPEDA was not to develop partnerships to improve a particular type of service, but rather to improve the delivery of all workforce development services through collaboration, leveraging of resources, and system building. The legislation mandated that the four agencies come together to establish an MOU, select and fund at least five regional collaboratives, and develop and implement an integrated state workforce development plan. According to the evaluation, the state-level collaborative was able to overcome several significant barriers, including the layer of bureaucracy established by the enactment of WIA in 1998, and to achieve successful collaboration. The Joint Management Team, established by the four agencies, was able to develop an integrated strategic workforce development plan that served to guide the state agencies and regional collaboratives (BPA, 2002).

The evaluation of RWPEDA, conducted by an independent consulting firm, found that successful collaborations at both the regional and state levels depended upon strong leadership, the involvement and support of key stakeholders, consensus decision making, a strong focus on the goal of system change, timely and consistent funding streams, and formal communication networks – all consistent with the Baldrige criteria. The state-level collaboration also benefited from developing a memorandum of understanding among the agencies. The more successful regional collaborations grew out of new collaborations instead of relying on existing ones, and they found that the process of applying to become a collaborative promoted collaboration (BPA, 2002).

National Governors Association's Policy Academy Initiative

Other states followed California's example to implement similar types of partnerships. For example, the National Governors Association (NGA) brought together six states committed to forging partnerships among workforce, economic development and education initiatives. The purpose of the year-long project was to assist governors in developing strategies for a global economy. The agenda included: 1) connecting workforce development to economic needs, 2) building a stronger educational pipeline to produce skilled workers, 3) expanding opportunities for continuous learning, 4) enhancing workers' abilities to manage their careers, 5) strengthening work supports to promote employment retention and career advancement, and 6) strengthening governance and accountability in the workforce system. Each of the six states approached these tasks in different ways, building upon their existing strengths and ongoing initiatives. For example, to connect workforce development to economic needs, Ohio has formed regional councils throughout the state to evaluate and address important workforce issues for key sectors in specific regions of the state. As another example, Missouri's Division of Workforce Development has collaborated with various private sector companies to develop career ladders for workers. The partnership with the private sector has been critical in helping the state identify the specific technical skills needed by businesses in the key sectors of biotech, healthcare, and information technology.

The lessons learned from the six-state project are similar to those from California. Partnerships must share a common vision, have strong leadership, develop trust among the partners through consensus building, develop and assign defined tasks and deliverables, maintain a focus on desired outcomes, develop measures to track the outcomes, and communicate the outcomes to all partners (NGA, 2004).

Federal initiatives promoting regional partnerships

The federal government has also initiated programmes to encourage effective partnerships among local businesses, workforce development, economic development and educational institutions. Specifically, the US Department of Labor has sponsored the Workforce Innovation in Regional Economic Development (WIRED) to support the development of a regional, integrated approach to workforce and economic development and education. The ultimate goal of WIRED is to expand employment and advancement opportunities for workers and catalyse the creation of high-skill and high-wage opportunities. Currently, the WIRED initiative consists of three generations of regional collaborations. The first generation of WIRED, which includes 13 regions, was announced in February 2006. Each first-generation WIRED region received USD 15 million over a three-year period. An additional 13 regions – the second generation of WIRED – followed in January 2007. After receiving a small planning grant, these regions will now receive an additional USD 5 million over the next three years, bringing the total investment to more than USD 260 million for the first and second generations.

Given that one of the significant goals for WIRED is to fully align the public workforce investments with a regional economic growth agenda, WIBs are integral to the programme's success. They are encouraged to work with governors on the application process and on implementation of the WIRED initiative. Regional partnership teams must include a senior representative of the workforce investment system within the region as the lead, or co-lead, with at least one other regional partner, for the region's WIRED grant activities.

Grand Rapids, Michigan received one of the first-generation WIRED grants. The collaborative comprises more than a dozen partners within a seven-county area of over 1.2 million people and focuses on developing and managing an innovations lab concept designed to spawn a wide range of innovations in the regional workforce development system. The collaborative pursues four categories of innovations.

1. Market intelligence initiatives are under way to understand better the detailed structure of regional employment clusters and the new requirements for the innovation economy. These include an analysis of the skill development needs of emerging life sciences, alternative energy and sustainable manufacturing sectors; analysis of the evolution of the global supply chains in the region's industries and how they affect the demand for workforce skill development; development of a strategy for attracting and retaining knowledge workers through new workplace designs; and a system for regional outreach and engagement.

2. The collaborative is also bringing together all of the region's other initiatives in order to focus on building awareness and knowledge about innovation and developing innovation skills in the current and emerging workforce.

3. An integrated workforce system for the emerging industries and their skill needs is another component of the initiative. Collaboratives are working to transform the workforce system by providing performance-based credentialing, developing a model global school, accelerating engineering programmes, implementing the manufacturing skills standards system, and other region-wide workforce development programmes.

4. The collaborative focuses on initiatives designed to stimulate entrepreneurship and new business creation in key sectors of the innovation economy.

The WIRED initiative is too new for evaluation, but it includes many of the features of the other programmes listed above with the addition of federal funds to help sustain the effort. Applicants who were successful in receiving funds had to demonstrate that their proposed regional initiative had the commitment of key leaders in the region; focused on the needs of businesses; integrated workforce development, education, and economic development efforts; established clear goals and objectives; aligned resources with those goals; developed and tracked performance measures; and set in motion ways to meld the cultures of the various organisations.

Local economic development organisations

Strategic planning and implementation for local economic development take place primarily at the local level, while much of the funding for economic development efforts originates at the national or state levels. In most instances, higher levels of government have more taxing authority and are better able to spread the financial burden across a broader population base. Yet, local organisations are closer to local businesses and residents in their areas and better able to assess their needs and direct resources to meet them. They can best determine the combinations of programmes that are best suited to target the needs of businesses and residents within their geographical area of concern.

The responsibility of designing and implementing local responses to economic development needs is shared by both government and non-government entities. In some instances, municipalities and other local government entities, such as counties and states, assume sole responsibility for administering certain programmes. Local elected officials see promoting economic development in their areas as one of their primary responsibilities.

Partnerships between economic development and workforce development organisations face the typical challenges of sharing common goals and objectives, aligning resources according to their goals, and tracking outcomes. For workforce development and economic development entities, an even more vexing challenge is the melding of two cultures. Workforce development organisations are accustomed to working with state and federal governments, which require strict accountability, transparent accounting and programmatic practices that are scrutinised closely by funding agencies. They have also fostered a paternalistic culture; they view their customers as needing assistance in understanding what is in their best interests. Economic development organisations, on the other hand – particularly the non-governmental ones – work behind closed doors in order to strike deals with private business entities. Businesses do not appreciate public scrutiny.

Thus, economic development organisations, which deal directly with businesses, are not accustomed to transparency and resist the oversight and accountability of government. They also have a culture of responding to the needs of business without question. In addition to cultural differences, they may have different goals from workforce development entities and may work at cross-purposes. For example, economic development efforts typically take a posture of reducing labour costs to attract and retain businesses. At the same time, lower labour costs may mean pursuing labour-saving strategies and opting for jobs with fewer worker benefits, and workforce development organisations strive to find workers jobs with decent pay and benefits. Obviously, a region's economic vitality is essential for a stable and healthy labour market, and *vice versa* .

An example of an economic development organisation that has successfully partnered with other local agencies is the Right Place Program in Grand Rapids, Michigan. It is a private, non-profit organisation focused on promoting economic growth in the urban core of a metropolitan area with a population of more than a million people. The Right Place provides the standard set of economic development services (*e.g.* information on industrial sites, tax abatements, statewide business incentives) and works closely with businesses to help them connect with the proper government agencies to receive the appropriate incentives and assistance. In addition, it has partnered with other organisations to offer several unique programmes. One such initiative, partnered with the City of Grand Rapids, is to redevelop abandoned industrial land in the inner city. Such a venture is risky, since companies looking to locate in an area are more attracted to undeveloped "greenspace" than to urban locations with uncertain payoffs.

The International Economic Development Council (IEDC), in collaboration with Georgia Tech University, recently conducted a survey of accredited economic development organisations (AEDOs) to assess their effectiveness, using a slightly expanded list of Baldrige criteria. In addition to the seven principles listed in Box 3.2, IEDC added partnerships and relationships. Each respondent self-assesses their organisation with a score between 0 and 5, with 5 the top rating. Results show that the highest-rated category is customer and market focus, receiving an average score of 4.4. The partnerships and relationships category tied for second (with the results category) with an average score of 4.3. Leadership and performance tracking systems are the two lowest-scored categories, receiving 3.9 and 3.3, respectively (Georgia Tech Enterprise Innovation Institute, 2006).

Within the partnership and relationship category, the top responses were related to the active involvement of board members in other community groups (4.6), the economic development organisation's effective relationship with local government which could include WIBs (4.6), and its effective relationship with state/regional partners (4.6). Its three lowest-ranked categories were its collaboration with other community-based organisations (4.1), its ability to expand resources through relationships (4.0), and its effective collaboration with other economic development organisations (3.9).

Requisites for effective partnerships

Observations of partnerships among workforce development, economic development and educational institutions point to several important lessons and challenges. These insights are listed according to the relevant Baldrige criteria.

Leadership

The first requirement for effective partnerships is strong leadership. Leaders must define the common purpose of the partnership and educate partners on the importance of cutting across the various boundaries that may separate their efforts. The benefit of turning disconnected specialised organisations into cross-functional teams is to create a system that serves workers and businesses holistically, cost-effectively, and creatively. It adds value that exceeds the capacity of each partner working alone.

Strong leadership is also required to mobilise resources within the community and within the partnering organisations in order to achieve the desired outcomes. Simply following formal procedures or interventions that have been adopted in other areas or that have been prescribed by higher levels of authority may not be sufficient for an effective delivery of services. It may take the abilities of a leader to motivate workers and other partnering organisations to make it all work. The need for strong leadership is particularly important for informal partnerships, in which the relationship is not based on a contract arrangement or a memorandum of understanding, but solely on the shared vision between the organisations.

Partnering organisations must also be advocates for their causes, such as workforce development agencies for workers and economic development agencies for businesses. This advocacy must be ongoing. Implementing a programme or set of programmes, which at the time are shown to be effective in serving the needs of workers, does not guarantee that the programme will continue to achieve the same desired outcomes in the same cost-effective manner. The circumstances of workers, the demand for their skills, and general economic conditions affecting the demand for workers with various qualifications all change over time. Unlike the case with businesses, there is no ongoing market test to indicate the benefit-to-cost ratio of these social programmes.

Leaders of partnering organisations should also be "cheerleaders" for one another, encouraging their organisation to pursue sound procedures and to adhere to rigorous performance goals. Each must recognise that the success of their partners enhances their own performance. With each organisation monitoring the performance of the other partners, a system of mutual accountability can be achieved, in which no central organisation would act as "principal", but rather a community of organisations that hold each other accountable for their actions and progress.

Shared vision of customers and their needs

Partnerships need to establish a shared vision of the customers they serve and the reason for serving them. Since each member may come to the alliance with a different customer base and purpose, it may be difficult to reach agreement on a shared set of objectives. For instance, even though workforce development and economic development organisations share a common vision of job creation and economic growth, their objectives may differ. Finding and retaining a job is a well accepted and desired outcome of employment policy. Yet, the dual objectives become less absolute when one adds to the outcome metric the goal of achieving relatively high wages. Economic principles dictate that the pursuit of high wages can compromise the goal of gaining employment for broad groups of workers. High wages may also discourage businesses from remaining in the area and new businesses from coming into a region. However, adding education to the partnership and setting as a goal the pursuit of a highly qualified workforce may help to harmonise the goals of these three entities.

Strategic planning and analysis

Once a shared vision has been established, local partnering organisations need to become problem-solvers. The first step in this process is to conduct research regarding the needs of the customers and the circumstances that account for such needs. This analysis should be based on accurate and objective information, and the research should be conducted in a rigorous and systematic manner. The next step is to use the information obtained to design a plan that serves the customers. The plan needs input and then endorsement from all parties in the partnership. It also needs explicit steps that attract, satisfy and retain partnering organisations. Proper metrics should be identified to track the progress of the initiatives; these include information on how customers are progressing in meeting their identified needs, and on the cohesion and effectiveness of the partnerships.

Human resource focus

Effective problem solving and advocacy requires an engaged and motivated set of stakeholders. These stakeholders – regardless of whether they represent business, social organisations, labour groups, or educational institutions – must be given sufficient authority to make "real" decisions. If decision making is only ritualistic and has little significant bearing on the type of services and the manner of delivering them, then the value of these partnerships are drastically diminished and the partnership is in danger of disintegrating. For example, Workforce Investment Boards risk losing qualified business leaders that assume active roles as members of boards unless the boards consider their input to be integral to the decision-making process. The same is true for the boards of non-profit organisations that partner in these efforts.

Process management

To be effective partners, organisations must also have competent staff who understand how the organisation fits within the goals and objectives of the partnership and then carry out their responsibility in that partnership. It is increasingly difficult to attract qualified workers as funding from the federal and state governments is cut and local organisations depend more and more on volunteers and part-time workers. Staff must therefore be trained not only in providing the services their particular organisation specialises in, but also in understanding how to be meaningful participants in a partnership arrangement. The "academy" established by the Minnesota Department of Employment and Economic Development to train state employees to provide better assistance to targeted industries is one example of a formal approach to educating staff to be better partners.

Information and ongoing analysis

Information is the glue that helps bond partnerships. Once obtained and validated, this information must be shared across partnering organisations, which means that these organisations must speak the same language in terms of purpose and performance outcomes, and must trust their partners in accepting their information to be accurate and their experience relevant. Establishing a common basis for defining purpose and objectives is not always easy, since different organisations may focus on different aspects of the challenges facing an individual who is pursuing employment options. Therefore, partnerships must continuously monitor the wellbeing of their respective constituents to assure that the programmes are meeting their needs. The monitoring should include rigorous and independent evaluations. There is a tendency for some service delivery organisations and even advocacy groups to get caught up in their own self-promotion, blindly accepting that the programme is effective without actually evaluating its merits.

Conclusion

Partnerships are constantly evolving as they try to position themselves to meet the changing needs of businesses and workers in order to generate or retain jobs for their constituents. Although there are few rigorous evaluations of the effectiveness of partnerships *per se*, it is widely accepted that bringing together key stakeholders and leveraging resources can be powerful catalysts for improved performance of local workforce development and economic development organisations, which in turn promotes local economic development.

Several lessons for successful partnerships have been gleaned from case studies of workforce development, economic development and educational institutions within the United States. The more pertinent ones for promoting economic development are: 1) business and workers, as customers, should be the common focus; 2) outcomes must be agreed upon, quantified, and tracked, 3) local organisations must become entrepreneurial and problem solvers, and form strong networks among the stakeholders; and 4) strong leadership is required to help define and advocate the common purpose and to mobilise community resources.

Achieving effective partnerships is a long, transformational journey. It involves increasing the ability to commingle individual funding sources, reducing programme restrictions, overcoming turf issues, collapsing hierarchies in order to empower those making decisions and providing the services, and providing continual feedback on the effectiveness of efforts. The reward for successful partnerships and the integration of the three functions of workforce development, economic development, and education is developing a workforce that is better prepared to meet the needs of local businesses and workers, and thus to meet the challenges of an increasingly competitive global economy that all local economies face.

Notes

1. The description of MOWD that follows is based upon a site visit by an OECD study tour that examined training programmes to upgrade the skills of low-qualified workers. This description appears in Eberts, 2006.

2. Statistics taken from a prepared statement by Jackie Edens, Commissioner of the Mayor's Office of Workforce Development, and transmitted to members of the Chicago City Council, 27 October 2003.

Bibliography

Baldrige National Quality Program (2001), "Criteria for Performance Excellence", US Department of Commerce, Washington, DC.

Barnow, Burt S. and Christopher T. King (2005), *The Workforce Investment Act in Eight States*, US Department of Labor Employment and Training Administration Occasional Paper 2005-01, Washington, DC, February.

Bauer, Paul W., Mark E. Schweitzer and Scott Shane (2006), "State Growth Empirics: The Long-run Determinants of State Income Growth", Federal Reserve Bank of Cleveland Working Paper 0606, May.

BPA (Berkeley Policy Associates) (2002), "Evaluation of the Regional Workforce Preparation and Economic Development Act: Final Report", June.

Briggs, Xavier de Souza (2001), "The Will and the Way: Local Partnerships, Political Strategy, and the Well-Being of America's Children and Youth", Working Paper, John F. Kennedy School of Government, Harvard University, November.

Eberts, Randall W. and George A. Erickcek (2001), "The Role of Partnerships in Economic Development and Labour Markets in the United States", *Local Partnerships for Better Governance*, OECD, Paris.

Eberts, Randall W. (2006), "Sectoral Initiatives to Train Low-qualified Incumbent Workers in the United States: Two Case Studies", *Skills Upgrading: New Policy Perspective*, OECD, Paris.

Georgia Tech Enterprise Innovation Institute (2006), "Benchmarking Survey of AEDOs" (Accredited Economic Development Organizations), Atlanta, GA.

Giloth, Robert (2004), *Workforce Intermediaries for the Twenty-first Century* (ed.), Temple University Press, Philadelphia.

Grubb, W. Norton (1996), *Working in the Middle: Strengthening Education and Training for the Mid-Skilled Labor Force,* Jossey-Bass Publishers, San Francisco.

Javar, Janet and Stephen Wandner (2004), "The Use of Service Providers and Brokers/Consultants in Employment and Training Programs" in Christopher O'Leary, Robert Straits and Stephen Wandner (eds.), *Job Training Policy in the United States,* W.E. Upjohn Institute for Employment Research, Kalamazoo, MI.

Kanter, Rossabeth Moss (1994), "Collaborative Advantage: The Art of Alliances", *Harvard Business Review*, July, pp. 1-13.

Macro, Bronwen, Sherry Almandsmith and Megan Hague (2003), *Creating Partnerships for Workforce Investment: How Services are Provided under WIA*, Berkeley Policy Associates, Oakland, CA.

Marano, C. and K. Tarr (2004), "The Workforce Intermediary: Profiling the Field of Practice and Its Challenges" in R. Giloth (ed.), *Workforce Intermediaries for the 21st Century*, Temple University Press, Philadelphia, pp. 93-123.

NGA (National Governors Association) (2004), "The Next Generation of Workforce Development Project: A Six-State Policy Academy to Enhance Connections Between Workforce and Economic Development Policy", Final Project Report, Washington, DC, December.

National Governors Association Center for Best Practices (2006), "State Sector Strategies: Regional Solutions to Worker and Employer Needs", Washington, DC, November.

ISBN 978-92-64-04327-5
More than Just Jobs:
Workforce Development in a Skills-Based Economy
© OECD 2008

PART II

Chapter 4

France: Bridging Regional Training and Local Employment

by

Xavier Greffe

In France, as in many other countries, devolution of labour market policy and training has been a continuous trend. During the past 20 years, statutory decisions and financing regulations intervened to give greater weight to the interventions of regional and local actors and to increase their level of responsibility in training and employment. But the French experience differs from that in other countries on a very specific point: the devolution of training policies there did not coincide with devolution of employment and labour market policies. The levels of responsibility do not correspond, since the former was organised on a regional level and the latter on a departmental or municipal level. The advantage of these differences is that the regional perspective widens the local prospects so as not to define in too narrow a way the needs for training of the workers – thus supporting their chances of later adaptation and mobility. Disadvantages include a top-heavy administration with overlapping and rather high organisational costs.

Introduction

Regional development and local employment development hold an increasingly important place in France. During the last 20 years, statutory decisions and financing regulations have intervened to give greater weight to the interventions of the regional and local actors and have even extended the scope of their responsibility in development and employment. The context has been one of ongoing decentralisation, much more in training than in employment (Greffe, 2005). In France, employment was always considered as a national issue, and employment policy was always considered a fundamental responsibility of the central authorities (Lothiois, 1996, IGTAS, 2002). Many experiments or initiatives collided with two facts:

- In France, the field of employment policy is mainly focused on the issue of international competitiveness, which has to be managed by the central state.

- In France, equality for all means that the rights have to be the same, whatever the territory or sector of the economy, which implies a centralised employment policy.

And yet, the relevance of the regional and local social environment has been progressively recognised (Greffe, 2004a):

- In a first phase the regional and local dimension were acknowledged but not given an essential role in the determination of employment policies. Local actors too were recognised, but not given a role in the decision process. Specific institutions were then organised and relevant employment territories defined statistically.

- In a second phase, extending from 1995 until now, the central state accords institutional and decision-making place both to regional and local actors. However, it does so in line with the principle of equitable employment policies. Central government has accepted the idea that local flexibility may be an opportunity to fight against unemployment, whereas traditionally flexibility was considered a threat to equal social treatment of unemployed people (Abens, 1999; DARES, 1995).

The result of this evolution is interesting from a strictly internal point of view. It is also significant for other experiments in terms of the institutional design of employment policies. In France, the devolution of the training policies did not correspond to the devolution of the employment and labour market policies. The levels of responsibilities do not correspond, since the former was organised on a regional level whereas the latter was organised on a departmental or municipal level, *i.e.* lower than regional. It is interesting to know why this choice, which does not appear coherent at the first glance, was made, and the advantages and costs.

The choice of different levels is explained thusly: training policies should not confine the workers within geographical or temporal horizons that are too narrow, slowing down their mobility. Then it is necessary to define training references, scopes and schemes in such a way that they address long-term prospects even if they must also answer constraints of the short term, *i.e.* adapt to needs that are immediate and locally specific.

The advantage of these differences is that the regional perspective necessarily widens the local prospects so as not to define in too narrow a way the needs for training of the workers – thus supporting their chances of later adaptation and mobility. Disadvantages include top-heavy administration with overlapping and rather high organisational costs (*idem*).

Regional mobilisation: The need for strategic management of the regions

Economic development does not occur at the same speed throughout the territory. This phenomenon is not new, but it has taken on a dramatic dimension during the past years.

The central government has long considered that unequal regional development could be eliminated through centralised voluntary actions. The corresponding policies relied on three instruments:

- Investment in heavy infrastructure and equipment such as motorways and high-speed trains that reduced the cost of transportation and did away with remoteness.
- Delocalisation of public companies and offices in order to create new growth poles (Renault, Electricité de France).
- Finance of local development through tax exemptions on a territorial basis.

These centralised policies have not been very efficient. After some years, their effects vanished. Inequality, in terms of both quality of life (Table 4.1) and rate of unemployment (Table 4.2), remained.

In the early 1980s, the central government recognised these failures and devolved new competencies to make the regions more active and so likely candidates for economic development. Regions had to organise both development schemes and training schemes. At that time the schemes were underpinned by a very traditional vision of growth, and it was easier for political bodies to invest in collective physical infrastructures. Progressively a more relevant view was adopted, recognising the endogenous character of growth and the role of intangible growth factors such as knowledge and organisation.

Table 4.1. **Regional gross product, 2002**

	RGP Millions of euros	RGP per inhabitant Euros	RGP per job Euros
Alsace	44 268	24 804	61 102
Aquitaine	66 717	22 475	56 926
Auvergne	27 586	21 011	52 520
Bourgogne	36 418	22 511	56 534
Bretagne	63 485	21 402	53 230
Centre	54 965	22 192	55 404
Champagne-Ardenne	30 839	22 926	57 643
Corse	5 052	19 133	52 484
Franche-Comté	24 727	21 897	54 510
Ile-de-France	430 183	38 739	79 453
Languedoc-Roussillon	46 121	19 416	55 761
Limousin	14 659	20 592	51 145
Lorraine	47 071	20 297	55 240
Midi-Pyrénées	57 577	22 025	54 565
Nord-Pas-de-Calais	79 931	19 835	55 355
Basse-Normandie	29 666	20 599	52 739
Haute-Normandie	41 479	23 013	59 402
Pays de la Loire	73 715	22 300	53 578
Picardie	37 482	19 932	55 791
Poitou-Charentes	33 887	20 325	52 127
Provence-Alpes-Côte d'Azur	105 826	22 901	61 051
Rhône-Alpes	145 427	25 153	60 426
Territories and departments abroad	22 891	13 375	45 882
Total	1 520 804	24 837	61 292

Source: INSEE, National Accounts, 2004.

Concentration and agglomeration of economic activities are now considered as having important positive characteristics for development in a global economy. Moreover, it seems that a country or a region that does not benefit from the presence of a metropolis faces difficulties in both capturing new ideas and exporting new products. Naturally, these concentration, agglomeration and metropolisation effects will be the results of the capacity of a territory to define and capture comparative advantages.

Therefore, the strategic planning of competitive comparative advantages has become a main factor of success for regions, which now have to define their strategies for economic development in an open and highly competitive context. In order to be competitive, these regions have to:

● Support the creation and sustainability of new enterprises.

● Allocate the regional collective goods that will be necessary for their development, beginning with good research and training systems.

● Regulate any fiscal competition between the municipalities.

Table 4.2. **Rate of unemployment per region**

Area	Unemployment rate, percentage
France	9.9
Alsace	8.3
Aquitaine	9.8
Auvergne	8.5
Bourgogne	8.5
Bretagne	8.0
Centre	8.6
Champagne-Ardenne	10.2
Corse	10.0
Franche-Comté	8.8
Ile-de-France	10.0
Languedoc-Roussillon	13.6
Limousin	7.6
Lorraine	9.6
Midi-Pyrénées	9.6
Nord-Pas-de-Calais	12.9
Basse-Normandie	9.2
Haute-Normandie	10.7
Pays de la Loire	8.2
Picardie	10.7
Poitou-Charentes	9.2
Provence-Alpes-Côte d'Azur	11.7
Rhône-Alpes	8.8

Source: INSEE, National Accounts, end-2004.

When these conditions are satisfied, it is possible to create competition between regions by organising and exploiting old and new competitive advantages. Strategic planning is a key component in managing the human capital of businesses and communities, and a critical engine in their drive toward progress. At this time, managers of big firms are used to competitive analysis but SMEs and public managers are not. Better use of the most up-to-date planning and information tools for defining adequate policies will provide a valuable advantage when it comes to designing efficient public policies in a world where the part played by immaterial inputs in development is growing.

Strategic and competitive analysis tools for regional development are used in diverse ways in the different French regions. Some regions are already deemed advanced while others lag far behind.

Different studies have been carried out during the past ten years in order to ascertain these different regional situations and needs. In a recent one, eight main factors have been screened: GNP per inhabitant (1); share of private research in the national product (2); share of public research in the national product (3); percentage of the population highly qualified (4); percentage of the population without any qualification (5); percentage of the population employed in highly technical manufacturing activities (6); number of patents per inhabitant (7); rate of unemployment (8) (ADIT, 2005).

A factor analysis shows the difference between the French regions (Tables 4.3 and 4.4).

Table 4.3. **Definition of the axes**

	Axis 1 (+41.7%)		Axis 2 (+23.2%)	
Positive contributions	Patents:	+21%	Public research:	+31%
	Private research:	+20%	Tertiary education:	+25%
	GDP per inhabitant:	+14%	Unemployment:	+18%
	High tech. employment:	+12%	Private research:	+1%
Negative contributions	Lower education:	−14%	Lower education:	−14%
	Unemployment:	−6%	High tech. employment:	−8%
			GDP per inhabitant:	−1%

Source: Agence pour la diffusion de l'information technologique (2005), *Regional Scientific Management in Europe*, Paris, p. 23.

Table 4.4. **Table of correlation**

	2	3	6	4	8	1	7	5
Private research	1.00							
Public research	0.20	1.00						
High employment	0.51	−0.32	1.00					
High qualification	0.18	0.44	−0.31	1.00				
Unemployment	−0.19	0.49	−0.22	0.26	1.00			
GNP	0.14	−0.11	0.34	0.02	−0.51	1.00		
Patents	0.63	0.06	0.49	0.14	−0.29	0.56	1.00	
Low qualification	−0.56	60.42	−0.07	−0.54	0.03	−0.15	−0.50	1.00

Source: Agence pour la diffusion de l'information technologique (2005), *Regional Scientific Management in Europe*, Paris, p. 28.

Four types of regions are identified (*idem*) (Figure 4.1).

● Type I regions: These benefit from a high standard of living, numerous patents per inhabitant and an important share of private research expenditures. Examples include Ile-de-France (IdF) and Rhône-Alpes (RA).

● Type II regions: These are characterised by an important share of public research expenditures, a well-trained population and a significant level of unemployment. Examples include Midi-Pyrénées (MP).

● Type III regions: These are characterised by a lower standard of living, low job qualification and a high rate of unemployment. Examples include Nord-Pas-de-Calais (NPC).

Figure 4.1. **Results of the factor analysis**

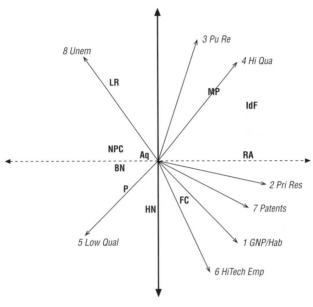

Source: Agence pour la Diffusion de l'Information Technologique (2005), *Regional Scientific Management in Europe*, Paris, p. 32.

- Type IV regions: These have both a high rate of activity in advanced industries and a low-qualified population. Examples include Franche-Comté (FC).

Closer examination reveals a strong dispersion, with two homogeneous groups: one group of leaders (Ile-de-France, Rhône-Alpes and Midi-Pyrénées) and one group of performing regions that nonetheless have high unemployment (Centre, Alsace, Franche-Comté).

Given the results of this statistical analysis and the lessons of the new economic geography, a number of instruments for growth can be identified:

- Training policies, in order to benefit from the relevant level of qualification.

- The development of new clusters localised in high-technology industries.

- Long-term or robust industrial strategies, to guarantee the availability of funds over many years.

- Equilibrium between transversal and sectoral strategies, in order to better disseminate the expected external effects of growth.

- A strategic marketing.

- Governance adapted to the nature of the regional social capital.

Local mobilisation: The need for a local governance of the labour market

During the past two decades the governance of labour policies has become more and more decentralised. Starting from a system where the decisions were taken by representatives of central government, we are now in a situation where very intensive local partnerships – involving public employees, local authorities and social partners – are really defining and implementing labour policy objectives. The general framework is still defined at the central level. But specification and adaptation of this general framework at the local level are now well recognised principles (Simonin, 2001; Vernaudon, 1997).

In the French economy there are many justifications for focusing specifically on local conditions for employment (Greffe, 2004b). One has to do with the multifaceted nature of employment problems. Today, many such problems involve much more than a mismatch between supply and demand, even if that is how they appear. The demand for employment is increasingly seen as predetermined by aspects involving training, housing or mobility, health care, minimum wage constraints, etc. These factors can in fact be identified and managed only in a precise manner and in proximity to the people involved, meaning that initiatives must be planned, carried out and co-ordinated at the local level. The supply of employment is, in most cases, only potential; it materialises only if other problems are solved – *i.e.* obtaining land or a loan, acknowledgement of intellectual property rights, etc. Problems of adjustment and co-ordination between these various dimensions must therefore be resolved if the supply of employment is actually to materialise – problems that to a large extent can only be solved locally. Fifteen years ago, some specific institutions were created, the Specific Agencies for Young People (*Missions locales pour l'emploi des jeunes*) for solving this specific problem. Now the *Maisons de l'emploi* – crossroads of training and trades – illustrates the need to supplement information with personalised advice, with respect to employers and jobseekers alike.

A second justification today stems from another characteristic of the French labour market. The duration of jobs is ever shorter, entailing increasingly frequent adjustments as evidenced by the predominance of fixed-term contracts, temporary employment, transitional jobs in the case of training leave arising from job rotations, etc. This employment "volatility" prompts labour market agents to seek the most direct channels of information and training, which renders local labour market organisation tremendously important. This organisation deals with not only information and transparency – challenges that to a great extent can be met thanks to the new information technologies – but the likely prospects of the choices to be made, both by jobseekers and by potential employers. The situation is even pushed to extremes in the case of adhocratic labour markets, *i.e.* markets in which employment lasts only as long as the single project for which a person is hired (ministère du Travail et de l'Emploi, 2002). Such is the case, for example, with artistic markets in which artists are recruited for a given product and the production structure is created for a single product only – another product entailing another structure and other employment contracts. In this specific context, buyers and sellers are prompted to come closer together and even to live in the same geographical space – hence the expression "cultural district" (OECD, 2005).

A third reason stems from the desire to make French employment policies active. At the national level, a distinction is traditionally made between so-called "passive" and "active" measures. Passive measures deal essentially with the labour market environment and with mechanisms to compensate for lost income. Active measures seek to make a more direct impact on the behaviour of market agents and thus to restore a greater reactive capacity. There are two prerequisites for the institution of such measures: their provisions must be diversified in line with the actual circumstances of a market, an industry or a company; and the groups that the measures are to target must be identified. In either case, active measures require a local approach – even if some of their principles must obviously still be laid down centrally, if only to justify budgetary choices and assess effectiveness.

A final reason is tied in with the particularities of certain territories. Here, islands or mountainous areas are generally cited as examples, because the severity of their problems precludes reliance on spontaneous labour market mechanisms, or on policies formulated far afield that do not take local particularities into account.

The efficacy of this local approach: the lessons of the Territorial Employment Pacts (TEPs)

In order to demonstrate the interest of a decentralised approach in employment policy, we may consider the lessons illustrated by analysis of the French Territorial Employment Pacts (Greffe, 2002). These were an instrument for organising co-ordination between vertical and horizontal partnerships at the local level. In fact, some partnerships were more vertically oriented, reflecting the traditional management of employment policies. Other partnerships were more horizontally oriented, underlying the new approach. These partnerships differed also according to the nature of the tools or instruments mobilised, as categorised below: Direct creation of jobs through the development of proximity services; direct creation of jobs through the creation of new enterprises; materialisation of jobs through a better match between demand and supply of labour.

A sample had been selected that included four representative TEPs (Albertville, Hérault-Montpellier, Saint-Herblain and Pays de Valois) (*idem*). Their employment efficacy was measured through three categories:

I: Direct creation of jobs through the development of proximity services.

II: Direct creation of jobs through the creation of new enterprises.

III: Materialisation of jobs through a better match between demand and supply of labour and creation of full-time jobs by employers' groups (*groupements d'employeurs*).

The findings are significant (Table 4.5):

- The results are very low for Montpellier-Hérault, which was a much bigger area. The relative effect in terms of jobs is approximately the same. This is to be expected, as the relative effect of a TEP will decrease with the size of the population.

- The effect pattern of the two TEPs supported by a local partnership (Albertville, Saint-Herblain) is both similar and very different from that of the two TEPs supported by local authorities (respectively, Montpellier-Hérault and Pays de Valois). The difference lies mainly in the relative importance of traditional employment actions.

- The distribution between active (I + II) and passive (III) labour market policy instruments is related to the nature of the industrial structure of the TEP: Albertville and Saint-Herblain are more actively policy-oriented than the two TEPs organised and steered by administrative structures (Montpellier-Hérault and Pays de Valois).

- In terms of development, which is mainly represented by the relative share of II, the two TEPs based on a more open partnership structure are more efficient, becoming so since they began promoting actions that are more promising in development terms than traditional actions.

The local employment development policy framework changed at the end of the Pact, since many more actions were undertaken after taking into consideration the four processes underlying the TEP. The partnership was

Table 4.5. **French TEPs' employment impacts**

	Number of jobs	I	II	III
Albertville	400 (0.04%)	140 (35%)	120 (30%)	140 (35%)
Montpel.-Hérault	1 042 (0.015%)	179 (17.1%)	162 (15.5%)	701 (77.4%)
Saint-Herblain	395 (0.05%)	138 (34.9%)	173 (43.7%)	84 (21.2%)
Pays de Valois	234 (0.04%)	10 (4.2%)	60 (25.8%)	164 (70%)

Source: Greffe, X. (2002), "L'évaluation des pactes territoriaux pour l'emploi: Le cas de la France", Rapport général sur l'évaluation des pactes territoriaux pour l'emploi, Bruxelles, Union européenne, Direction générale de l'Emploi, p. 80.

unanimously considered a good opportunity. We can say that in a sense, a new employment culture has been created by the TEP. But this is probably much more true in the case of the larger TEPs than in the case of the smaller ones, which have not experienced this change (Greffe, 2002; Barbier et Sylla, 2001).

Bridging regional development and local employment: The issue of training

Regional development does not automatically generate employment at the local level, for three reasons. First, some forms of regional development may be very capital-intensive and create more activities than jobs. Second, it is sometimes possible to create local employment without regional development by satisfying certain new needs. But these are short-term views. In the long run it is impossible to stabilise local employment without an influx of new jobs and incomes; regional development will appear through the creation of diverse enterprises and jobs. Finally, the lack of qualification can prevent the transformation of regional incentives into job creation. This is why training has become a main lever of regional development strategies (Greffe, 2001).

When new regional investments are considered for a certain territory, availability of specific skills acts as a positive determining factor. In areas deprived of educational and training resources, this lack impedes such investments; a local dynamic is needed in order to fit the arrival of new investments and the creation of new skills. Moreover, people are better suited to partake in a Knowledge Society economy if they possess the corresponding skills and abilities.

Training is no longer a phase or privilege occurring at a given point in a person's life but a permanent element in a person's life cycle. The idea of equal opportunity, long restricted to basic formal education (and considered justification for a centralised approach) is now enlarged to include continuous training systems.

In France, three specific factors have created an incentive to substitute regional for national management of training policies (idem).

- The local SMEs face many difficulties in attempting to adapt themselves to the Knowledge Society. Training is not their major concern and their needs are, at best, expressed in connection with other needs deemed to be more urgent. SMEs are frequently too short of funds and time to take this need into consideration. Their "training" environment thus has to be redefined.

- These difficulties also exist on the worker's side. In deprived areas, investing in new training sounds the knell for the skills they have acquired, since their old skills formed the basis of a social fabric. Other factors act negatively: the training proposed is often lengthy, the associated costs are high and the risk of failure is immense.

- The traditional training supply may be inadequate for assuming such stakes. Many constraints conflict with the training institutions' own time frame. Too many resources are first of all mobilised to train the trainers. And finally, in the most deprived areas, training institutions no longer exist and opportunism rather than efficacy dominates the training market.

Furthermore, four conditions must be satisfied for training actions to be effective:

- Mapping and implementation of training must be carried out simultaneously.
- Training must be based on a project approach in order to teach trainees how to sustain or join in a project, i.e. to be self-reliant and innovative.
- The conducting of training requires a multidimensional approach, since the training problems of excluded persons are invariably linked to other living-condition problems.
- Regional and local trainers must exist, be available, and have their qualifications permanently updated in order to satisfy the need for training.

Such conditions call for a regional approach to training.

Centralised frameworks and processes very often have perverse effects due to their lack of precision in diagnosing problems, their systematic use of top-down organisation hindering adaptation, and the exclusion of specific SMEs and target groups whose needs cannot be analysed except at local level.

On the other hand, overly local approaches may be inefficient and prevent facility of mobility. Moreover, the cost of organising specific training for a very limited number of people could be onerous, and prevent the existence of economies of scale and scope.

This is why as early as 1983, the law defined the competency of the regions for planning and organising the delivery of qualification.

For ten years this policy was not very efficient since the national education system – that represented approximately 70% of the training potential – did not co-operate willingly with the regional councils. Now things have changed, and the regional councils are actually responsible for training, mobilising either public or private institutions.

This is why regions have competencies in terms of both economic development and training, whereas lower levels of local government share with the central government and regions responsibilities for organising the labour market.

New competencies and instruments at the regional level

Regional economic development schemes

As early as the mid-1980s, regions were asked by the central state to set forth regional economic development schemes (*Schémas de développement économique régionaux*), for a five- to eight-year period. Once these schemes were defined, there was an agreement between the central government and the regional council concerned for implementing the objectives (Secrétariat général aux Affaires régionales de la Région Poitou-Charentes, 2001). In 2004, a new law modernised the process.

The main features of that process are as follows (Greffe, 2005):

1. The aim of these regional development schemes is to establish a strategic economic basis in order to promote development, to create and/or attract new activities, and to prevent job destruction and delocalisation.

   These schemes are prepared and decided by the regional council or government after a wide consultation with the economic and social actors at the different levels of local governance (*départements, municipalités, bassins d'emploi*). However, whatever the domain, the regional council is considered to be the leader and will represent the local governments. A failure of the previous system lay in the fact that many local governments directly weaved links and agreements with the central government, which weakened the role of the regional council. The term "scheme" has been preferred to the term "project" in order to demonstrate that the final objective is more to create a new positive environment than to attain predefined quantitative objectives.

2. In order to define the scheme, the regions have to offer a cogent diagnosis of their own situation. In order to realise their objectives, regions use SWOT analysis (strengths, weaknesses, opportunities and threats) to some extent, but a self-diagnosis of governance implies involving a very great number of actors.

3. The scheme has to define "domains of strategic activities", i.e. domains where a region benefits from a capacity for action, considering the market, the competition and the quality of the actors. Some are vertical, such as clusters or branches; others are horizontal, such as communication networks and enterprise creation. Once these domains are identified, the scheme has to consider the relevant tools for defining their sustainable development.

4. During this process, regions can mobilise specific regional development agencies that have been created to organise permanent channels and platforms between business companies, civil society and local governments.

5. When the regional government adopts this scheme, it will in effect have a new competency: to allocate the financial support and instruments that the central government has defined in favour of the enterprises. This aspect is very important since it prevents discrepancies between the central and corresponding regional policies.

6. Finally, there may be an agreement between the regional and central governments to define the relative size of the financial effort that the two parties will provide. There are two reasons why central government has to fund some of the regional initiatives:

    • Some regional projects create positive external effects throughout the economy, and they may benefit other regions as well.

    • Some regions are financially too weak to implement the required projects. In France this last dimension is very important: it is recognised that the central government has to spend more resources in the poorest regions than in the richest ones. This may create a kind of moral hazard issue, but the concept of equality is always at the core of the French public management, whatever the level or the entity.

Poles of competitiveness

In 1998, The National Agency for Regional Development and Planning (DATAR) began a policy aimed at supporting clusters (or *systèmes productifs locaux*, SPL, as they were called) (DATAR, 1999). France did not have industrial districts, as Italy did. However, in France as elsewhere, local clustering of enterprises clearly generated reciprocal external benefits. Then some areas benefited from fuller local development. The enterprises intending to create a cluster had to build up a common structure; they could then benefit from some public tools and incentives. This policy had mixed results. On the one hand, one hundred SPL have been created; on the other, some of them have only been created to take advantage of this national programme. Today it appears that the most efficient SPL are those initiated by private companies that have not necessary benefited from these public supports. By contrast, the voluntary bodies created by the central authorities have not been very successful.

Nevertheless, this policy has been redefined in 2006 (Secrétariat général du Gouvernement, 2006). The main difference with the previous cluster policy lies in the importance given to the innovation process. Clustering is not enough; new links have to be created between companies, research centres, training institutions and other stakeholders. The creation of new activities producing real benefits is stressed. Sixty-seven projects of competitiveness poles have been selected out of an eligible hundred. They have to organise a follow-up committee and will benefit from financial support. Moreover, three specific programmes have been defined to create a positive environment: a financial fund for supporting venture capital; very high-speed connection networks; and a programme to put the real estate to best use. Finally, the enterprises that will locate new research projects into these areas will benefit from large fiscal expenditures. Some "super poles" have been defined, such as the pole of Cadarache in the south of France where the ITER project will be implemented (New Experimental Thermonuclear Process). These poles have scattered all over the territories but are mainly concentrated where important resources already exist in order to sustain their viability.

In defining and implementing these poles, central and regional government act as partners. At the start this was not a clear-cut matter because the central government was obliged to select some strategic poles that can only exist in one or two places, certainly not anywhere within the 22 regions. But progressively it became clear that the financial commitment to implement such poles had to be shared between the two levels of administration.

Regional training plans

In France, the policy of vocational training was gradually transferred to regions – at first for adults in 1983, then for young people in 1993. Regional governments establish multi-year programmes of training and produce a map of the specialisations supplied (Regional Training Scheme or *Schéma régional des formations*). These maps are rather flexible because diplomas of local interest can be created in connection with the needs of a local employment market for longer or very short periods, according to that market's evolving characteristics. Other texts have intervened to strengthen the competence of regions since, but some difficulties remained.

The policy of vocational training greatly depends on the training supply of the Department of Education, which is highly centralised. It was thus necessary to effectuate difficult transfers of competencies, and even today these transfers depend on solid co-operation between the Department of Education and the regional governments. Interaction among the other actors – training schools, apprenticeship centres, centres of adult training – takes place more easily.

The efficiency of these policies collides with a difficulty unanimously recognised: the separation of competencies relative to employment, training and inclusion. The employment competence, as already underlined, depends on the central government. The inclusion competence mainly depends on the municipalities. The training competence is thus separated from the employment and inclusion competences, and the dynamics of training may not correspond to the requirements of inclusion. This risk especially holds for the young people emerging from the secondary educational system.

Sharing of the financial cost of training is an issue as well. Very often the regions are obliged to mobilise the Department of Education institutions, and the latter then ask for a budget surpassing the cost of the specific training programme. This is a shortcut to receiving money that the central government does not want to give to its own institutions for financial reasons. It is a permanent issue, and some regions prefer to create their own training structures rather than to mobilise existing structures. The result is inevitably a waste of funds. But in the long run, better co-operation can be expected due to cultural changes initiated by the managers of such institutions.

Some regions have created their own system for observing and defining new qualifications. This too is costly and it may be better to have a more powerful instrument at the local level. In fact the central government has changed the management of some of its forecasting resources, such as the Research Centre on Qualification (*Centre d'études et de recherche sur les qualifications,* or CEREQ). These institutions now work in partnership with the regions, but that took around 15 years to happen – again, mainly because the required cultural change took that long.

New competences and instruments at the local level

In parallel with the increasing regionalisation, the tools used to increase the efficacy of the local labour market are progressively being transformed. Some initiatives are focused on the administrative organisation of the employment service, whereas others are creating new instruments for integrating the long-term unemployed.

The local public employment service (LPES)

The LPES, an instrument funded by central government, was organised to co-ordinate the actions of:

- the Local Office of the Ministry of Employment (*Direction départementale de l'emploi*, DDE);
- the Local Agency for Employment (*Agence locale pour l'emploi*, or ALE);
- and the Agency for the Vocational Training of Adults (AFPA).

The difficulties come from the fact that the levels of organisation of these three pillars are not the same, so they are never totally in phase. Besides, the internal delegations of power are not the same: they are stronger for the services of both agencies than for those of the state. Nevertheless, many efforts are being made to increase their effectiveness (ministère du Travail et de l'Emploi, 2002).

Today the LPES elaborates local diagnoses and local plans, and is in charge of synergising all the existing tools. The experience of the European

TEPs, where they existed, allowed for a better understanding of the partnerships required. This was notably the case in Saint-Herblain, where the TEP really played a major role and stimulated the establishment of the Local Action Plan for Employment (LAP) of the city of Nantes and then of the Loire-Atlantique *département*.

Municipal plans for inclusion

The core of this policy is the Local Plan for Inclusion (PLIE, *Plan local d'insertion par l'emploi*), called since the Law of 29th July 1998 Local Plan for Inclusion and Employment (*Plan local d'insertion et d'emploi*).

These action plans have to be elaborated on the initiative of the municipalities; they aim to put back into employment persons who had lost their jobs and accumulated health problems, professional/social handicaps, etc. The plans are generally established for a three-year duration and seek the support of partnerships and other local governments (*départements*, regions). Their objective is to manage within six months to place the person in a fixed-term labour contract (Ville de Grenoble, 2002; Ville de Roubaix, 2002).

The plans follow a set procedure. First, a municipality or grouping of municipalities establishes the location of districts or sites requiring action. This location is ascertained with the co-operation of the central government administration and the consultation of the local council for inclusion (*Comité départemental d'insertion*). This shared diagnosis paves the way for the project, and then a protocol is established associating the various partners. A pilot committee and a technical committee are set up. The financing comes from various contributions, national and local; that of the European Social Fund is in conformance with Objective 3. If the ESF participates, funds other than the ESF will have to represent at least 55%. There are two other constraints: a ceiling for the contribution of private companies of 10%; and a limitation of the running costs in percentage of the eligible expenditures (10%) (Centre d'études de l'emploi, 2002).

There are approximately 200 PLIE, and the average number of persons that they assist varies between 70 and 300. Between 1996 and 2000, 130 000 persons were concerned. The rate of return to employment is of the order of 60%.

New services and new jobs

Since 1990, first in an experimental and then statutory way, initiatives have been taken to connect on a large scale the satisfaction of new needs and job creation, notably for the benefit of young people. The year 1997 saw the launch of a very important programme, eventually named "New Services – Jobs for the Young People" (*Nouveaux services, emplois-jeunes*). Its objective was to create 700 000 jobs, half in the public or associative sector and half in the private sector. The device used was particularly interesting: the jobs were paid at the minimal wage, the national insurance contributions were taken care of by the state, and specific training had to be set up so that at the end of five years the possibility of durable inclusion is actually realised. In fact and from the beginning, the for-profit private sector did not agree to participate. But the other part of the programme worked well and the announced objectives were effectively reached (350 000 jobs were created). At the end of the five years, two-thirds of the young people found permanent jobs. The government took measures to pursue the programme, although these measures will probably be less favourable than they were in the past (Greffe, 2005).

Here we cannot speak strictly in terms of local employment, since it is a centralised system. But the majority of the jobs created related to proximity services and were created by local partnerships and governments or associations that intended to respond to local needs. So this programme became a "local" programme. The Local Public Employment Office mobilises with local governments to diffuse the information, screen the new services and solve the implementation problems. The 2002 National Action Plan for Employment presented this programme in conformity with the momentum toward localising employment policies (ministère du Travail et de l'Emploi, 2002).

Clustering the employers around a job

Groupings of employers were created in 1985 and revised several times since. Their object is to allow the creation of a "real job", knowing that this job cannot lean on a single activity or a single type of employer. Various employers are therefore grouped in an association, which signs a contract with a worker who aggregates various quantities of activity and so benefits from full-time employment on an annual basis.

This need for employer grouping (*groupement d'employeurs*) can be explained in three ways (Greffe, 2004a).

- There are seasonal activities, and the passage from one to the other allows certain persons to benefit from a regular activity all year round. This type of grouping was thus especially useful in the field of the agriculture: today there are 2 700 such groupings with approximately 5 000 workers.

- Certain permanent activities are not of sufficient scope for an employer to create a full-time job. It may then be relevant to add these small quantities of work, and then to associate some of these employers.

- A third type of employer grouping appeared recent years: That for inclusion and qualification. These groupings organise pathways of inclusion involving work periods in different companies. Roughly 80 in number, they are gathered in a national association (the CBCE-GEIQ) and benefit from a subsidy of the order of 400 euros for every job so created. Some exist in the field of artistic activities: in Lyon, three theatrical companies joined in a GEIQ to recruit 20 artists. These young artists devote three-quarters of their time to their activity and one-quarter to training.

This policy is considered as a positive driver of local employment development because it mobilises local networks and needs to activate territorial bodies in place.

First results, main issues

These transformations have taken place over the past ten years. It is still difficult to arrive at a precise estimation of the benefits such reforms yield. Moreover, it is one thing to transform institutions and rules of the game, and another to transform the underlying cultural references of the public employees involved in such institutions. This section points to some of the difficulties now being faced.

1. A first difficulty relates to how the economic development process is perceived. Too often, analysis of the Knowledge Economy is formal and the local actors do not consider its implications. The equilibrium between tangible and non-tangible infrastructures is still biased in favour of the former.

2. A second difficulty arises in implementing training strategies; the sound partnerships needed for implementing these strategies are formed slowly. The training system's traditional actors, again, have a supply-driven orientation and find it difficult to take into consideration the demand of enterprises.

3. The third relates to the misuse of regional contracts, mainly due to the behaviour of the central government. Contracts between regions and the central government were presented as the most powerful support mechanism for the current efforts of the local governments (in partnership with the social partners) to maintain and create some jobs at the local level: "*The contract defines programmes of action on the scale of the region contributing to economic development.*" These programmes finance the engineering and implementation of actions that can find financing within the framework of national devices. They also finance the implementation of projects to develop the territory, the transfer of good practices, etc. The contract thus serves simultaneously as the framework for the project's development, as clarification of the actors' respective roles and as the financial plan. Nevertheless, the central state has modified the logic of such a system. It makes the region participate in disproportionate measure in the realisation of national objectives in exchange for its financing of regional objectives (Commissariat général du Plan, 1999).

4. The relevance of local employment policies is recognised. Yet, everything takes place as if the subject of local employment policies had acquired its legitimacy and as if the main actors were persuaded. While at first the local focus was considered the consequence of the multifaceted approach to unemployment, it is considered today as generating real added value for the identification and creation of new jobs. However, it does not create a strong dynamic and continues to arouse the scepticism of certain actors. Trade unions are still very reluctant to adopt this new approach.

5. The distribution of competencies is not conducive to good synergy between the actors. The central government remains responsible for employment; regional governments are responsible for initial and vocational training; local governments (*départements* and cities) are increasingly responsible for inclusion programmes. Thus allocation is not totally logical since it is difficult to unbundle employment, training and inclusion. Regions complained that they had not been consulted on some programmes of inclusion, such as TRACE, even when these programmes had a training dimension. An optimal allocation of competencies appears inconceivable. The current distribution generates complex situations, and increases costs.

6. There are very powerful mechanisms of re-centralisation. Policies of fiscal exemptions and subsidies imply strict controls on behalf of central government. At the level of information, the central government remains much attached to the unemployment rate indicator, the production of which it pilots and the readings of which it currently interprets.

7. There is always a certain tension between two views of the local dimension. One comes from the centre and mobilises local actors only to improve the efficacy of its interventions on the labour market. The other comes from the local base and supports local employment development.

   • In the first case, the intervention and the means are concentrated on precise target groups to favour both their qualification and their access to employment; in the second case, it is a question of dealing with an integrated view of local economic and social development.

   • In the first case, it is a question of the state operating a policy elaborated and piloted from the central level (downward logic); in the second, it is a question of the state taking into account projects to create activity that are carried by local actors (horizontal and ascending logic).

   • In the first case, the local area is perceived as the administrative space for application of a national policy; in the second the local area is perceived as the economic and social space of development.

8. A dominant part of employment and labour policies is based on equal rights for all. The rights to employment, work and replacement income are construed differently from one country to another. But wherever they are

affirmed, such as in France, decentralisation movements will be suspected of introducing variations in the effective enjoyment of such rights (and thus they will be limited). It is therefore not surprising that the devolution of powers has not been as great in the realm of training.

9. The term "local" must be used very carefully, as here there can be confusion between an employment approach that is conducive to decentralisation, and the geographical limits of local territories, which are necessarily restricted from an institutional standpoint. An employment approach necessarily seeks to enhance coherency between participants in the employment system, at a level that is as close as possible to the sources of their information and their projects. The local focus must be construed here as a method rather than an end in itself, because very few employment trends are shaped by territorial factors alone. While that may be the case for certain neighbourhood services, it would be better to consider it an exception rather than the rule. When speaking of local employment or local employment policy, the approach should be to stress the extent to which local factors shape employment problems and not the notion that jobs depend exclusively on decisions that are taken locally.

10. While evaluation is already complex at the national level, it is even more so at a decentralised level. When the effectiveness of the policies they implement is wanting, the local authorities (or local employment services) can always contend that such policies only influence the choices of labour market agents, and that the effects of those policies are filtered or even thwarted by economic trends, decisions taken with regard to other territories, or changes in people's behaviour.

Another difficulty is that of setting objectives. If the objectives of employment policies are set at the central level, no one contests the fact that the choices involved are those of the central authority, lest the debate be opened on the nature of the chosen objectives. Turning to the setting of the public employment service objectives, if it is decentralised, the problem becomes more complex: in addition to objectives received from the centre and related to the missions of the public service, there is a need for indicators related either to conditions specific to the territory in question, or to additional policies for that territory.

Conclusion

The experience of regionalisation and municipalisation makes clear the desire to bring development, training and employment governance more closely in line with contemporary economic development and labour market trends, and to make it more efficient from the standpoint of resource utilisation. To succeed, governance must enhance the strategic content, flexibility and accountability of development and employment policies deployed at the local level. Can it be said today that these movements have in fact succeeded?

First, regionalisation of training and municipalisation of social inclusion are supposed to enhance the strategic dimension of policies by incorporating a large number of agents representing diverse dimensions of development and employment issues. By doing so, they can lead to joint actions and create synergies in time and space between separate initiatives, thereby improving effectiveness and efficiency.

However, things are not always perceived that way in the field. There may appear to be a loss of means, a dilution of responsibility or – what is worse – the creation of jobs but not of sustainable employment, which does not correspond to the intended strategic goal. This raises a number of questions: does decentralisation succeed in persuading the agents to work with the local authorities? In particular, does it successfully bring economic agents into strategic initiatives? Does it have local information systems capable of yielding relevant assessments?

Second, regionalisation of training and municipalisation of inclusion are supposed to give policies the flexibility they lack when they are centralised, by enabling a sharper identification of needs, responses that are more relevant, and the participation of target groups in the implementation of initiatives for their benefit.

Here too, the reality has been different. It often takes a long time to set initiatives in place, and employment policies at the local level focus on the least difficult or least risky actions. This is reflected in a bias concerning the indicators used, with indicators of means tending to take precedence over indicators of results. As a result, several questions arise: is it effective to devolve powers? Can the resources allocated be used flexibly, which might run counter to auditing requirements or requirements for the allocation of public appropriations? Are local authorities prepared to run "the risk of flexibility", with all its implications? Do capture effects exist at the local level, on the part of certain employment system agents if not of the target groups?

Third, regionalisation of training and municipalisation of inclusion must be accompanied by a clarification of responsibilities in order to be effective and sustainable. Because new agents and new resources are harnessed, it is essential to clarify responsibilities in order to avoid a shortage of these in the future. Decentralisation places the responsibilities of local authorities centre stage without necessarily doing away with those of the central authorities, and it adds interfaces with numerous decision centres controlled by neither group.

In this situation three instruments appear essential if responsibilities are to be clarified:

- A clear statement of comprehensible and feasible objectives.

● Establishment of a system of indicators regarding these objectives.

● Implementation of agreements between the agents destined to become partners in such policies.

Insofar as this implementation is difficult and entails a gradual learning process, pragmatic initiatives, in which contracts can play a role, ought to be adopted. This requires a new culture on the part of local authorities and centralised authorities alike – one very different from the traditional cultures of public management: if regionalisation of training and municipalisation of inclusion are to make a difference, regional and local authorities must consider themselves here to be civic innovators, and the central authorities as support instruments.

Bibliography

Abens, J. (1999), "L'effort financier des collectivités locales dans la lutte contre le chômage et pour l'aide à l'emploi", Rapport à la DARES, ministère du Travail et de l'Emploi, Paris.

ADIT (Agence pour la diffusion de l'information technologique) (2005), *Regional Scientific Management in Europe*, Paris.

Barbier, J.-Cl. and N.D. Sylla (2001), "Stratégie européenne de l'emploi: Les représentations des acteurs en France", Rapport à la DARES, ministère du Travail et de l'Emploi, Paris.

Centre d'études de l'emploi (1983), "Colloque : Une stratégie locale pour l'emploi", ministère du Travail et de l'Emploi, Paris.

Centre d'études de l'emploi (2002), "La mise en œuvre du programme d'objectif 3 du FSE: Contribution aux réalisations et l'impact du programme en France", ministère du Travail et de l'Emploi, Paris.

Commissariat général du Plan (1999), "Rapport du groupe interministériel sur la définition des contrats de villes du XIIe plan", Paris.

DARES (1995), "L'implication des collectivités locales dans la lutte contre le chômage", premières synthèses, No. 77, ministère du Travail et de l'Emploi, Paris.

DATAR (Délégation à l'aménagement du territoire et à l'action régionale) (1999), "Les systèmes productifs locaux", Paris.

Greffe, X. (2001), "Devolution of Training: A Necessity for the Knowledge Economy", *Devolution and Globalisation: Implications for Local Decision Makers*, OECD Publications, Paris.

Greffe, X. (2002), "L'évaluation des Pactes territoriaux pour l'emploi dans le cas de la France", Rapport à la Commission européenne, DG Emploi, Brussels.

Greffe, X. (2003), "Decentralisation: What Differences does it Make? A Synthesis", *Managing Decentralisation: A New Role for Labour Market Policy*, OECD, Paris, pp. 31-64.

Greffe, X. (2004a), *Le développement local*, Éditions de l'Aube, Paris.

Greffe, X. (2004b), "National Policies for Local Development" in European Union (2004), *Horizontal Evaluation of Local Employment Development*, DG Employment, Brussels, pp. 59-89.

Greffe, X. (2005), *La Décentralisation*, La découverte, Paris.

IGTAS (Inspection générale du travail et des affaires sociales) (2002), *Politiques sociales de l'État et territoires*, ministère du Travail et des Affaires sociales, Paris.

Lorthiois, J. (1996), *Le diagnostic local de ressources*, ASDIC editions.

Ministère du Travail et de l'Emploi (2001), "Loi organique du 2 août 2001", Paris.

Ministère du Travail et de l'Emploi (2002), "Plan National d'Action pour l'Emploi", Paris.

OECD (2005), *Culture and Local Development*, OECD Publications, Paris.

Secrétariat général aux affaires régionales, région Poitou-Charentes (2001), "Rapport d'évaluation de l'objectif II pour l'année 2000", préfecture de la Vienne, Poitiers.

Secrétariat général aux affaires régionales, région Poitou-Charentes (2002), "Rapport d'évaluation de l'objectif II pour l'année 2001", préfecture de la Vienne, Poitiers.

Secrétariat général du gouvernement (2006), "Circulaire du 25 novembre 2006 relative à la mise en œuvre de la politique des pôles de compétitivité", Paris.

Simonin, B. (2001), "Politiques de l'emploi : La territorialisation en chantier", *Problèmes économiques*, No. 2706, pp. 10-3.

Vernaudon, D. (1997), "La territorialisation des politiques de l'emploi", Université de Paris XII.

Ville de Grenoble (2002), "Le projet d'agglomération et le programme Urban", mairie de Grenoble.

Ville de Roubaix (2002), "Le plan de développement économique et social", mairie de Roubaix.

ISBN 978-92-64-04327-5
More than Just Jobs:
Workforce Development in a Skills-Based Economy
© OECD 2008

PART II

Chapter 5

Germany: The Local Impact of Labour Market Reforms

by

Hugh Mosley and Petra Bouché

The recent reform of the public employment service has greatly expanded the role of the local authorities in providing comprehensive labour market services for unemployed welfare recipients. It does not, however, create a unified local job centre as initially envisioned, but in fact splits the delivery of employment services into two organisational units based on benefit entitlement rather than on their service needs. In addition, the focus of the reform is on the governance or mode of implementation of labour market programmes and not on innovation in programmes with a regional development focus. In this context, special intermediary organisations at regional level play a useful role in enhancing the institutional capacity to assist with the practical implementation of various programmes for promoting employment. The most important tasks these organisations have are to provide the actors of labour market policy with professional consulting services and to work at the state level to co-ordinate programmes and projects co-funded through the ESF.

Introduction

The recommendations of the Hartz Commission on "Modern Services in the Labour Market" in 2002 and the subsequent wave of reform have transformed the public employment service (PES) – its internal organisation, its management strategy, the portfolio of active measures and the unemployment benefit system.[1] It has also greatly expanded the role of the local authorities in providing comprehensive labour market services for unemployed welfare recipients. The labour market programmes of the German states also play an important role in the co-ordination of labour market and employment policies at the regional level.

The first section of this chapter briefly surveys the labour market situation in Germany; it is followed by a section that discusses the multi-level institutional framework of local employment policy in German federalism; the chapter then describes the new one-stop-shop "Jobcenter" approach to providing services for unemployed on social assistance adopted in the Hartz reforms; this is followed by a discussion of the role of the German states as regional co-ordinators of labour market policies, illustrated by a case study of consulting and mediation services in North Rhine-Westphalia, Germany's largest federal state. A summary and conclusion are presented in the final section.

The German economy and labour market

The Germany economy has had one of the lowest growth rates in the OECD area since the mid-1990s, and there has been a marked secular increase in unemployment levels over the past 30 years. The overall unemployment rate (8.4%) is high in comparison with the rate for the EU15 (7.4%), the United States (4.6%), Japan (4.1%), Korea (3.5%) and the average for OECD countries (6.0%).[2] There is, moreover, a high incidence of long-term unemployment, with over one-third of the figure unemployed for 12 or more months, and with large regional disparities between eastern and western Germany and within western Germany. Thus in June 2007 the unemployment rate in eastern Germany was 14.7%, in comparison with "only" 7.3% in western Germany.[3] Within western Germany there is a North/South divide between older industrial areas in the north and the more dynamic economies of southern Germany. While the unemployment rate exceeded 9% in Bremen, Hamburg and North-Rhine Westphalia in mid-2007, it was markedly lower in Bavaria

(4.8%) and Baden-Württemberg (5%). These regional disparities, especially between east and west, are the most acute labour market problem facing Germany today.

Unemployment rates by skill levels also diverge markedly: unskilled workers have a rate more than twice the general unemployment rate. However, unemployment rates are relatively high for skilled workers, even those highly educated. Germany's labour market problems are primarily a consequence of slow growth and lack of aggregate demand, and not of skill shortages.

There has been a relatively heavy reliance on labour market programmes as a buffer to absorb surplus labour in Germany. If this hidden unemployment is counted, German unemployment is actually 10-15% higher than the official statistics report. The most important programmes in western Germany are short-time work, subsidised employment and labour market training. The most dramatic use of labour market programmes to absorb labour surplus was in East Germany, in response to German unification, where special early retirement programmes also played an important role.

The institutional framework for economic development and labour market policy

Responsibility for local economic development and employment promotion in the German federal system is divided between the German states (*Bundesländer*) and the national government. The central government is primarily responsible for labour market policy – including the local implementation of labour market programmes through the national public employment service – whereas the 16 German state governments, together with some 450 local authorities (county and city governments), are responsible for local economic development. Typically, the local agencies for economic development (*Wirtschaftsförderungsgesellschaften*) are organised as public-private partnerships with representatives of the local business community and trade unions, and chaired by a leading local government official. Their focus is on the promotion of new businesses, advisory services to existing businesses, public relations, etc.[4]

Co-operation at the local level between the national public employment service and local economic development agencies is widespread but largely on an informal and *ad hoc* basis. PES training and employment programmes especially are a potential resource for regional economic development strategies. However, the client orientation of the PES programmes makes it difficult to link them with regional economic development. In that regard the PES has been most active in response to mass layoffs and plant closings (*e.g.* short-time work, transitional "employment companies" and other adjustment assistance), rather than in supporting existing industries and attracting new ones. Finally, the PES's status as an agency of the federal government does not foster close integration with local economic development.

The German state governments engage in a wide variety of activities to promote local employment and economic development – such as promotion of entrepreneurship, skills training in small and medium-sized companies, and training for young people. They are also responsible for education, including vocational schools and universities, which has important links to local economic development strategies. Moreover, they have developed special labour market programmes for target groups such as women, youth and the long-term unemployed that complement those of the national PES. These activities are financed from their own revenues as well as from the European Social Fund, which allocated *circa* EUR 5.6 billion for German federal and state programmes in the 2000-2006 period.

The German federal government addresses regional disparities in employment and living standards – especially the regional crisis in eastern Germany – in a number of important ways:

1. The programme "Improvement of the Regional Economy" is a principal tool for overcoming regional disparities; it creates favourable conditions for private investment by investing in infrastructure and in human capital in structurally weak regions (see Box 5.1). Since target regions are defined on the basis of employment, unemployment and income, most funding goes to regions in eastern Germany. In 2003 EUR 1.7 billion in subsidies is reported to have leveraged a total of EUR 8.8 billion in private investment. An additional EUR 500 million was invested in subsidies for infrastructure (Federal Ministry for Economics and Labour, 2004d, p. 41).[5]

2. Through interregional revenue transfers. A noteworthy feature of the German federal system for offsetting regional disparities is the "revenue equalisation system" (*Länder Finanzausgleich*), which provides for substantial transfers to financially weaker German states with the aim of providing the latter with approximately the average per capita revenue base of all German state governments. In 2004 about EUR 43.5 billion was transferred to the new German states through this programme.

3. Target 1 regions in eastern Germany receive most of the EUR 14.5 billion allocated by the European Structural Funds (especially the European Regional Fund) to Germany for the 2000 to 2006 period.

4. Diverse other federal government programmes – for example, PES active programmes and highway and rail transportation infrastructure investments – have disproportionately targeted support to the eastern region.

5. Special tax subsidies are available to promote business investments in eastern Germany.

> ### Box 5.1. **"Improvement of the Regional Economy" – programme activities**
>
> - Regional Management partnerships between all relevant stakeholders at the local level.
>
> - Promotion of business-related investments for research departments and labs.
>
> - Support of research- and technology-based businesses and investments of industry that strengthen the regional potential for innovation.
>
> - Promotion of consulting measures as well as applied research and development (R&D) for small and medium-sized enterprises, and training measures for their employees.
>
> - Promotion of industrial investments in vocational training centres of enterprises and in vocational training, further training and retraining facilities.
>
> - Promotion of R&D in innovative organisations with a potential for growth in disadvantaged regions.
>
> - The programme "Learning Regions – Promoting Networks" supported 74 networks with approximately EUR 116 million until 2006.

The public employment service

The public employment service (*Bundesagentur für Arbeit*, hereafter PES) is a quasi-independent administrative agency under the jurisdiction of the Federal Ministry for Labour and Social Affairs (BMAS). It is responsible both for the implementation of active employment programmes and for the administration of unemployment benefits. The ministry appoints its managing director after consultation with the agency's tripartite advisory council *(Verwaltungsrat)*. The PES is organised into ten regional directorates and 180 local PES district agencies. These agencies are to a great extent autonomous, within the budgetary and legal framework established by the national employment service and social security law.

In contrast to trends in a number of other, larger OECD countries that have adopted decentralised strategies for implementing employment programmes (*e.g.* the United States, Canada, Italy, Spain), the German PES remains a relatively centralised, national organisation. Since 1998 it has, however, undergone a major transformation influenced by new public management models – especially that of management by objectives – that gives greater flexibility to local PES offices within the framework of nationally set performance targets.

The first step in this decentralising reform was to merge line item budgets for active measures into a single budget: the so-called "reintegration budget". While the local PES districts are still obliged to offer all types of measures, they are free to determine the mixture of these measures. Up to 10% of the reintegration budget can now be allocated to innovative measures, *i.e.* measures not defined in the standard portfolio. On the face of it, the reforms represent a considerable step forward in terms of managerial decentralisation.

"Hartz" reforms

In 2003 and 2004 an even more fundamental series of PES reforms were adopted. The Hartz reforms were based on proposals put forward by the 2002 Commission on Labour Market Reform chaired by Peter Hartz, the personnel chief at Volkswagen, Europe's largest automobile firm.

The major elements of this modernisation strategy in placement services, which represents a belated adoption of approaches already widespread in other OECD countries, are:

- An emphasis on activating the unemployed.
- Profiling and segmentation of services by client groups.
- Emphasis on improvement of services to employers and job-matching.
- Increased reliance on outside provision of placement services.
- Merger of previously fragmented service provision for jobseekers on social assistance in one-stop-shops, the new Job Centres.

Although the principal focus here is on the new Job Centre approach to local employment promotion, the remainder of this section briefly sketches the other major elements of the reform in placement services.

The activation strategy represents a paradigm change for German active policy. Under the motto *fördern und fordern*, which roughly translates as "assistance and responsibility", the unemployed are to receive more intensive and individualised assistance, but they will also become subject to increased pressure to search for and accept any available employment. This is to be achieved by increasing the frequency and quality of contacts with the unemployed, especially through reduced caseloads for placement counsellors, as well as by improved IT systems and streamlined work organisation. Specific changes also include, for example, mandatory early contact with the PES for persons given notice of termination or on temporary contracts; stricter regulations requiring the long-term unemployed to accept any job offer; shifting the burden of proof to the unemployed and more flexibility in applying sanctions; and greater availability of self-service information facilities.

A combination of quantitative and qualitative *profiling* is to be used to divide jobseekers into client segments (job-ready, in-counselling, and intensive service clients) according to their distance from the labour market. This classification serves as a basis for individual action plans and for allocating labour market services.

Improved placement services for employers, including special services for "premium" clients, faster reaction times, screening of prospective jobseekers before referral, referral of only a limited number of qualified jobseekers, follow-up contact with the employer, an improved database on job openings and monitoring of adherence to these quality standards. The central goal is to achieve an improved image among employers and a higher market share of notified vacancies.

Outsourcing of placement services is promoted through new programmes that permit the PES to contract out partial or complete responsibility for reintegration of the unemployed to third parties. Two innovations of particular interest are the personnel service agencies (PSA) and the placement voucher. The PSA is a temporary work agency for the unemployed that is established on a contract basis with a local service provider, in many cases from the temporary work industry. The placement voucher is issued to persons who have been unemployed for more than six weeks. The private agency is paid a maximum of EUR 2 000 for placing the unemployed person in employment of at least 15 hours per week: EUR 1 000 after an employment duration of at least six weeks; and an additional EUR 1 000 after a duration of at least six months.[6]

"Hartz IV": Establishing local Job Centres for the long-term unemployed

The labour market reform legislation on Basic Income Support for Jobseekers that came into effect in January 2005 ("Hartz IV") provides a framework for the integrated provision of benefits and labour market services to the long-term unemployed and other employable social assistance recipients in local Job Centres. To understand the Hartz reform of local employment promotion, it is useful to recall the problem it was intended to resolve. In Germany, responsibility for labour market programmes for social assistance recipients was previously divided between a nationally financed and PES-administered means-tested system of "unemployment assistance" for those who had exhausted their regular benefit on the one hand, and labour market programmes financed and administered by local authorities for social assistance recipients on the other.

Under the new legislation, all needy unemployed persons not eligible for unemployment insurance benefit are eligible for the new Unemployment Benefit II. This is a consolidated benefit near the social assistance level, which is to be funded by the federal government and administered by the PES in co-operation with the local authorities. The basic benefit is EUR 345 per month for single persons, with additional benefits for dependent children (60% or 80% of basic benefit) and spouse (90%) plus a housing allowance.[7] Unemployment Benefit II recipients who were previously eligible for the regular unemployment insurance benefit (usually paid for 12 months) receive a temporary degressive benefit supplement for the first two years, which partially offsets the decline in benefits payments.[8]

The actual impact of the changes on the household income of benefit recipients depends on the type of household and the previous net income. In general, for benefit recipients with a previous income around or below the average gross earning in Germany of EUR 2 200, there is little or no loss in benefit level as a consequence of the reform. For households in which the unemployed had above-average earnings of EUR 3 000, there is a stepwise reduction in benefits over three years of about 25% for singe-person households and of *circa* 8% for a household with two adults and two children. In the latter case benefit is actually higher in the second year of unemployment and lower only in the third and subsequent years. Furthermore, due to more stringent rules for counting the income of other household members, some individuals may no longer be eligible.[9]

The new Job Centres are responsible not only for providing the new Unemployment Benefit II but also for active programmes to all recipients of this means-tested benefit, including social services provided by the local authorities. While there was broad agreement on the need for integrated services for this target group, there was an intense political debate between government and opposition over whether the PES or the local authorities should be responsible for the integrated services, and over how the municipalities are to be compensated for the services they provide. The previous government of the Social Democratic and Green parties favoured giving primary responsibility to the PES, with the local authorities providing supplementary services on a contract basis. The Christian Democratic Party opposition favoured giving the local authorities the option of assuming primary responsibility for administering benefits and labour market services for this target group.

From a policy perspective, the advantage of assigning the PES responsibility for the unemployed on social assistance (Unemployment Benefit II) is that of having a single agency provide integrated services for all unemployed persons. This would avoid the stigmatisation to which a separate agency run by the local authorities might lead. The local option, to the extent that it is exercised, means that there will not be a uniform delivery system for services for the long-term unemployed, but a system where local authorities run their own service centres in some localities while in others the PES is responsible for this clientele. On the other hand, the PES in its current situation (it is undergoing a major reform of all its services and programmes) is in the short run clearly overburdened by the additional task of assuming responsibility for up to one million new social assistance clients. Moreover, in many areas the local authorities have developed excellent reintegration services for welfare clients, whereas the PES has in the past been focused more on the job-ready unemployed. The PES management itself initially preferred to leave the local authorities with responsibility for this target group but was overruled by the responsible government minister.

The final legislation passed gave primary responsibility to the PES but required the PES to co-operate in joint agencies with the local authorities. It also permitted 69 local authorities (municipalities and counties) to assume full responsibility for placement and active programmes for this target group, as well as for benefit administration on a local option basis. The legislation defines this local option as a limited experiment for a period of six years.[10] In 354 local areas, so-called joint agencies ("*Arbeitsgemeinschaften*"), one-stop-shops in which there is a close co-operation between local social agencies and the PES, were established. Nineteen other localities have not agreed to form a joint office with the PES and will continue to administer their local services for this target group (housing and heating allowances, counselling) separately. This compromise means that there will be separate specialised agencies providing labour market services and administering benefits for the unemployed on social assistance parallel to the PES's own service centres (*Kundenzentren*) for job-ready clients, instead of comprehensive job agencies for all unemployed persons as originally envisioned by the Hartz Commission. The remainder of this section will focus on the Job Centre model, in which the PES together with the local authorities forms a joint agency, the so-called "*Arbeitsgemeinschaft*" (or "ARGE"; see Figure 5.1).

The *Arbeitsgemeinschaft* is established on the basis of a formal agreement between the local authority and the local PES. Its legal form is that of either a public authority or a private corporation. The appointment and powers of the chief operating officer of the ARGE, and of his or her deputy, are regulated by agreement between the contracting parties. An advisory body consisting of local actors in labour market and social policy can also be established.

In the Job Centre of the ARGE there is a clear division of labour: the PES is responsible for the administration and financing of active measures and for Unemployment Benefit II. The social agency of the local authority is responsible for the administration and financing of:

● Rent subsidies and heating costs.[11]

● Initial furnishing of living quarters, including appliances and clothing.

● Subsidies for school trips for dependent children.

Figure 5.1. **The multi-level governance with Job Centre as joint operative agency of PES and local authority**

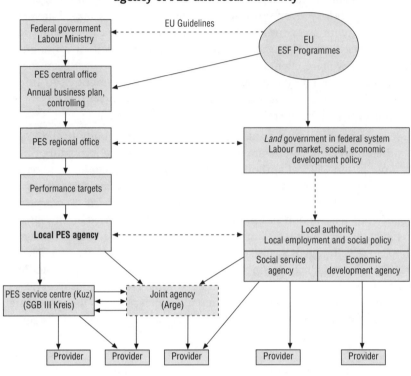

- Care for minor or handicapped children, home care of dependent relatives.
- Debt counselling.
- Socio-psychological counselling.
- Drug counselling.

The relevant legislation also requires that clients in the ARGE be given a personal counsellor (*i.e.* case manager) and that a reintegration agreement be concluded with the client. Except for the need for an appeals procedure and the division of labour between the partners noted above, the details of the work process are at the discretion of the local parties. For example, the local authorities can carry out their responsibilities directly or delegate them to third parties. The ARGE has no employees of its own but is staffed with personnel from the local PES and social agency temporarily assigned to it.

The actual organisation of front and back office work processes is largely at the discretion of the local contracting parties, the PES and the local authority. Three hypothetical models are conceivable: 1) a fully integrated organisational model, in which front office services for clients depend solely on client needs; 2) a fully separated model, in which the PES and the ARGE operate fully independently, duplicating services and programmes for their respective clientele of benefit recipients; 3) a semi-integrated, co-operative model in which some services and programmes are carried out jointly and in other cases a specialisation and division of labour is agreed based on client needs. Model 1 probably fails to reflect sufficiently the special needs of the long-term unemployed and the interests of the local authorities in maintaining a visible, if reduced, role in local employment promotion, as well as the importance of those authorities' contribution. Model 2, with its strict division of clientele and services according to the type of benefit received, would hardly merit the name Job Centre. It is in fact close to the local option model that is being implemented in 69 localities. The authors assume that Model 3, the semi-integrated co-operative model, is the model of the future. The key question then is which placement services and programmes should be integrated and how is co-operation between separate activities to be organised in the interest of the efficiency and effectiveness of the Job Centre and customer service.

Capacity building at the regional level: the role of intermediary organisations in implementing and integrating policies in Germany's federal states

The importance of labour market policy in Germany's 16 *Länder* has increased immensely since the 1990s as a consequence of the regionalisation strategy funded by the structural funds of the European Union. To cope with their new responsibilities, most of the states have created new intermediary organisations to assist the traditional ministries and support regional and local actors involved in implementing labour market policy. These consulting companies or service providers perform a primarily advisory and co-ordinating function rather than a political one. They exemplify the building of institutional capacity at the state level – a key requirement for the practical implementation of an integrated regional policy on the labour market and employment. This section compares the development of these intermediary organisations and their activities in the 16 states. But first it provides an outline of the regional policy framework and compares the various states.

Labour market policy at the regional level

The labour market policies of the states complement those of the federal government in various ways. The states develop programmes for target groups that have only limited, if any, access to PES labour market measures: long-term unemployed persons, recent immigrants, women, and young people entering the labour market. The states also provide services or pursue goals that the PES does not provide (*e.g.* childcare, business consulting, and special programmes for women). In addition, state policies reflect each state's own emphasis on certain target groups or issues – for example, industrial restructuring in North Rhine-Westphalia – and are an important source of innovations in German labour market policy, such as transitional "employment companies" as a response to plant closures, temporary work agencies for unemployed persons, and wage-plus-top-up benefit models (Blanke, 2002). Moreover, the states themselves are largely responsible for the implementation of European Social Fund (ESF) programmes, for which they develop and co-ordinate with the EU Commission the state-level programmes. They thus play a lead role in co-ordinating the joint activities of the EU, federal programmes, and state[12] and local actors in their regions.[13] Finally, the states are also simultaneously responsible for related policy areas, especially regional economic development and other structural policies. They are therefore, in principle, in a good position to develop a more integrated approach to labour market and employment policy.

The increasing importance of state labour market policies in many of Germany's states is closely related to the rise in mass unemployment, but also to the growth of EU funding resources after 1988; the latter impose special responsibility for programme planning, tendering, controlling and evaluation at the state level. In the ESF funding period (2000-06), the EU's most important instrument of labour market policy, resources were directed to three target areas:

- **Category 1 target areas:** Regions lagging economically far behind the EU average [less than 75% of the average gross domestic product (GDP) per capita]. Through 31 December 2005, only the five new federal states in eastern Germany and former East Berlin were in this category.

- **Category 2 target areas:** Regions with major problems with adaptation, such as former coal or steel districts and very rural regions.

- **Category 3 target areas:** These regions are all those not classified as Category 1 (former West Germany).

Germany received approximately EUR 12 billion from the ESF for the funding period ending in 2006. Depending on the region, no more than 75% of a project's total costs can be paid with ESF money (up to 75% in Category 1 target areas, otherwise up to 50%). Federal, state, or local government co-funding must be arranged to cover the rest of the costs. ESF funding for active labour market policy totalled about EUR 20 billion for the period 2000 through 2006 – a substantial sum, but relatively small in comparison to federal spending.[14]

Because the funds are disbursed according to the priority of the target region areas, their significance is considerable to some states and certain target groups. As Category 1 target areas, the eastern German states receive a greater share of the ESF money than areas in the other two categories do. Moreover, on the basis of a national formula, the east German states themselves administer about 75% of the ESF funds to which Category 1 target areas are entitled (as opposed to only 50% of the corresponding funds in former West Germany). The ESF funding for Category 2 target areas goes mostly to North Rhine-Westphalia, Lower Saxony, Schlesweig-Holstein, Saarland, Rhineland-Palatinate, and the city-states of Berlin and Bremen. The urgency of the problems and the importance of ESF co-funding in these states make the role of labour market policy more salient, the planning and administration of policy more complex, and the need for intermediary institutions correspondingly greater than in other western German states.

Diversity of state employment programmes

Years of high unemployment and low economic growth, coupled with the Hartz IV reforms under former Chancellor Gerhard Schröder, have confronted the governments of Germany's 16 federal states with new responsibilities in labour market policy. Most of the state governments have responded by developing and implementing their own new initiatives in the fields of regional and local policy. In particular, the creation of the new local Job Centres for the long-term unemployed under the auspices of the federal government after January 2005 has led to a wave of changes in the orientation and organisation of state labour market policies. Fresh strategies have been elaborated and new, more clearly focused programmes introduced. New policy instruments have been developed, including the establishment of new intermediary organisations. At the very least, programmes have been adapted, priorities shifted, and the allocation of resources to the regions revised. Drawing on previous literature and a review of all 16 of Germany's states, this section gives an overview of trends in state programmes.[15]

The states' active labour market policies are based on a mixture of strategic concepts, programmes and priorities. A number of factors account for this heterogeneity, such as the goals of the regional restructuring process; the existence of industrial agglomerations with large firms; a prominent sector of small business and industry; and a well-developed service sector. Five strategies are followed, either individually or (in many states) in combination:

- Activating measures to promote labour market integration.
- Preventive measures designed to avoid unemployment.
- Measures for specific target groups and equal opportunity.
- Improved design of programmes to fit the needs of participants and the programme goals.

● Professionalisation of the monitoring and controlling of programmes and projects.

Some German states have consolidated their array of measures into "state programmes" under their own names, giving their foremost objectives finely differentiated subprogrammes and subprojects, including pilot projects. Bremen's new *Beschäftigungspolitisches Aktionsprogrammem* (BAP), or Employment Policy Action Programme, is one of the most exemplary in terms of goal clarity, transparency, strict standards, practicability, and close correspondence with the employment policy objectives of the ESF (Senator, 2006a). Similar initiatives are being taken by Mecklenburg-Vorpommern with its *Arbeitsmarkt- und Strukturentwicklungsprogramme* (Labour Market and Structural Development Programme, ASP), Rhineland-Palatinate with a reorientation of its programmes, and North Rhine-Westphalia with its differentiation of subprogrammes addressing priority goals. By contrast, Baden-Württemberg, Bavaria, Saarland, and initially Hesse and Hamburg as well, have made little effort to build sophisticated state programmes. This reflects the lower priority accorded labour market policies in these states, though the latter two have systematically developed their state programmes since 2005 and 2006, respectively. All these cases of policy activism obviously relate to the unemployment rate, the resulting political pressure for action, the overall political orientation of each state, the existence of intermediary organisations and their activities, and the volume of available funding (see Schmidt, Hörrmann, Maier and Steffen, 2004).

Intermediary organisations: the federal states compared

The role of intermediary organisations is to co-ordinate and support the implementation of labour market policy. Intermediary organisations exist in the vast majority of the states, though in different legal forms and with different responsibilities (see Table 5.1). Only Bavaria, Baden-Württemberg and Saarland have no such organisations; functions are performed by the competent state ministries and economic development agencies. As Table 5.1 shows, these entities had not existed until just recently in Hamburg, Hesse, Bremen and Mecklenburg-Vorpommern. Their creation is evidently a response to the new situation confronting the states since the Hartz IV reform in 2005 (Hamburg and Hesse) and to a new emphasis on an integrated regional labour market policy (Bremen and Mecklenburg-Vorpommern). The oldest and most experienced institution is by far the GIB (Gesellschaft für Innovative Beschäftigungsförderung, or Organisation for Innovative Employment Promotion), in North Rhine-Westphalia, established in 1986.

Most of the states have established these organisations as their own limited liability consulting companies. The three exceptions are Rhineland-Palatinate, Schleswig-Holstein and Saxony, where private companies are

Table 5.1. **Intermediary organisations as actors of labour market policy in Germany's federal states, 1991-2006**

State	Intermediary organisation	Year of creation	Special characteristic	Framework labour market policy programmes	Unemployment rate June 2007
Bavaria	None Responsible: State Ministry of Labour and Social Affairs, Family, and Women Administers funding instrument: Labour market funds	...		Labour market policy subprogrammes	5%
Baden-Württemberg	None Responsible: State Ministry of Labour and Social Affairs	...		Labour market policy subprogrammes	4.8%
Berlin	Arbeitsgemeinschaft Servicege sellschaften Berlin GbR as a holding of: • Consult GmbH, • GSUB mbH • Zukunft im Zentrum GmbH	2001 1991 1991 1991	Performs state functions	4th Framework Policy Programme (ARP) for the Labour Market and Vocational Training Bezirkliche Bündnisse für Wirtschaft und Arbeit (BBWA, Local Pacts for Business and Employment)	16.6%
Brandenburg	Landesagentur für Struktur und Arbeit GmbH (LASA)	1991		State programme Qualification and Work for Brandenburg INNOPUNKT Pilot funding for innovative projects	15.5%
Bremen	Bremer Arbeit GmbH (BAG)	2001		Beschäftigungspolitisches Aktionsprogramm (BAP)	12.7%
Hamburg	Hamburger Arbeitsgemeinschaft (ARGE) SGB II "Team.Arbeit.Hamburg"	2005		Hamburg model for employment promotion	9%
Hesse	HA Hessen Agentur GmbH	2005		Hessisches Aktionsprogramm Regionale Arbeitsmarktpolitik (HARA) Hessisches Aktionsprogramm Regionale Arbeitsmarktpolitik "Passgenau in Arbeit" (PiA)	7.4%
Lower Saxony	Landesberatungsgesellschaft für Integration und Beschäftigung mbH (LaBIB)	1991		Labour market policy subprogrammes addressing priority areas: • Preventive labour market policy • Labour market policy for youth and long-term unemployed persons	8.5%
Mecklenburg-Vorpommern	Gesellschaft für Struktur- und Arbeitsmarktentwicklung mbH (GSA)	2004		Arbeitsmarkt- und Strukturentwicklungsprogramm (ASP)	15.8%

Table 5.1. **Intermediary organisations as actors of labour market policy in Germany's federal states, 1991-2006** (cont.)

State	Intermediary organisation	Year of creation	Special characteristic	Framework labour market policy programmes	Unemployment rate June 2007
North Rhine-Westphalia	Gesellschaft für Innovative Beschäftigungsförderung mbH (GIB)	1986		Labour market policy subprogrammes addressing priority areas: • Integration into the labour market • Youth and vocational training • New work in North Rhine-Westphalia: Promotion of employability	9.5%
Rhineland-Palatinate	Rhineland-Palatinate Advisory Office: Arbeitsmarktintegration Benachteiligter – Technische Hilfe zum Europäischen Sozialfonds (RAT)	1992	Private company	Labour market policy subprogrammes addressing priority areas: • Youth and training • Labour market integration of special target groups • Monitoring of structural change	6.3%
Saarland	None Responsible: State Ministry of Economics and Labour	...		Labour market policy subprogrammes	8.3%
Saxony	Institut für Innovation und Arbeit Sachsen GmbH (IAS)	2006	Private company	State programme "Work and Qualification in Saxony"	14.2%
Saxony-Anhalt	Trägergesellschaft Land Sachsen-Anhalt mbH (TGL)	1992	Private company	Individual programmes addressing priority areas: • Long-term unemployed persons • Older workers • Youth • Women • People starting up a business	15.5%
Schleswig-Holstein	Beratungsstelle für Beschäftigung Schleswig- Holstein GmbH (BSH)	1991	Private company performing state functions	Arbeit für Schleswig-Holstein (ASH) 2000 (Work for Schleswig-Holstein)	8.2%
Thuringia	GFAW Gesellschaft für Arbeits- und Wirtschaftsförderung mbH	1994	Performs state functions	Individual programmes addressing priority areas: • Long-term unemployed persons • Older workers • Youth • Women • People starting up a business • Part-time training	12.6%

Source: Bouché, 2006. Monthly unemployment rates as reported by the Federal Employment Agency, June 2007.

commissioned to carry out these services. In any case, the principal contractor is the responsible state ministry. Additional possible contractors include other labour market policy actors such as business associations, chambers and occupational associations, the regional employment services, and unions. The state ministries also determine and assign the range of the tasks, which vary from state to state. Six tasks have been assigned to the intermediary organisations in most states:

- Internal consulting services for the state ministry in matters of a) programme development or direct development of programme proposals for state labour market policy, b) reform of the state's policy and funding instruments, and c) the selection of providers of labour market or industrial policy programmes and projects.

- Co-ordination of the co-operation between the state ministries, regional PES agencies, and other local labour market policy actors; development and maintenance of Internet-aided project databanks.

- External consulting services and support – substantive and legal counsel, including assistance with grant application – for, e.g., local actors planning or conducting projects, providers of further training, outplacement companies, businesses, business start-ups and individuals.

- Internal research and communication, expert reports, and organisation of public hearings as well as external publications and public relations.

- Continuous monitoring of the labour market, internal controlling and evaluation of programmes, including budgets and expenditure.

- State functions in special cases: independent administration and disbursement of programme and project funds and all funds from the ESF.

In some of Germany's states, the mandate for both internal and external consulting is very broad, as with the GIB in North Rhine-Westphalia and the Gesellschaft für Arbeits- und Wirtschaftsförderung mbH (GfAW) in Thuringia. In other states the practice is more restricted. The extent of external consulting differs, with the GIB, the GfAW and the *Arbeitsgemeinschaft Servicegesellschaften* Berlin GbR providing a high level of services. The GIB and the GfAW are also extremely active with regard to external communication and publications. They offer an impressive range and depth of information (the GIB's Internet presence is exemplary) that is easily accessible in a well-maintained databank. A number of intermediary organisations have databanks, but none that matches that of the GIB. The emphasis on monitoring and controlling likewise varies widely. The GIB and the GfAW are fully engaged in these tasks as well.

The innovative aspect of what these institutions do is not to be underestimated. Their activities have already given rise to a variety of new ideas and pilot projects in North Rhine-Westphalia. Other examples are the Innopunkt pilot projects in Brandenburg and the GAP employment projects in Mecklenburg-Vorpommern, and the local employment initiatives Bezirkliche Bündnisse für Wirtschaft und Arbeit (BBWA) in Berlin. Three states – Berlin, Schleswig-Holstein and Thüringia – have given these institutions the authority to administer and disburse programme funding on their own. The GfAW in Thuringia has the greatest authority in this regard, having been entrusted with the entire administration of the state's ESF funding. That arrangement is an exception, however.

Cross-sectional objectives such as a better integration of labour market, economic development and structural policies, as well as gender-mainstreaming and coping with demographic change, have been embraced by most of the states in their regional policy. That holds true for, *inter alia,* Bavaria, Baden-Württemberg, and Saarland, states with no intermediary organisations and whose governments have in some cases developed other structures. Bavaria, for instance, has its own state labour market fund (financed through the proceeds of state privatisation). Baden-Württemberg sets its priorities differently, and with good reason: enjoying both the lowest unemployment rate of all the federal states in Germany and a well-established, innovative small-business sector, it relies more on technical qualification and market forces than on classic state labour market programmes.

Integrating regional labour market policy in North Rhine-Westphalia

This section examines in depth the role of GIB in co-ordinating and implementing policy in North Rhine-Westphalia, which is as an example of good practice in Germany.

North Rhine-Westphalia's socio-economic context

With approximately 10% of Germany's total area and 18 075 million inhabitants, North Rhine-Westphalia is Germany's most populous state. The Ruhr District in North Rhine-Westphalia is one of Europe's largest industrial agglomerations, and has an impressive history. From the onset of the industrial age through the 1970s, it was marked by the rapid development of industrial technologies and a steady growth in the production of coal, iron ore, steel and chemicals. But that prosperity ended when demand for coal plummeted in the late 1960s and the steel industry began a structural decline in the 1970s and 1980s. Coal production dropped from 125 million tons in 1956 to 51 million tons in 1993, leading to the closure of 78 coal mines by 1968 and the loss of about 80% of the jobs in that sector. Steel production shrank from

75 million tons in 1974 to 18 million tons in 1988, a decrease of 76%. Whereas 20 independent smelting plants were still operating in 1975, only eight were left by 1988, an employment loss of 55% (Ditt, 2004). The decline of the traditional industrial base led to a secular increase in unemployment: North Rhine-Westphalia was long considered one of the nation's problem regions with a difficult labour market.

Nonetheless, successful change in its economic infrastructure, particularly in the 1990s, made the Ruhr District and North Rhine-Westphalia less dependent on coal and steel. The North Rhine-Westphalian industries with the highest sales at this time are chemicals (Bayer, Henke and BASF); machine-building (Thyssen-Krupp Technologies, SMS, Claas, and Deutz); steel production (Thyssen-Krupp); automotive manufacturing (Ford and Thyssen-Krupp Automotive); metalworking (Thyssen-Krupp Steel, HydroAluminium, and Mannesmann); coal- and petroleum-processing and energy production (RWE); and electronic engineering, electronics, and food production (Dr. August Oetker). In addition to manufacturing and the extractive industries, the service sector is enjoying robust growth. Regional industrial policy in North Rhine-Westphalia is today aligned more closely with the dictum of "making strengths stronger" than to the previously dominant approach of balancing different living conditions. In other words, innovation and competitiveness are to be promoted in those economic areas with prospects of above-average growth rates. This perspective lies at the centre of the project entitled "Initiative Zukunft Ruhr" (Initiative for the Future of the Ruhr) that has been developed for the Ruhr District. It is scheduled to supersede the "Wachstums- und Beschäftigungspakt Ruhr" (Ruhr Growth and Employment Pact), and will continue supporting selected clusters only (Bosch and Nordhause-Janz, 2005; Ministerium für Wirtschaft, 2006).

With an unemployment rate of 9.5% in June 2007, the state ranks in the median range of a comparison of Germany's federal states, a scale that extends from the low unemployment rate of 4.8% in Baden-Württemberg to the high of 15.8% in Mecklenburg-Vorpommern (Table 5.1). This relatively high unemployment rate is a late consequence of the region's still incomplete structural transformation.

Regionalisation was introduced in North Rhine-Westphalia in the 1980s as an approach to management and problem-solving within a modernisation strategy and is currently the favoured policy model at the state level. The labour market policy of North Rhine-Westphalia's Ministry of Labour, Health, and Social Affairs is committed to regionalised and integrated promotion of the labour market and employment, and aims to tie the various policy areas – economic, industrial, labour market, and technology policy – more closely together than in the past. One of the actions taken to follow through on this intention was a statewide reorganisation that replaced the region's

30 secretariats with 16 regional agencies corresponding to districts of the chambers of industry and commerce. These are to serve as linchpins between the State Ministry of Labour, Health, and Social Affairs and the individual regions. The regional agencies have steering committees in which the key local co-operation partners (chambers of industry and commerce, employers' associations, unions, local employment services, providers of initial and further training, and representatives of equal opportunity policy) consult on and propose strategic guidelines for the region, appropriate regional conceptions, and oversee their implementation. The regional agencies are expected to promote the development of regional networks for labour markets and employment, and thereby to enhance links between the ministry and the regional actors in order to respond to changes in regional and local conditions as quickly and flexibly as possible (GIB, 2004a, 2005a).

Within this regional framework the State Ministry of Labour, Health, and Social Affairs implements programmes in three priority areas (Ministerium für Arbeit, 2006a):

- Integration into the labour market – perspectives for special target groups.

- Youth and vocational training – orientation for the future.

- New work in North Rhine-Westphalia – promoting employability.

North Rhine-Westphalia receives and administers substantial ESF funding under the guidelines governing Category 2 target areas (change of industrial structure in agglomerations and structurally weak regions) and (especially) Category 3 target areas (modernisation of vocational training and employment), which require 50% co-funding. From 2000 through 2006, approximately EUR 1.8 billion were available for ESF Category 2 and 3 programmes in North Rhine-Westphalia. About EUR 0.9 billion of that sum come from ESF co-funding. The necessity of co-financing ties up a major part of the state's funds for active labour market policy, and so state policy is largely identical with the ESF programme. The expanded financial scope of state employment policy through ESF co-funding entails enormous political and administrative responsibility. Of the total amount, 80% was used in around 13 000 regional projects and 20% in statewide implementation of about 900 projects (Ministerium für Arbeit, 2006b).

Establishing GIB

Implementation of well-conceived programmes in the labour market policy of Germany's states generally depends on the activity of intermediary organisations, with functions and responsibilities that neither federal agencies nor their state counterparts can fulfil adequately. The function of these organisations is to support as effectively as possible the responsible state ministry and local actors on the labour market acting as organisers, mediators, consultants and planners. For many years now, these tasks in North Rhine-Westphalia have been performed by the GIB regional agency (*Gesellschaft für Innovative Beschäftigungsförderung*), whose development and activity is examined in the following sections.

The 1980s in North Rhine-Westphalia were a period of steadily rising unemployment rates to which the state government responded with a number of exemplary labour market policy initiatives and projects, some of them with substantial funding. In addition, there emerged a host of unconventional self-help projects and initiatives to create employment for target groups in the regular and alternative economies in problematic regions, and in university towns. It was in this context that the GIB was founded. As a publicly funded but legally independent state consulting organisation affiliated with the North Rhine-Westphalian State Ministry of Labour, Health and Social Affairs, its task was to analyse and co-ordinate the goals and programmes of these new currents and movements against unemployment.

Just a few years after the creation of the GIB, its focus changed. Since the early 1990s, it has shifted from the selective funding of numerous separate initiatives and projects to regional or local integrated approaches to labour market policy. The spectrum of clients greatly expanded as actors of employment policy (*e.g.* local authorities, trade associations, chambers of commerce, enterprises and providers of vocational and further training) displaced the self-help groups. Moreover, the emphasis shifted from the sole priority of consulting on projects to additional key responsibilities such as further training, providing information on statewide programmes and projects, and legal counselling. In the mid-1990s the state ministry assigned the GIB the function of advising on and co-ordinating the programme relating to the ESF's Category 2 target areas ("change in industrial structure in agglomerations and structurally weak regions"; GIB, 1994).

Mission and functions

The GIB's mission is to provide information, co-ordination, counselling and project support for regional and local labour market policy actors in conjunction with the goals and strategies of the state's economic, industrial, and regional policy. Its principal functions, which have emerged over the 20-year development of the GIB as an intermediary organisation, are:

- Planning and development of ideas, models and concepts of labour market and employment programmes for the state Ministry of Labour, Health, and Social Affairs.

- Co-ordination, co-operation, and facilitation pertaining to the implementation of labour market policy programmes and projects by various actors.

- Consulting services for and support of project management, providers of further training, business start-ups, companies and other actors.

- The gathering, processing and dissemination of information as databanks, publication series and further training.

- Monitoring and controlling – that is, long-term observation of the labour market and the success of programme and project implementation.

- Early recognition of changes in factors relevant to labour market policy (target groups, fields of employment, funding concepts and organisational structures).

A relatively new and distinct task the GIB has acquired since 2004 is technical consulting with and co-ordination of the regional agencies of the state Ministry of Labour, Health, and Social Affairs, with the aim of developing regional networks for promoting labour market and employment policy. The GIB's overview and experience as an organisation operating statewide and co-operating with a vast spectrum of clients can provide valuable support (GIB, 2003, 2004b, 2005b).

To support structural change in North Rhine-Westphalia through innovations in employment promotion, the GIB sets itself the task of functioning as an intermediary at the state, regional and local levels. It advises regional policy makers, companies, providers of further training, and public corporations in matters bearing on the implementation of the state programmes supporting the labour market. Conversely, the GIB can, on the basis of its rich practical experience in working together with regional and local actors, advise the state Ministry of Labour, Health, and Social Affairs, helping to improve the state's policy initiatives.

Current organisational structure, fields of activity and funding

The GIB has the legal status of a fully state-owned limited liability company (GmbH). Its activities are overseen by a supervisory board representing three North Rhine-Westphalian state ministries (Labour, Health, and Social Affairs; Construction and Transport; and Economics, Small Business and Energy), the state's regional headquarters of the Federal Employment Service, and the mayor of Bottrop. To plan and conduct the activity of the GIB, the organisation and the supervisory board agree on annual goals, which are accompanied by corresponding tasks that lead to the formation of "work packages". In 2006 there were projects in six areas:

- Integrating unemployed persons.

- Helping young people with entry to their training and occupation.

- Promoting business start-ups and young business organisations.

- Enhancing employability.

- Assisting employees and companies during corporate crises.
- Working on issues that cut across goals.

    These projects are pursued at four levels:

- Development of individual and integrated projects (local level) – approximately 55% of the services.
- Support of regional consulting structures and partnerships (regional level) – approximately 15% of the services.
- Development and implementation of statewide programmes and initiatives (state level) – approximately 30% of the services.
- Encouragement of cross-border innovation transfer (national and international level) – approximately 5% of the services.

The GIB's financial resources consist of state institutional funding (around 20), additional state contracts and market revenues from third-party contracts. Turnover totals approximately EUR 5.5 million. The total number of employees in 2006 was 67 as compared to 30 in 1994. Figure 5.2 shows the allocation of GIB's services across four work goals and the levels of action as compared to the corresponding information from 2004 and 2005.

Figure 5.2. **Services of the GIB by goals and levels of action, 2004-2006**

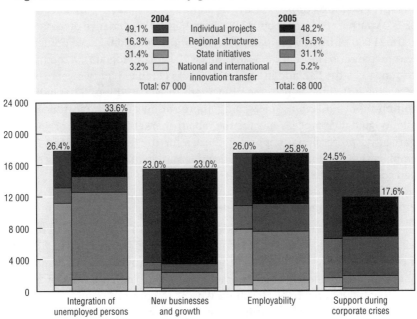

Source: GIB, "Bericht an den Aufsichtsrat für das Jahr 2005" (Report for the Board of Directors for 2005), Bottrop, 2006.

Examples of GIB projects

The GIB performs widely recognised work on the implementation and support of many programmes, projects and initiatives for the Ministry of Labour, Health, and Social Affairs. This section cites a few examples illustrating such good practice.

The state programme "Youth in Work Plus"

The North Rhine-Westphalian state initiative "Jugend in Arbeit plus" (Youth in Work Plus), part of the *Land* programme "Youth and Training", encompasses an offer of employment for young people up to 25 years of age who have been unemployed for six months or more. The Ministry of Labour, Health and Social Affairs, the regional headquarters of the Federal Employment Service, the business associations, the local authorities, and the welfare organisations co-operate on the programme to improve the chances of this age group on the labour market. For 12 months the participants in the initiative receive a job with standard wages, gain vocational experience, raise their level of vocational training, and thereby increase their prospects of finding a regular job. The employer receives a 50% wage-cost subsidy for one year. The programme, launched in 1998, is considered one of Germany's most successful measures for promoting youth employment. Since the beginning of the programme, approximately 350 advisors have contacted some 48 500 youths, of whom about 43 000 have begun the guidance process. By late 2004, 21 000 of them were placed in jobs and a vocational development plan was prepared for more than 39 000. Since 2003, this programme too has been co-funded by the ESF, and in early 2006 it was extended for two years because of persistently high youth unemployment in North Rhine-Westphalia. This commitment reflects an increasing appreciation of the importance that a quality guidance process has for the labour market integration of youth. As part of its professional support activities for the programme, the GIB has emphasised quality standards and documentation of the counselling services and controlling (GIB, 2005b, 2005d).

Promotion of women's employment

"Regionen Stärken Frauen" (Regional Women's Initiative) – part of the *Land* programme "Promotion of Employability" – was inaugurated in 2004. It is a response to the fact that, although men's and women's vocational qualifications are nearly equal, women's participation in the workforce is still inadequate, not only in North Rhine-Westphalia but in Germany as a whole. This initiative therefore addresses women who are employees as well as potential employees – such as women re-entering the workforce, taking parental leave, starting up new businesses, or seeking work but not entitled to active employment promotion or benefits – and female migrants.

About 200 subprojects have been funded since 2005, through 37 medium- and long-term, regional, sector-specific co-operative activities with companies, training providers and equal-opportunity offices, with the goal of fostering the compatibility between family and career – and hence women's participation in the labour market – partly by offering childcare arrangements. Modern design of work processes and flexibility in working time are intended as primary vehicles for enabling women to reconcile career advancement, family life and child-rearing. The RSF initiative was one of the GIB's special focal activities in 2006. It is supported primarily by in-depth guidance services and project monitoring, training proposals and coaching (GIB, 2005e).

Increasing the competitiveness of small business: "Consulting for Potential"

"Potenzialberatung" (Consulting for Potential), part of the Land programme Consulting Services for Enterprises, is an advisory instrument co-funded by the ESF that has existed since 2000. It offers companies and their employees one-on-one coaching aimed at optimising operational processes through analysis of strengths and weaknesses, followed up with an evaluation by external consultants in order to foster modernisation. Subsidies covering 50% of the costs (not exceeding EUR 500 per day of coaching) are granted for this purpose. That arrangement holds for a maximum of ten coaching days for small businesses with up to 49 employees, and 15 coaching days for those with 50 employees or more. By 2005 more than 6 800 companies, most with less that 100 employees, had participated in the programme. The consulting and developmental processes initiated by this instrument have proved highly useful to the companies. Ninety-nine per cent of them have claimed that most if not all of their expectations have been met; only 1% of the companies have been dissatisfied with the result. Other studies by the GIB indicate that the companies enjoyed significantly better-than-average development after participating in the programme, and that they posted employment increases ranging from 1.6% to 4.3%. These outcomes have been reported by companies in almost all sectors, especially those in metalworking, machinebuilding, services, or construction. For this programme the GIB conducts regular information meetings for enterprises, consulting firms, and local economic development agencies. It also provides further training for employees of the regional employment and economic development agencies (Hermann and Kratz, 2004; GIB, 2004b, 2005b).

The ARBID initiative promoting intergenerational employment structures in companies

The number of young and middle-aged gainfully employed persons in Germany will plunge by approximately 5.5 million in the next ten to 15 years. The ARBID initiative – "Arbeit und Innovation im demographischen Wandel" (Work and Innovation in Demographic Change) – was introduced in 2004 to help North Rhine-Westphalian companies cope with the impacts of demographic change and to assist them in shaping age-appropriate working and employment conditions consistent with the common interests of entrepreneurs and employees. The intention behind ARBID is to facilitate the rethinking that has become imperative in companies and business associations facing the reality of increasingly scarce skilled labour and an ageing workforce. Recommended options for the business community are:

● To activate the 40- to 50-year-old employees through further training so as to make better use of their potential.

● To reduce prejudice against the capabilities of older members of the workforce and to design age-appropriate jobs and work processes.

● To promote the transfer of practical knowledge between the various age groups and to systematically use the complementary age-specific skills of younger and older members of the workforce.

● To design transparent and binding specialist and management careers, broaden the strategies for recruiting women and older unemployed persons, and achieve balanced employee age structures in order to avoid waves of retirements and similar problems.

The GIB supports the activities of enterprises to cope with demographic change. It provides comprehensive information, consulting and training to consulting firms and other business-related actors on the availability of financial support for the development of firm-specific solutions (Hermann and Kratz, 2004; GIB, 2003b, 2004b).

Controlling programme implementation and expenditure

Since 2000, the implementation of the North Rhine-Westphalia state programmes, including their co-funding by the ESF, is controlled by the Ministry of Labour, Health, and Social Affairs by means of a monitoring system. Since 2004, control of ESF-co-funded state programmes has centred on programme- and project-specific goals. The goals must be precisely represented in a controlling system. For this purpose, the GIB must continually adapt and develop its methodological instruments for preparing standardised reports and the necessary software, and for providing quantitative and qualitative information and advice on programme implementation. The goals formulated in the framework of the individual projects are squared with the results at prescribed intervals through the use of programme monitoring data and GIB's own survey data. The key qualitative instruments are content analyses, written surveys, semi-structured interviews and case studies.

Since 2000, the GIB has regularly evaluated the results of its own activity. It does so by comparing its use of resources against the number of services rendered and by conducting surveys that have the various groups of clients rank the quality of the services according to innovativeness, practical relevance, and gain in competency. Evaluating the quality of service implies measuring the subjective effect on or utility to labour market policy actors and individual users. As an intermediary organisation, however, the GIB is not in a position to measure the impact indicators of paramount public interest, such as the rates of job placement or the number of jobs created. In other words, the impact of GIB's activity on the labour market and enterprises is not directly measurable (GIB, 2004b, 2006b).

Conclusion

Preliminary assessment of the Job Centre model

Since the Job Centre only became fully operational in the course of 2005 and systematic evaluation results are not yet available, at this time it is only possible to assess its broad design features. Still, a number of potential strengths and risks are apparent.

The Job Centre model does not create a unified local job centre as initially envisioned by the recommendations of the Hartz Commission, but in fact splits the delivery of employment services into two organisational units based on benefit entitlement rather than on their service needs: the PES service centre for those on unemployment insurance benefit, and the new Job Centre for all unemployed on the means-tested Unemployment Benefit II.

The focus of the reform is on the governance or mode of implementation of labour market programmes and not on innovation in programmes with a regional development focus. The Job Centre reform is primarily aimed at resolving a structural problem of fragmentation in the delivery system between the employment promotion activities of the PES and those of the local authorities for the unemployed on social assistance. The institutional merger in a formal, co-operative structure became necessary after a voluntary and co-operative approach had failed.

The most important shift in the programme portfolio has been away from expensive temporary public employment programmes in "real" jobs towards "workfare" ("one-euro jobs"), in which Unemployment Benefit II recipients are expected to work up to 30-hours per week for a small hourly supplement to their benefit payments. This was previously only selectively practiced in local social assistance agencies, but not by the PES.

The Job Centre model may actually reinforce the basic pattern of a centralised labour market policy within a national organisation (the PES), since the role of the local authorities in employment policy – except for the 69 local option authorities – is now reduced to provision of auxiliary services. Although Germany has a strong federal system of government, decentralisation of responsibility for labour market policy to the *Bundesländer* or states was not seriously considered as an option.

The Job Centre model does not address the isssue that PES employment promotion treats unemployment primarily as an individual problem rather than one of regional economic development. The recommendation of the Hartz Commission that the ten regional offices of the PES should become "Competence Centres" for promoting regional employment and economic development was not adopted. The limitations of this supply-side approach are most apparent in eastern Germany, where large amounts of funding have been channelled into labour market programmes that have had little longer-term impact on the employment prospects of participants or on regional economic development.

The Job Centre model perpetuates the structural problem in active policy it was intended to overcome: a division of labour based on the type of benefit received rather than on the labour market needs of clients. What is required is a common port of entry that steers clients toward appropriate services based on initial screening, but the design of the Job Centre segments clients primarily by the type of benefit for which they are eligible. In fact many unemployed not eligible for unemployment insurance have relatively good labour market prospects (*e.g.* youth – especially those with higher education – women re-entering the labour market, highly qualified immigrants) and some unemployment benefit recipients may face a high risk of long-term unemployment (*e.g.* older displaced workers). How in practice the Job Centre copes with this heterogeneity in its clientele remains to be seen.

The splitting of employment services into two organisational units based on benefit entitlement rather than on their service needs could entail a great deal of inefficient duplication between programmes under the auspices of the PES Service Centres (*Kundenzentrum*) and similar activities by PES in the ARGE, unless co-operative solutions are found; one such solution could be the joint planning of programmes for both clientele groups. Necessary co-operation is at the very least rendered more difficult by the fact that services for the two types of clients are financed from separate budgets.

Capacity building through intermediary organisations

The labour market policy of Germany's federal states makes an important contribution to implementing European employment strategy. Within the regional networks of economic and labour market support over the past 15 years, the creation of special intermediary organisations has increased the institutional capacity to assist with the practical implementation of various state programmes for promoting employment. The most important tasks these organisations have are to provide the actors of labour market policy with professional consulting services and to work at the state level to co-ordinate programmes and projects co-funded through the ESF.

State labour market programmes are strongly dependent on financial support through the EU's structural fund, especially in this field of policy. Because of the accession of ten new members, the volume of ESF funding available to Germany will be shrinking anywhere from 20% to 30% during the new funding period (2007-13). The old member states shall receive 53% of the structural funds and the new member states 47%, although the latter account for only 20% of the population (Kjellström, 2006). This redistribution, based on the principles of European solidarity, requires of Germany's states far more careful planning of the priority areas in order to provide sufficient funds for the necessary projects.

Germany's states differ in their understanding and implementation of regional labour market policy. There is a strong relationship between the level of economic development and unemployment and the pressure for policy action. This has led to a more or less strong development of regional labour market programmes and to the need for capacity-building intermediary organisations that support the development and implementation of state labour market policies.

Implementing a regionalised and integrated labour market policy since 2000, in conjunction with a sizeable increase in the volume of ESF funding, has brought about a strategic, institutional, and practical change in North Rhine-Westphalia. This change has meant gradual growth in the status and discretionary latitude of regional actors but also, because of the expanding range of tasks they are taking on, greater responsibility as well. In this context the competence, professionalism and experience of the GIB as an intermediary state-consulting organisation has played a pivotal role.

Meeting these goals will require a long-term policy perspective accompanied by continuous supervision, monitoring, and adaptation to contemporary developments. In the process, intermediary organisations such as the GIB will continue to increase in importance as institutions whose primary functions are consulting and mediation, especially if the present problem with mass unemployment remains unsolved.

ESF funding in North Rhine-Westphalia as a Category 2 and Category 3 target area from 2007 through 2013 has recently been officially extended by the relevant policy-making bodies. In this period there will be a continuing need for the support of GIB (and similar organisations in other states) for developing and implementing regional labour market policies. The GIB can serve as a model for regional organisations working in a similar capacity in other countries.

Notes

1. The authors would like to thank Günther Schmid for helpful comments on an earlier version of this report.

2. OECD standardised unemployment rates for 2006.

3. The German national unemployment statistics reported here are based on registered unemployment rather than on ILO definitions, and are consistently higher than the OECD standardised unemployment rates for international comparison.

4. A recent survey of local economic development agencies in German cities and counties in 2002 indicates that the most widespread organisational form is that of a local agency incorporated under private law (30%). Other typical forms are local public agencies (26.8%) and special staff units in local government (19.1%). The average agency size raged from two to five persons for small towns and counties to 11 for larger entities with over 250 000 inhabitants; the largest had almost 70 employees. Most personnel were specialists (*e.g.* business school graduates, engineers, economists) and only a minority (30%) had a background solely in public administration (ExperConsult 2002).

5. A much smaller amount (circa EUR 500 million in total) was allocated for regional assistance in western Germany.

6. The description of the placement voucher is based on changes that came into effect in January 2005.

7. The PES also becomes responsible for social benefit (*Sozialgeld*) payments for family members of the unemployed.

8. The supplement amounts to two-thirds of the difference between Unemployment Benefit I and II in the first year and one-third in the second year. In contrast to the low flat-rate benefits under Unemployment Benefit II, the regular unemployment benefit compensates two-thirds of previous net wages (60% for single individuals).

9. These are model projections reported by the Federal Ministry for Economics and Labour (2004a). No empirical studies on the actual impact of the reforms are yet available.

10. The legislation also foresees an evaluation of the changes before a final decision is made on the mode of implementation.

11. Ca. two-thirds of these costs are borne by the local authority.

12. At the state level itself, the activities of various ministries must be harmonised.

13. The complexity of the implementation process is illustrated by the number of actors involved in financing state labour market programmes. For example, from

2000 through 2006, the ESF provided 34% of funding for the measures of the current labour market programme run by the state of Schleswig-Holstein. The state government covered 20%; the federal government, 21%; local authorities, 12%; and private sources, 13% (Schleswig-Holstein Landtag, 2006).

14. Expenditure of the German federal government in the same period totalled more than EUR 100 billion.

15. For previous literature, see in particular the highly instructive review by Schmidt, Hörrmann, Maier and Steffen (2004) and similar earlier works (Schmidt and Blanke, 1998, 2001) that provide detailed comparative analyses of state labour market policies in German federalism.

Bibliography

Berthold, Norbert (2005), "Arbeitsmarktpolitik in Deutschland – grottenschlecht oder nur schlecht?", *Wirtschaftswissenschaftliche Beiträge* No. 81, Bayerische Julius-Maximilians-Universität Würzburg.

Blanke, Susanne (2002), "Politik-Innovation im Schatten des Bundes. Eine Untersuchung von Policy-Innovation und –Diffusion an Hand der Arbeitsmarktpolitik der Länder", Tübingen, dissertation.

Blancke, Susanne and Josef Schmid (1998), "Die Aktive Abeitsmarktpolitik der Bundesländer im Vergleich: Program, Konzepte, Strategien", *Europäisches Zentrum für Föderalismus-Forschung*, Occasional Papers No. 18, Tübingen.

Bosch, Gerhard and Jürgen Nordhause-Janz (2005), "Arbeitsmarkt in NRW: Entwicklungen und Herausforderungen" in *Jahrbuch 2005*, Institut Arbeit und Technik Gelsenkirchen, pp. 47-64.

Bouché, Petra (2006), "Intermediäre Organisationen zur Umsetzung regionaler Arbeitsmarktpolitik in den deutschen Bundesländern. Die GIB in NRW als Beispiel für gute Praxis", Wissenschaftszentrum Berlin, unpublished manuscript.

Czommer, Lars and Claudia Weinkopf (2005), Beschäftigungsförderung für gering Qualifizierte: Erfahrungen und Ergebnisse der Modellprojekte im Rahmen des "Bündnis für Arbeit NRW", IAT Working Paper 2005-02, Gelsenkirchen.

Czommer, Lars, Matthias Knuth and Oliver Schweer (2005), "ARGE: Moderne Dienstleistungen am Arbeitsmarkt", Working Paper 104, Hans-Böckler-Stiftung, Düsseldorf.

Ditt, Karl (2004), "Westfalens Wirtschaft im 20: Jahrhundert – Vom Vorreiter zum Nachzügler", Westfälisches Institut für Regionalgeschichte, unpublished manuscript.

ExperConsult (2002), "Wo Steht die Wirtschaftsförderung in Deutschland? Befragung 2002", ExperConsult, Dortmund.

Federal Employment Agency (2005), "SGB II Zahlen, Daten, Fakten: Halbjahresbericht 2005", Federal Employment Agency, Nuremberg.

Federal Ministry for Economics and Labour (2004a), "Erste Basisinformationen zur Grundsicherung für Arbeitsuchende", Berlin.

Federal Ministry for Economics and Labour (2004b), "Merkblatt für zugelassene kommunale Träger der Grundsicherung für Arbeitssuchende gemäß 6a SGB II", Berlin, August.

Federal Ministry for Economics and Labour (2004c), "German National Action Plan for Employment Policy", Federal Ministry for Economics and Labour, Berlin.

GIB (Gesellschaft für Innovative Beschäftigungsförderung) (1994), "Geschichte, Selbstverständnis und Praxis der GIB", Bottrop.

GIB (2003a), "Kompetenzzentrum Beschäftigungsförderung NRW", GIB Report 2002/3, GIB, Bottrop.

GIB (2003b), "Arbeitsmarkt und Beschäftigungsfähigkeit im demographischen Wandel", GIB-Info 3/2003, Bottrop.

GIB (2004a), "Neue Strukturen in der Regionalpolitik NRW", GIB-Info, 1/2004.

GIB (2004b), "Kompetenzzentrum Beschäftigungsförderung NRW", GIB Report 2003/4, GIB, Bottrop.

GIB, (ed.) (2005a), "Neue regionale Strukturen zur Förderung von Innovation und Beschäftigung", Neue Arbeitspolitik in NRW: Beispiele guter Praxis, CD-ROM No. 4, GIB, Bottrop.

GIB (2005b), "Kompetenzzentrum Beschäftigungsförderung NRW", GIB Report 2004/5, GIB, Bottrop.

GIB, (ed.) (2005c), "Berichte über die Praxis von Projekten und Förderinstrumenten", Neue Arbeitspolitik in NRW: Beispiele guter Praxis, CD-ROM No. 4, GIB, Bottrop.

GIB (2005d), "Modellprojekte zur Beratung von Jugendlichen im Kreis Höxter", Neue Arbeitspolitik in NRW: Beispiele guter Praxis, CD-ROM No. 4, GIB, Bottrop.

GIB (2005e), "Die Initiative Regionen Stärken Frauen 2005", Neue Arbeitspolitik in NRW: Beispiele guter Praxis, CD-ROM No. 4, GIB, Bottrop.

GIB (2006b), "Kompetenzzentrum Beschäftigungs-förderung NRW", GIB Report 2005/6, GIB, Bottrop.

GIB (2006c), "Bericht an den Aufsichtsrat für das Jahr 2005: Ressourceneinsatz, Dienstleistungen und ihre Wirkungen", Bottrop, mimeograph.

Herrmann, Gerhard and Arnold Kratz (2004), "Arbeitsmarktpolitische Instrumente zum Beschäftigtentransfer", Working Paper 8, edited by Gesellschaft für Innovative Beschäftigungsförderung, GIB, Bottrop.

Jann, Werner and Günther Schmid, (eds.) (2004), Eins zu eins? Eine Zwischenbilanz der Hartz-Reformen am Arbeitsmarkt, Edition Sigma, Berlin.

Kißler, Leo, Ralf Greifenstein and Elke Wiechmann (2003), Kommunale Bündnisse für Arbeit, Edition Sigma, Berlin.

Kjellström, Sven (2006), "Moderne Arbeit und der Lissabon-Prozess: Rede auf der Fachtagung 'Moderne Arbeit – Wettbewerbsfähige Betriebe'", Bochum, 24 April, www.arbeitsmarkt.nrw.de/aktuelles/material/moderne-arbeit-kjellstroem.pdf.

MAGS (Ministerium für Arbeit, Gesundheit und Soziales) des Landes Nordrhein-Westfalen (2004), "Zur Zukunft der Europäischen Strukturpolitik. Positionspapier des Ministeriums für Wirtschaft und Arbeit NRW" in Gesellschaft für Innovative Beschäftigungsförderung (ed.), Neue Arbeitspolitik in NRW: Beispiele guter Praxis, CD-ROM No. 4, GIB, Bottrop.

MAGS des Landes Nordrhein-Westfalen (2006a), Arbeitsmarktpolitische Landesprogrammeme.

MAGS des Landes Nordrhein-Westfalen (2006b), Bilanz 2005-2006, MAGS, Düsseldorf.

MAGS des Landes Nordrhein-Westfalen (2006c), "ESF-Kofinanzierte Arbeitspolitik des Landes NRW Landesbericht über die Umsetzung im Zeitraum 1.1.2004 bis 31.12.2005", MAGS, Düsseldorf, May.

MWME (Ministerium für Wirtschaft, Mittelstand und Energie) des Landes Nordrhein-Westfalen (2006), *Wirtschaft in NRW 2006: Statistischer Anhang*, MWME, Düsseldorf.

Mosley, Hugh (2005), "Job-Centers for Local Employment Promotion in Germany" in Sylvain Higuère and Yoshio Higuchi (eds.), *Local Governance for Promoting Employment*, JILPT, Tokyo, pp. 165-178.

Mosley, Hugh (2003), "Flexibility and Accountability in Labour Market Policy", *Managing Decentralisation: A New Role for Labour Market Policy*, OECD, Paris, pp. 131-156.

Mosley, Hugh and Holger Schütz (2001), "The Implementation of Active Policies in the German Regions: Decentralisation and Co-operation" in Jaap de Koning and Hugh Mosley (eds.), *Labour Market Policy and Unemployment: Impact and Process Evaluations in Selected European Countries*, Edward Elgar, Aldershot.

Ombudsrat (2005), "Zwischenbericht", Berlin, June.

Reis, Claus *et al.* (2003), *JobCenter: Organisation und Methodik*, Ministerium für Wirtschaft und Arbeit Nordrhein-Westfalen, Düsseldorf.

Reis, Claus *et al.* (2005), "Leistungsprozesse im SGB II. Anregungen zur organisatorischen Ausgestaltung von Arbeitsgemeinschaften und Optionskommunen. Endbericht zum Pilotprojekt 'Arbeitsgemeinschaften' und Modellprojekt 'JobCenter in Kreisen'", Fachhochschule Frankfurt am Main.

Schleswig-Holstein Landtag (2006), "Kleine Anfage und Antwort der Landesregierung", Drucksache 16/876.

Schmidt, Josef and Susanne Blanke (1998), "Die aktive Arbeitsmarktpolitik der Bundesländer im Vergleich", Europäisches Zentrum für Föderalismus-Forschung, Tübingen, mimeograph.

Schmidt, Josef and Susanne Blanke (2001), "Arbeitsmarktpolitik der Bundesländer: Chancen und Restriktionen einer aktiven Arbeitsmarkt- und Strukturpolitik im Föderalismus", Edition Sigma, Berlin.

Schmidt, Josef, Ute Hörrmann, Dirk Maier and Christian Steffen (2004), Wer macht was in der Arbeitsmarktpolitik? Maßnahmen und Mitteleinsatz in den westdeutschen Bundesländern, LIT, Münster.

Schulze-Böing, Matthias (2004), "Erfolg ohne Mandat: Die Kommunen als arbeitsmarktpolitische Akteur in Deutschland", Offenbach.

Senator für Arbeit, Frauen, Gesundheit, Jugend und Soziales des Landes Bremen (2006a), *Aktive Arbeitsmarktpolitik des Landes Bremen*. Bremen.

Senator für Arbeit, Frauen, Gesundheit, Jugend und Soziales der Freien Hansestadt Bremen (2006b), "Informationen zum Arbeitsmarkt im Juni 2006", Bremen.

ISBN 978-92-64-04327-5
More than Just Jobs:
Workforce Development in a Skills-Based Economy
© OECD 2008

PART II

Chapter 6

The United Kingdom: Boosting the Role of Cities in Workforce Development

by
Dave Simmonds and Andy Westwood

It is in cities that full employment will ultimately be achieved or missed. Full employment in our largest cities will create the most socially inclusive society. To be in a position to achieve this outcome, cities need local government to have more powers over the processes that drive economic competitiveness and social cohesion. These needs are reflected in the government agenda for cities, employment and skills governance in the United Kingdom, which is changing rapidly with major reviews and announcements. Yet the changes to be made are significant and have implications for the way policies are designed and implemented across several government departments, and involve regional and local organisations. It is clear that major policy changes are being implemented, but the United Kingdom also needs to learn directly from best practice in other countries as new policy frameworks are developed and implemented.

Introduction

"The English are town-birds through and through, today, as the inevitable result of their complete industrialisation. Yet they don't know how to build a city, how to think of one, or how to live in one." – D.H. Lawrence, quoted in Asa Briggs, *Victorian Cities*.

"The majority of European citizens live in urban areas. Cities are centres of economic growth, but at the same time face concentrations of social, environmental and economic problems." (OECD, 2003)

Cities are where most people in the United Kingdom, Europe and the West now live and work, but are also places where most people who are not working live. With a concentration of key socioeconomic changes, the urban dimension is of increasing importance to both national and local politics. As a result cities are the focus for policy makers in the drive towards full employment.

Not unlike many other cities, cities in the United Kingdom have had to endure rapid and deep-seated economic and labour market changes in the past few decades. There may be little doubt that recent economic stability in the United Kingdom has provided some of the necessary conditions for an urban renaissance, and yet the overwhelming view is that this has benefited some areas much more than others. Many of the United Kingdom's major cities are still struggling with their collective legacy of de-industrialisation, major population shifts, low infrastructure investment and the consequences of mass unemployment.

Opinions in policy-making circles about the role of cities in driving the UK economy are sharply divided. Some consider city regions as key in driving higher national levels of innovation and competitiveness – while others are deeply suspicious of the capacities of local government and are unconvinced of the ability of our largest urban areas to drive even their own local economies. Such disagreement is not limited to the United Kingdom alone. Joseph Rykwert has recently described this polarisation of thought on the economic role of cities:

... critics of the city, economists particularly, have recently moved to a more radical argument: were cities after all, a real stimulus to economic and social growth or were they rather a parasitic excrescence on market economies that would have flourished even more without them? (Rykwert, 2004)

The drive, entrepreneurialism and networks within cities have brought with them large numbers of dependants and problems. This paradox, sharply evidenced in the United Kingdom, is where economies are at their most vibrant but also where they are at their weakest. Cities are highly heterogeneous places – with diverse populations and economies – but also with complex forms of social exclusion and poverty. The challenge then is to develop effective local policies for cities where economic opportunities exist alongside significant disadvantage, typically expressed in low employment levels and high concentrations of people with low or no formal qualifications. In the United Kingdom, these socioeconomic disparities have always been the basis for political disagreement rather than consensus.

Under the Conservative governments of Thatcher and Major (1979-1997), local city councils throughout the whole of the United Kingdom had their power drained to the centre. Major resources such as business rates were nationalised and new sources of local funding such as the poll and council taxes were introduced. Above all, the process of centralisation was a political one – most city councils were led by local Labour politicians and the removal of power (such as the closure of the Greater London Council in the 1980s) undoubtedly had a political objective. Alongside this process, de-industrialisation and high unemployment created major social problems in our cities, culminating in widespread rioting in the 1980s.

Much may have changed since 1997 with a Labour government, a stronger economy and lower unemployment, but the divided and haphazard approach to cities has continued. Devolution was a major theme of Labour's early years in government but mainly to countries and regions rather than to local government in cities. The one great experiment for cities was the introduction of the London Mayor and the (re)creation of the London Assembly. However, the election of the then independent candidate Ken Livingstone swiftly curtailed a wider expansion of the mayor and city devolution programmes. Only recently has this begun to change again. New powers for cities and local government are being considered alongside powers for devolved administrations in Scotland, Wales, Northern Ireland and London. Major reviews of skills policy have taken place alongside significant reforms to the UK welfare system. This chapter describes the performance of UK cities and their infrastructure for delivering skills and employment services. It also summarises the range of current and planned policy initiatives that are focused on improving city performance in one or both of these areas.

How policy is currently developed and delivered

According to HM Treasury and the Office of the Deputy Prime Minister (ODPM) (2003), "The Government's central economic objective is to achieve high and stable levels of growth and employment. An essential element of that objective is to improve the economic performance of every part of the United Kingdom, both for reasons of equity and because unfulfilled economic potential in every nation, region and locality must be released to increase the long term growth rate in the UK." Paul Krugman, a leading international economist, has said that: "One of the best ways to understand an economy is to study its cities" (Krugman, 1991). Likewise, the business analyst and Harvard academic Michael Porter has highlighted how the geographical clustering of industries helps to explain both the competitive performance of those industries, and the success of the regions and cities in which those clusters are located (Porter, 2003).

The views of both Krugman and Porter testify that, to succeed at the global level, the United Kingdom's exporting industries need to have successful cities in which to locate. That is because, for any business or industry, success generally depends on the ability to exploit increasing returns to scale – and these increasing returns are strongly dependent on the type of geographical agglomerations that cities offer (Krugman, 1991; Fujita, Krugman and Venables, 1999). This realisation of the role of cities as drivers of the UK economy is relatively new and a developing foundation for policy making and place-based policy. While there may be consensus among some urban economists and geographers, there appears to be little agreement amongst UK politicians and policy makers. To many, the UK cities are a reminder of industrial and social decline, economic dislocation and ineffective local government. Those convinced of the role of cities in a knowledge- and service-driven economy are starting from a very low evidence base. Little agreement, little power and fewer resources currently reside in UK cities. In comparison, the approach in France has been rather different where autonomous, localised decision making has led to the regeneration of French regional cities.

Decentralisation has thus far been confined to countries within the United Kingdom and to executive agencies acting at the local or regional level such as the Learning and Skills Council and regional development agencies. London has been the exception, but its powers are a result of pragmatic politics rather than planned decentralisation. London has whetted the appetite of other UK cities and regions that want more power. For the United Kingdom to be able to compete in the global economy[1] cities need to develop their competitiveness by being given increasing control over decision making and expenditure. This urban competitiveness is crucial for meeting the needs of the industries that will be driving the global economy forward over the long term.

Parkinson *et al.* (2004) show that strategic decision-making capacity is one of the five key drivers of urban competitiveness. It is also one of the most significant distinguishing features between high-performing continental

European cities and the larger cities in England – often described as the (English) Core Cities.[2] The complete list of the factors driving urban competitiveness are as follows:

- Innovation.
- Quality of the workforce.
- Sectoral diversity and specialisation.
- Connectivity.
- Strategic decision-making capacity.
- Quality-of-life factors.

In the United Kingdom, local city governments tend to have little direct control over many of these factors. In comparison with other OECD countries, the United Kingdom has the lowest level of local spending financed through local taxation. Le Galès estimates that French cities are responsible for approximately 70% of all public expenditure, whereas the figure in the United Kingdom is around 30%.[3] In Germany the figure is 35% and in the United States it is 42% (Simmie *et al.*, 2004). England has one of the most centralised systems of government in Europe; this results in the majority of strategic decisions being taken by central government, although local, regional and devolved tiers of government all exist. Employment services are almost exclusively delivered centrally for the whole of the United Kingdom and while skills are devolved to the different UK countries, most policy is still managed centrally by each country's administration.

In England, the governance framework is managed through public service agreement (PSA) targets for each department of state, including those with principal responsibility for cities, employment and skills. Until June 2007 these departments were the Departments for Trade and Industry (DTI); Education and Skills (DfES); Work and Pensions (DWP); and Communities and Local Government (DCLG), formerly the Office of the Deputy Prime Minister (ODPM). In June 2007, under the premiership of Gordon Brown, two of these departments were restructured. The DTI was renamed the Department for Business, Enterprise and Regulatory Reform (DBERR), and the DfES was split into two departments: the Department for Children, Schools and Families (DCSF) and the Department for Innovation, Universities and Skills (DIUS).

The new Department for Business, Enterprise and Regulatory Reform will take the lead in "creating the conditions for business success" and promoting "productivity and enterprise". The department will lead also on making sustainable improvements in the economic performance of the regions, and will provide support to the new Business Council for Britain. The department will also work closely with the new Department for Innovation, Universities and Skills (DIUS).

DIUS takes over some responsibilities from the former DTI, such as science and innovation, and others from the former DfES, including further and higher education and skills. With the overall aim of building a dynamic knowledge-based economy, DIUS will be responsible for improving Britain's global position for science, research and innovation, and for delivering the stated ambition of a world-class skills base. The DCSF will co-ordinate youth and family policy and will have specific responsibility for pre-19 education. It will also drive forward the government's Every Child Matters agenda.

Department for business, enterprise and regulatory reform (formerly DTI)

Policy developments in DBERR can be seen as relevant to the performance and governance of UK cities. The department has responsibility for several areas that impact on the overall competitiveness of cities such as economic diversity, but its mandate also covers skills; it is responsible for the Regional Development Agency network, and the Skills for Business Network that comprises of Sector Skills Councils that are designed to represent employer interests in the skill system, advising on labour market data, qualification content and other matters that employers see as priorities. DBERR also acts as a conduit for some European Union funding.

Public service agreement targets

The DBERR has 11 targets for 2004-08; at the time of writing, these remain the same as the former DTI targets. Several have a clear relevance to competitiveness in cities and many to employment and skills criteria in particular. They include:

- To demonstrate further progress on raising the rate of UK productivity growth over the economic cycle and improving competitiveness (a joint target with HM Treasury).
- To improve the relative international performance of the UK research base and the overall innovation performance of the UK economy.
- To help to build an enterprise society in which small firms of all kinds thrive and achieve their potential.
- To deliver measurable improvements in gender equality as one of the government's objectives for equality and social inclusion.
- To promote ethnic diversity, co-operative employment relations and greater choice and commitment in the workplace.
- To make sustainable improvements in the economic performance of all English regions and reduce the persistent gap in growth rates between regions (a joint target with DCLG and HM Treasury).

This last regional target involves improving Gross Value Added (GVA) per capita for each region, but also narrowing the gap between the North and South. Measures to bring about improvements include national, regional and sub-regional programmes that may be supported by European Structural Funds. Others measures may be local, including those aimed at neighbourhood renewal and raising enterprise and employment rates in deprived areas.

The major expenditure headings include small firms and enterprise, innovation, and regional development. Regional Selective Assistance and Enterprise Grants are targeted particularly at the problem areas of the six English regions. The DBERR target is to use such aid to lever in over GBP 3.75 billion of capital investment and create or safeguard 75 000 jobs by 2008.

Regional Development Agencies

Eight Regional Development Agencies (RDAs) became operational in April 1999, and the London Development Agency was established in 2000. They have a target to "provide the strategic framework to improve sustainable economic performance of each region, measured by the growth trend of GVA per capita, while also contributing to broader quality of life in the region". DBERR is lead sponsor for the RDAs and the portfolio of activities includes economic development and regeneration, promoting business efficiency, investment and competitiveness, and promoting employment and skills development.

Regional Economic Strategies – some looking forward to 2016 – detail the targets and spending programmes of the Regional Development Agencies' substantial budgets. This funding provides preferential support for the regions containing England's largest cities; the RDAs represent an important opportunity for support for developing entrepreneurial cities and city regions.

The Department for Communities and Local Government (DCLG)

DCLG is one of the government departments with the greatest potential for impact on city competitiveness. Its policies cover not only regeneration, spatial strategies, planning and local government but also the governance structures for regions and cities and consequently, their decision-making ability.

Selected DCLG targets

The significance of DCLG for competitiveness criteria is underlined by an examination of the department's targets and objectives. The overarching aim is to create thriving, inclusive and sustainable communities in all regions and to increase social inclusion, neighbourhood renewal and regional prosperity.

DCLG also aims to provide for effective devolved decision making within a framework of national targets and policies. Its ten targets include:

- Tackling social exclusion and delivering neighbourhood renewal by working with other departments to help them meet their floor targets.

- Making sustainable improvements in the economic performance of all English regions and reducing the persistent gap in growth rates between the regions (a joint target with the DBERR and HM Treasury).

- Improving the effectiveness and efficiency of local government in leading and delivering services to all communities.

- Improving the condition of social housing, particularly in deprived areas.

In addition to the PSAs, particular policy areas within DCLG that are of importance to city objectives include urban development, planning controls, policies on regional governance and sustainable communities. In addition there are many area-based initiatives, such as the New Deal for Communities, Urban Regeneration Companies and the Neighbourhood Renewal Fund, which impact on cities.

Department for innovation, universities and skills

As skill levels have been identified as a key component of regional competitiveness, the Department for Innovation, Universities and Skills has a key role to play in promoting the city agenda. It is also the second-biggest-spending government department. Given the importance of skills to city competitiveness, this section also considers the Learning and Skills Council (LSC), which is under the direct control of DIUS.

The aims of DIUS are to:

- Sustain and develop a world-class research base.

- Raise and widen participation in higher education.

- Raise participation of and attainment by young people and adults in post-16 education and learning.

- Tackle the skills gap among adults.

Learning and skills council

The Learning and Skills Council (LSC) is a semi-autonomous agency funded by government with responsibility for further education and adult- and employer-based learning. The LSC has a national council and 47 local councils – along boundaries that don't always match city or city region boundaries. While Greater Manchester provides a good city template, other cities have to depend on local LSCs that follow old boundaries and have yet to adjust to the city-region. The national LSC has the following objectives:

- To extend participation in education, learning and training.
- To increase the engagement of employers in workforce development.
- To raise the achievement of young people.
- To raise the achievement of adults.
- To raise the quality of education and training and user satisfaction.

Funding

The LSC was allocated GBP 10 billion for 2006/07 and it is also a recipient of European funding for education and training. Due to this funding injection through local Learning and Skills Councils, most cities do relatively well in terms of funding flows on a per capita basis.

Department for children, schools and families

This new department was created to bring together services for children and young people, with the broad aim of securing integrated children's services and educational excellence. In addition to its direct responsibilities, the department will lead work across government to improve outcomes for children, including work on children's health and child poverty. This integration of various policy streams has been carried out in order to enable government to cohesively deliver on the principal aims contained in its strategy called "Every Child Matters". DCSF's public service agreement targets are similar to the former Department for Education and Skills, but concentrate on policy and outcomes for the under-19s.

Selected DCSF targets

The DCSF has the following broad targets. Specific targets within them can be found in its Annual Report:

- To safeguard children and young people, improve their life outcomes and general wellbeing, and break cycles of deprivation.
- To raise standards and tackle the attainment gap in schools.
- To ensure that all young people reaching 19 are ready for skilled employment or higher education.
- To tackle the adult skills gap.
- To raise and widen participation in higher education.

These targets should benefit the cities by improving educational attainment and participation in further and higher education. However, these are national policies aimed at all areas of the country. If all areas show the same level of increase, then the relative disadvantage of cities will remain.

Funding

Overall government spending on education allocated for 2006/07 was nearly GBP 676 million and is set to rise in the years to 2010. Roughly half of this amount is controlled directly by DCSF and half is channelled through Local Education Authorities (LEAs). Although this suggests that there is significant devolution to local authorities and to cities, this spending only applies to schools and not to the skills infrastructure, which is mainly governed through the Learning and Skills Council (LSC).

Department for work and pensions

DWP targets are geared to ensure that there is full opportunity for everyone. Broadly, they may be expected to press policy in a direction that should help the major cities with their concentration of deprivation and disadvantage. Government policy has, however, drives that are not reflected in the targets. It is therefore much harder to be certain as to whether real overall policy tends in this direction across the board – for example in pensions policy, benefits policy and other areas.

DWP targets

Objective I – Ensure the best start for all children and end child poverty in 20 years.

- The broader target is to halve child poverty by 2010 and eradicate it by 2020 (joint target with HM Treasury).
- Double the proportion of parents with care on Income Support and income-based Jobseekers' Allowance who receive maintenance for their children to 65% by March 2008.

Objective II – Promote work as the best form of welfare for people of working age, while protecting the position of those in greatest need.

- To demonstrate progress in increasing the employment rate, in particular for disadvantaged groups, and to reduce gaps in employment rates for different groups (joint target with HM Treasury).
- To reduce the proportion of children in workless households (joint target with DCSF through the Sure Start Unit).
- To increase the employment rate of people with disabilities, and to improve the rights of disabled people and remove barriers to their participation in society.

Objective III – Combat poverty and promote security and independence in retirement for today's and tomorrow's pensioners.

● To increase pension credit payments to pensioner households.

Objective IV – Modernise welfare delivery so as to improve the accessibility, accuracy and value for money of services to customers, including employers.

Devolved administrations

The Labour government elected in 1997 created new devolved governments in Scotland, Wales and Northern Ireland. Education and skills were one of the areas of policy devolved to the new administrations. Some economic powers were also devolved such as limited tax raising powers. The Scottish system, particularly the education system, has traditionally been very different to that in England. Devolution has resulted in further divergence, with different higher education tuition fee policies, a merged further and higher education funding body, and changes to qualifications. Scottish cities, in theory, have no more power than cities in England, with a largely similar system of local government. However, with the Scottish Government now based in Glasgow and Edinburgh, devolution has lent an air of greater power to these two cities and provided significantly easier access to national politicians.

The same structure of local and regional government is broadly repeated in Wales and Northern Ireland, with a range of similarly "centralised" agencies and departments managing skills and economic development. However, one interesting aspect of the four UK systems is that the Skills for Business Network (comprising the 25 Sector Skills Councils) has a United Kingdom-wide brief. This creates some confusion over what is and what is not devolved to each UK country. It is felt that a sectoral approach has more relevance across the whole of the United Kingdom than uniquely to each constituent country.

Despite the complex web of local, regional and national government tiers, the emerging picture shows that UK cities do not feature prominently in governance hierarchy. Resources are limited at the local level, powers over both skills and employment are marginal, and devolution thus far has not led to significant changes at city level. The exception is London. It has a mayor and considerably enhanced powers over transport, skills and influence over employment policies. Partly, this has been because London has been viewed as a region rather than a city, and powers devolved to Regional Development Agencies in the rest of England have also been granted to the London region.

The UK policy context: What has – and has not – worked for cities?

A skilled workforce is a critical feature of competitive cities. Modern economies increasingly depend upon knowledge intensive sectors, even within manufacturing ... It was rated the most significant single factor by the private sector. (Parkinson *et al.*, 2004)

> If the resident employment rates in cities were raised to the overall national rate (without being reduced in other parts of the region), the entire region's employment rate would in most cases also be raised to the national average. (DWP and HM Treasury, 2003)

There are stubborn pockets of the United Kingdom where unemployment and low skills remain disproportionately high. Unemployment problem areas are more starkly apparent given the overall high UK employment rate. These relatively high employment rates compare well with other OECD countries, whereas skill levels tend to compare much less well. However, many of these places where skill levels are lowest and where unemployment or inactivity is highest are in the largest cities, the vast majority of which have resident employment rates below the current overall UK rate, approaching 75%. There are exceptions: both Bristol and Leeds perform above the UK average. At the other end of the scale, Liverpool, Birmingham and Manchester show the largest shortfalls, and London the largest overall.

Reflecting this, ILO unemployment rates vary widely across the largest cities and their wider regions. In 2001 Liverpool had the highest unemployment rate (11.5%), more than twice the UK average. Following Liverpool is Birmingham, with an unemployment rate of 9.2%, and Inner London with 8.5%. At the other end of the spectrum is Bristol with the lowest rate of ILO unemployment at 3.2%.

The UK economy has long been associated with having high employment rates – a relatively high proportion of people of working age are in employment. Much the same can be said for the city regions surrounding the other UK cities. Only Liverpool and Newcastle city regions had a lower employment rate than the OECD average in 2001.

The Department for Work and Pensions has provided estimates for the increase in the number of employed necessary to bring up the performance of each city to the national average employment rate. Perhaps surprisingly, the number of people working required to bring about the increase in Inner London is estimated to be 207 000 – considerably above that required in other cities. The DWP acknowledges that this required increase in employment rate in cities should be considered alongside the government's aim to close the employment rate gap for disadvantaged groups. In other words, the policy is not just about increasing employment but also about *how* it is increased. Additionally, the Department for Work and Pensions and the Treasury point out that cities provide the most important focus for getting employment and regional policy right:

> If the resident employment rates in cities were raised to the overall national rate (without being reduced in other parts of the region), the entire region's employment rate would in most cases also be raised to the national average. (DWP and HM Treasury, 2003)

Figure 6.1. **Employment rise required in selected cities**

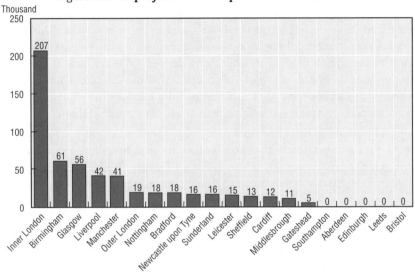

The problem of worklessness – as represented by the experiences of the main disadvantaged groups – is mainly concentrated in five of the United Kingdom's biggest cities: London, Birmingham, Glasgow, Liverpool and Manchester. Some of these cities also have major problems replicated in their surrounding city regions (Knowsley in Merseyside, for example). However, the problem in overall volume terms is essentially a city one; this is especially true in the North West region, where the shortfalls in Liverpool and Manchester are larger than the shortfall for the region as a whole.

The government has taken a predictably tough public line on the problem. In a piece entitled "Labour to Tackle Inner-city 'Culture of Worklessness'" (Denny, 2004), the *Guardian* reported the comments of the then Minister for Work, Des Browne. According to Browne, this "culture of worklessness endemic in many inner city neighbourhoods is marring Britain's enviable employment record".

However, solving what is essentially a set of city-based problems is not as politically straightforward as one might assume. Firstly, there has been a long-standing centralisation of political power in the United Kingdom;[4] local city authorities have little practical power or resources – and a fraction of those enjoyed by continental cities. The role of local authorities has remained limited under the New Labour government.

Labour's pre-1997 promises of devolution have been applied in the main to Scotland, Wales and Northern Ireland and more recently to the English regions, via the creation of Regional Development Agencies. Regional data on vacancies have underpinned the DWP's assessments of the healthiness of local labour markets; there have been numerous announcements about the level of vacancies created in previously depressed regions, and speeches stating that there are "more jobs than residents" in each of our larger cities. None of the announcements appears to fully capture the nuances of city regions and the complex labour markets that operate within them.

Cities instead have been the focus of numerous centrally led initiatives covering regeneration, education, transport and of course employment, through the creation of Jobcentre Plus and its raft of active labour market policies. Even where resources and decision making have been partially devolved to new local bodies such as Regional Development Agencies or local Learning and Skills Councils, the appointments have been directly controlled by central government and often devoid of local authority representation. This approach has not been without significant new sources of government funding, but none (with the rather tenuous exceptions of the New Deal for Communities and the Neighbourhood Renewal Fund) has come with any significant role for local city authorities.

The 2004 "Inner City Guarantee", pledging more jobs in Britain's deprived urban areas, indicated that creating the conditions for full employment will be a consistent major theme for Labour's policies:

> So to create jobs in the inner cities, we are creating an Inner City Guarantee, with our five point plan to refocus urban enterprise, training, employment and regeneration policies. Further measures to bring jobs and training to Britain's remaining areas of high unemployment will be a major theme of this summer's spending review. And our radical manifesto for a third term will set out tough new reforms to move Britain closer still to full employment. (Saturday, 29 May 2004 – See Inner City Guarantee on BBC Online)

The five-point plan included the creation of "enterprise areas" to boost local regeneration, a GBP 2 billion New Deal for Communities, a further GBP 1.8 billion urban regeneration push, more help for the unemployed, and specific help for people from ethnic minorities.

All of these elements demonstrated that the government was becoming more serious about reconstructing the conditions for full employment in even the most deprived urban areas, but may not necessarily allow cities to lead the process themselves. All of the measures in the Inner City Guarantee package were directly controlled and administered by central government departments or by agencies or quangos that report directly to them. This started to raise questions about where the best local knowledge and capacity resides – with local authority officers, or national agency staff, or indeed private sector providers.

In the United Kingdom there has been much debate about a "new localism" and "double devolution" and with these, the government's interest in the smallest of neighbourhood areas and the public services within them. Too often however, the analysis skips the importance of the city as a functional economic area. The rejuvenation of the largest UK cities may be continuing apace – and local authorities are leading the way – but UK cities still have little control over how their labour markets develop. The Local Government Act 2000 granted local authorities some economic responsibilities for promoting the "economic wellbeing" of their areas, and they have demonstrated that they have the capacity to both make decisions and deliver profound change for their cities.

There is then an opportunity for local and national governments to work together by combining Jobcentre Plus expertise with that found in town halls. In 2005 the national government signed an Accord with local government:

> In support of the national strategy, national and local government in England have agreed to work together on a number of shared priorities, one of which is promoting the economic vitality of localities by providing positive conditions for growth and employment, improving adult skills and helping the hardest to reach into work – the Partnership Accord between DWP, Jobcentre Plus and the Local Government Association commits the signatories to working together more strategically to increase employment rates and remove barriers to work – specifically through the use of innovative, flexible and collaborative working at a local level.[5]

This was, at the time, a big leap forward and was a clear pointer to how local flexibility and autonomy might practically work. It was especially important that the Accord was meaningful in the largest cities, where the biggest unemployment and inactivity problems exist. This has provided the basis for Local Strategic Partnerships and Local Area Agreements, and also for the 2006 launch of City Strategies.

Delivery of welfare reform in UK urban centres has had mixed results. Sometimes the services delivered or managed by Jobcentre Plus are performing most poorly in our largest cities.

Unemployment and Jobcentre Plus Performance

As mentioned above, the vast majority of the large UK cities have resident employment rates below the current overall UK rate of almost 75%. Variations in Jobcentre Plus performance between cities and other districts show that performance is vastly better in smaller towns but generally below average in the larger cities. Only Sheffield outperforms the UK average, with some – such as London, Liverpool and Birmingham – significantly underperforming compared to the average.

Table 6.1. **Jobcentre Plus district job outcomes**

	Lone parents	Sick and disabled	Long-term unemployed
Birmingham	1.9	0.2	10.9
Central London	1.4	0.2	9.3
City and East London	1.1	0.2	9.7
Leeds	3.2	0.3	17.0
Liverpool	3.1	0.3	10.8
Manchester	2.6	0.4	17.3
Newcastle	2.9	0.7	16.9
Nottingham	2.6	0.3	16.3
Sheffield	3.4	0.6	19.4
UK average	**3.3**	**0.5**	**17.6**
Wakefield	4.7	0.6	37.0
Wigan	4.5	0.3	18.7
Doncaster	4.6	0.4	31.2

Source: Jobcentre Plus job outcomes (1st Quarter 2004-05) – percentages of entire client groups.

Skills strategy

In his Pre-Budget Report delivered in December 2003, the then Chancellor introduced a policy that attempted to bring together the skills agenda with active labour market programmes such as the New Deal. In March 2004 the government pledged skills advisers in every Jobcentre Plus as well as further extensions of the existing Employer Training Pilots scheme.[6] Specifically, with the New Deal:

> The Government will ensure that its skills and employment services are restructured around the consumer rather than the producer, giving a stronger voice for employers, particularly through the work of Sector Skills Councils; clearly set out rights and responsibilities for individuals and employers in return for Government help; and support clear pathways for progression beyond subsidised training towards higher skills levels. (HM Treasury, 2004)

The government's Skills Strategy is an ambitious attempt to draw together many wide-ranging policy initiatives across several different government departments into a single coherent framework for skills and workforce development. The Department for Innovation, Universities and Skills and the Department for Work and Pensions have the most practical responsibility, through the Learning and Skills Councils and the Jobcentre Plus networks. The Strategy's main objectives are to improve national productivity and the strength of the economy while simultaneously improving the abilities of and prospects for individuals in both the labour market and organisations, specifically:

- To address skill shortage problems (especially at intermediate, technical and management levels).

- To give employers better support and information, greater choice and control over publicly funded training.

- To give individuals of any age a new entitlement to free learning at Level 2 (in particular sectors and regions – extended to Level 3 where appropriate).

- To develop new forms of financial support for learners.

- To further reform the qualifications system.

- To launch National and Regional Skills Alliances, comprising trade unions, business organisations and agencies of government (including Jobcentre Plus) to deliver the strategy.

- To provide better co-ordination and joint working among agencies of government involved with improving skills such as the Learning and Skills Councils, Jobcentre Plus, etc.

The challenge of improving the skills base of the UK workforce – and the provision of new skills for those in insecure work, unemployment or economic inactivity – are therefore likely to cut across a number of government departments. Specifically, welfare-to-work and skills policies will need to be delivered via a closer collaboration between the Department for Work and Pensions and the Department Innovation, Universities and Skills.

But in terms of cities there is a very long way to go. Just like the "work rich" and the "work poor", the lowest- and highest-qualified people tend to live side by side in our largest cities. Similarly, newly created employment opportunities remain to a large extent out of the reach of our most disadvantaged individuals and neighbourhoods. Too few city residents from disadvantaged groups or with low skills are able to compete with commuters from within the larger regions for the jobs that are currently being created. The case for change is compelling – for both social and economic reasons:

> I know that we cannot talk of real prosperity for all of Britain if thousands are left behind on the margins; that for economic efficiency and social justice reasons Britain needs an economy that works not just for some people some of the time but for all of the people all of the time.[7]

The fact is that people with better skills are more likely to be in work – and to hold on to it in the future. People with poor basic skills are five times more likely to be unemployed or totally out of the labour market than those with such skills. Men with good reading skills are over twice as likely to get promoted than those without (63% of men with poor reading skills have never been promoted, compared to 31% of men with good reading skills), and men and women with poor basic skills are over twice as likely to be sacked or made redundant than those with good skills (Healey and Engel, 2003). However, these conditions are expected to deteriorate still further and Digby Jones, the outgoing Director General of the Confederation of British Industry (CBI), famously claimed in 2004 that unskilled work would completely disappear in the United Kingdom within ten years.

Research by the Institute for Employment Research (IER) indicates that the growth in skilled work is expected to match a decline in unskilled jobs, and this evidence is further supported by the government's annual skill survey. However, there is uncertainty about how such decline and expansion in unskilled and highly skilled jobs will play out in the cities and regions of the United Kingdom, with currently more people with no qualifications employed in Northern cities and other regional towns and cities than in some parts of the South East.

Education levels in major English cities

Schooling is compulsory in England until the age of 16. Year 11 in secondary school is when most 15- to 16-year-olds sit their GCSE (General Certificate of Secondary Education) exams in a range of subjects. The percentage of secondary school pupils achieving a minimum of five GCSE passes at grades A-C is the benchmark at which educational performance at age 16 is measured across the country.

The educational achievement levels of both young people and those already of working age living in UK cities are poor. Typically, the number of young people living in the major English cities and attaining qualifications has been lower than both the national and regional averages. Of all Year 11 pupils taking GCSEs in the cities in 1994, 30.8% achieved five or more passes at grades A-C – some 12.3 percentage points behind the 1994 English average of 43.3%. In the same year, 13.5% of Year 11 pupils in the core cities – almost 5 500 young people – failed to pass any GCSEs at all, compared with the 1994 English average of 7.7%.

In the decade since, the national picture in cities has improved considerably, with some 51.6% achieving grades A-C and the share of those failing to get any GCSEs at all dropping to 8.6%. Each of the English major cities has also made significant improvements in their own educational performances. The most dramatic changes have taken place in Liverpool and Birmingham, where the number of Year 11 pupils earning grades A-C has risen by 15.0% and 14.2%, respectively.

Beyond the compulsory schooling age, 56.7% of 16- to 19-year-olds in core cities were in full-time education and training compared to national average of 57.4%. Some cities, for example, Liverpool, Manchester and Sheffield – have higher-than-average staying on rates. However, in all cases the performance of young people in the cities is below the regional average as well as the national levels. With a view to improving the skills across England and to tackle educational underperformance and reduce the number of young people leaving school at 16 with few or no qualifications, the government has published proposals recommending an increase of the compulsory education age from 16 to18.

The poor qualification levels of young people currently entering the workforce are generally matched by the poor skill levels of those already there. By and large, the stock of people of working age already in each of the core cities' workforces demonstrates lower-than-average qualification levels at virtually every point of the national qualifications framework.

There is a general tendency for the core cities to have: higher proportions of residents with no recognised qualifications; roughly average or slightly below-average achievement for those with low qualifications; average achievement for those with five GCSEs; and a general shortfall of people with graduate and postgraduate qualifications. (The performance of London accelerates away from the average because of the stronger graduate labour market.) The position at the top of the qualification structure has continued to improve. More people are achieving degrees and postgraduate qualifications and more of them are choosing to live in the core cities. However, the unqualified proportions have remained much more static.

The improvement in performance across cities has been uneven, with some cities doing better than others. Firstly, there are increasing numbers of graduates in some places (Manchester, Sheffield, Newcastle, Birmingham) as those economies continue to grow and they retain graduates. At the unqualified end of the spectrum, Leeds now has less than the national average and Sheffield has shown a dramatic 7 percentage point improvement in the numbers without a formal qualification. However, most other cities have seen little change or even an increase in the proportion of unqualified residents.

Educational performance and skills levels are therefore as significant (and interconnected) an issue as worklessness. While policy will need to move the skills and employment systems closer together, the priority of doing so in the larger UK cities will have to provide the testing ground.

What is changing in the United Kingdom?

As discussed, the UK policy framework for cities, employment and skills is rapidly developing. Cities, fuelled by a highly visible urban renaissance, are gaining new influence and powers. Following the 2005 General Election, new powers for London were to be followed by a "New Deal" for other cities in England. This potential devolution was touted by the then Minister for Communities and Local Government, David Miliband. In his consultation on additional London powers he embarked on a major policy review and tour of England's cities, asking each to make a case for greater powers.

A new Local Area Agreement[8] framework has provided the vehicle for putting a new wave of devolution in place – but with national government still retaining control through the target-setting framework. On top of these sometimes complex and *ad hoc* city governance arrangements comes a new raft of proposals and policy initiatives, including the potential for newly delegated powers, City Strategies from DWP, and a reorganisation of the skills system. Time will tell whether these initiatives clarify the landscape and improve conditions and resources within cities, or merely add new dimensions to the complexity and confusion surrounding the delivery of skills and employment services in UK cities.

London powers

In 2006, the government held a public consultation on the powers of the Mayor in London following a manifesto commitment during the 2005 General Election. "Skills" was one of the functions reviewed, along with housing, planning and waste. The outcome of the review has been that Ken Livingstone, the Mayor of London, has established a new London Skills and Employment Board that has developed a strategy and an annual plan for adult skills. These two documents inform the LSC on its adult skills expenditure in London. Delivery of the strategy and plan is the responsibility of the LSC; its job in London stays the same, namely to use the funds it receives from government to promote and deliver world-class skills to the individuals, employers and communities of London.

This sounds like a major devolution process for skills strategy; however, it falls short of what the Mayor requested. The strategy in London will still have to take its overall targets and responsibilities from the national objectives for the LSC. Furthermore, the Mayor only received powers over adult skills (from 19 years of age), so the settlement does not include 14-19 skills, which covers the majority of LSC funding throughout the country and in London. On top of that, while the Board's remit refers to employment, there are no clear responsibilities for employment devolved from DWP. Nevertheless, the new arrangements do have implications for the governance of the LSC in London.

These implications are being considered as part of the work the LSC, DCSF and DIUS are doing across the country on streamlining accountability structures.

This announcement is still good news for London, providing the Mayor with a new strong strategic role in skills. Under his responsibility, the Board will determine the London strategy for post-19 adult skills, building on and working within the framework of national skills targets, to address London's specific needs and drive the spending decisions of the LSC in London. The LSC is supposed to work closely with Jobcentre Plus and other partners in London, just as in the rest of the country. The strategy focuses on training and skills for adults in the labour market and those seeking to re-enter the labour market, and on the needs of London employers, large and small. It makes a strong link to jobs, tackling worklessness by ensuring people without jobs in London are helped through training to gain access to good jobs, and by integrating skills with business support. The Board is meant to ensure a close link between training and employment, particularly to help those without work gain productive employment. However, from the target and management processes described earlier we can see that these systems often have conflicting targets. Predominantly, one is driven by achieving qualifications and the other is about getting people into jobs that sometimes only last a short time. Expecting that the Mayor will somehow knit together these national systems and incentive structures is optimistic.

City strategies

DWP's City Strategy was initially announced in the Green Paper "A New Deal for Welfare in 2006", and is based on the recognition that to improve welfare-to-work outcomes, local consortia are needed. This responded to developments in other parts of government such as DCLG and also the new powers for London in skills, as well as to pressure from cities. City Strategies guidance states that "a central element of these proposals is a new strategy to tackle the highly localised pockets of worklessness, poverty, low skills and poor health that can be found across the United Kingdom, many of them within major towns and cities". City Strategies are based on the premise that local stakeholders can deliver more if they combine and align their efforts behind shared priorities, and are given more freedom to innovate and to tailor services in response to local needs. This is a big step for the centrally driven DWP and Jobcentre Plus structure, given that it has primarily tackled worklessness and benefits across the whole of the United Kingdom from a centralised structure governed directly by Whitehall civil servants and policy makers.

The then Secretary of State, John Hutton MP, described this as "a new contract between state and communities", pioneering modern forms of welfare delivery and offering freedom to innovate and flexibility. The City

Strategies will be an opportunity to pool funding from multiple funding streams at the end of the agreement. These are warm words and laudable ambitions but time will tell how much flexibility and innovation is allowed at the city level.

The selected areas cover most of the major UK cities and, not surprisingly, concentrate on those with the most stubborn problems of worklessness. This rules out cities such as Leeds, Bristol, and Cardiff as they typically have employment rates (and performance) at or above the national picture already. It also focuses some of the decision making at non-city areas such as in Rhyl – a coastal town in North Wales, and Heads of the Valleys – an old mining area in South Wales.

Speaking at the announcement of the winning cities, John Hutton said: "We are replacing the old one-size-fits-all welfare state that was run entirely from Whitehall, with tailored help for individuals and local initiatives. Harnessing the leadership our cities are providing will be a key part of this in years to come."[9] Delivery plans are intended to focus in particular on individuals who are currently farthest from the support available from the welfare state. The pattern of benefit receipt and disadvantage will vary from area to area, but this is likely to include incapacity benefit claimants, lone parents, older people and those from ethnic minority groups as well as those with low levels of formal qualifications. It is expected that consortia will join up the work of Jobcentre Plus and the Learning Skills Council to ensure that access to support is less complicated for individuals. Consortia will also be expected to ensure that the provision available better meets the needs of local employers, offering a clearer route from training and skills development to the workplace.

DCLG white paper and the Sub-national Review

There have been two recent important reviews on local issues: the Sub-national Review, jointly managed by Treasury and DCLG, about the optimal spatial frameworks for economic policy making; and the Lyons Review on local government finance.

Lyons inquiry into local government and the Sub-national Review

The Lyons Inquiry into Local Government explores the role and purpose of local government in England and the financial resources necessary at a local level. This independent inquiry began in 2004 to consider the case for changes to the present system of local government funding in England and make recommendations, including on the reform of council tax.[10] In September 2005 the government announced an extension to the Inquiry's terms of reference to cover questions relating to the function of local government and its future role, as well as how it is funded. The Review described economic development (or "place-shaping") as a major function of local government, with an associated need for influence over skills, employment, planning and regeneration policy.

In July 2007 the Treasury, along with the newly formed DBERR and the Department for Communities and Local Government, published the Sub-national Economic Development and Regeneration Review. To encourage economic growth, the Review sets out recommendations for the decentralisation of powers and responsibilities. The Review announced that the government will:

- Consult on the possible creation of a focused statutory economic development duty. This would require local authorities to carry out an assessment of the economic circumstances and challenges of their local economy. The assessment could cover the local labour market, skill levels and the condition of and planned investment in local infrastructure.

- Ensure that Local Area Agreements include a clear focus on economic development and neighbourhood renewal.

- Reform current arrangements for neighbourhood renewal funding by more intensive targeting of the Neighbourhood Renewal Fund, and consider introducing a reward element.

- Following machinery of government changes, transfer responsibility for funding 14- to 19-year-olds' skills policy from the Learning and Skills Council to local government.

- Consider options for supplementary business rates, working with local government, business and other stakeholders.

- Bring forward options for reforms to the Local Authority Business Growth Incentive (LABGI) scheme to produce a simpler, more certain scheme with a clear focus on growth.

- Work with the Regional Development Agencies so that they play a more strategic role, delegating responsibility for funding to local authorities and sub-regions where possible (unless there is a clear case for retaining funding at the regional level or there is a lack of capacity at lower levels).

Leitch Review of skills

The government announced in the 2004 Pre-Budget Report that Lord Leitch[11] had been asked to lead an independent review to examine the future skill needs of the UK economy. Specifically, the Review considered the skills base that the United Kingdom should aim to achieve in 2020 to maximise growth, productivity and social justice, and addressed the policy implications of achieving the level of change required. In particular, it examined the problems created by the separation of employment and skills systems and presented recommendations for better integration.

The Leitch Review of Skills published its interim report "Skills in the UK: The Long-term Challenge", setting out its analysis alongside the Pre-Budget Report in December 2005. Launching the Interim Report, Lord Leitch said:

Skills present a formidable challenge and a brilliant opportunity. They matter fundamentally for the economic and social health of the UK. Despite recent improvement there is consensus that we need to be much more ambitious and a clear message that the UK must "raise its game". This is an urgent task. The scale of the challenge is daunting. Delivering current plans will be difficult. Even then, it will not be enough to supply the skills that employers, employees and our nation needs in order to advance. The UK must become world class on skills – for all of our sakes.

The final report – Prosperity for All in the Global Economy – World Class Skills, published in December 2006 – points out that the United Kingdom is in a strong position with a stable and growing economy and world-leading employment rates, but that it also has persistently poor productivity rates trailing many OECD comparators. The report also found that over the last decade, the skills profile of the United Kingdom has improved because of a good higher education system, reforms to vocational training, and a more effective schools system. However, despite these improvements, there are still real weaknesses:

● Over one-third of adults of working age do not have a basic school-leaving qualification – double the proportion of Canada and Germany.

● Five million adults have no qualifications at all.

● One in six adults do not have the literacy skills expected of an 11-year-old and half do not have those of functional numeracy.

● Overall, the UK skills levels are not world-class; this is a key contributor to the United Kingdom's productivity gap and has a direct effect on social disparity.

The report sets out a compelling vision showing that the United Kingdom must urgently raise achievements at all levels of skills, and recommends that it commit to becoming a world leader in skills by 2020. It stresses that the responsibility for achieving this ambitious aim of doubling attainment at most levels of skills should be shared between government, employers and individuals. The main recommendations of the Review include:

● Increase adult skills across all levels – the raised ambitions will require additional investment by the state, employers and individuals.

● Strengthen the employer voice: rationalise existing bodies, strengthen the employer voice and better articulate employer views on skills by creating a new UK Commission for Employment and Skills.

- Launch a new "Skills Pledge" for employers to voluntarily commit to train all eligible employees up to medium-level skills in the workplace.

- Increase people's aspirations and awareness of the value of skills to them and their families.

- Create a new integrated employment and skills service, based on existing structures, to increase sustainable employment and progression.

- Establish a universal adult careers guidance service.

The Freud Review

The Freud report on welfare reform commissioned by the Department for Work and Pensions (DWP, 2007) has also set the stage for greater personalisation of employment support, with higher financial incentives for organisations to target resources at the hardest-to-help who need more support before they are ready to return to work. It suggests a rebalancing of rights and responsibilities – matching increased support with greater obligations on claimants to look for work. In particular, it recommends placing greater responsibilities on lone parents with older children to look for work once their youngest child reaches 12, rather than the current age of 16. This is certainly in line with recommendations in the governmental response to the Harker Report on child poverty, "Working for Children" (DWP, 2006). This response, published by the DWP in March 2007, refocuses GBP 150 million toward measures to provide greater support to families. The central objective stated in the report is to get more parents into work with the aim of reducing child poverty in the long term.

The government's response to Leitch

In July 2007 the government produced its response to the Leitch Review, "Implementing the Leitch Review in England". This report, published by the newly formed Department for Innovation, Universities and Skills (DIUS), sets out how the government has accepted the majority of the Leitch Review's recommendations, including the establishment of a UK Commission for Employment and Skills. There are plans for legislative reform to give adults the legal right to free training; alongside this choice, people will be given greater choice in their learning and will be offered tailored employment and skills advice. In turn the UK Commission for Employment and Skills will be the voice for employers, giving them more leverage over the content and delivery of skills and employment programmes. Critically the proposal for a new adult careers service was also accepted and will be formed by bringing together existing providers of information, advice and guidance on skills.

The response to Leitch was published alongside the Department for Work and Pensions report "In Work, Better Off: Next Steps to Full Employment". This report sets out proposals to deliver a step change in the support offered to those who are most disadvantaged in the labour market. Key proposals include:

- A new social contract with lone parents that increases rights and responsibilities to find work.
- A more personalised, flexible and responsive New Deal for unemployed people, delivering support that is right for the individual.
- A more integrated skills and employment system.

Also proposed is a new "jobs pledge", which will build on the Local Employment Partnerships announced in the 2007 Budget. The aim is for major employers to offer a quarter of a million job opportunities to the long-term out-of-work. At the launch of the report the Secretary of State for Work and Pensions, Peter Hain MP declared:

> The publication today of both our Green Paper In Work Better Off and the Leitch Implementation Plan spells out our aim to hit an employment rate of 80%. Eradicate child poverty and build economic prosperity and a fairer society.[12]

What will happen next?

Clearly the government agenda for cities, employment and skills governance is changing rapidly with major reviews and announcements in 2006 and 2007. This has meant a reallocation or refocusing of resources in the government's Comprehensive Spending Review, which will cover all spending for the period 2008-11 and the next phase of government policy during that time.

It is clear that major policy changes are being implemented, but the United Kingdom also needs to learn directly from best practice in other countries as new policy frameworks are developed and implemented. While each of the different government departments, agencies and policy areas may be doing this independently, lessons are being learned across boundaries. The point is that cities matter. It is in them that full employment will ultimately be achieved or missed. Equally, the ambitions for skills set out in the Leitch Review will not be met unless the resident populations of our largest cities, and the employers based there, begin to raise their collective sights.

City economies matter too. As leading European and North American cities show us, strong urban areas make up strong and productive regional and national economies. Cities also matter for social and political reasons; full employment in our largest cities will create the most socially inclusive society and the strongest evidence that politicians representing these areas are really working in their constituents' main interests. In the long term it may well be that local government requires major reform before it is able to take up fully these kinds of economic and social challenges. Cities need local government to have more powers over the processes that drive economic competitiveness – and as London has proved, it is better to have such government than not.

Notes

1. In addition to place competitiveness, determinants of national competitiveness include a stable macroeconomic policy framework conducive to business confidence and investment; policies that promote effective competition between enterprises; and high rates of investment at the national level in education, skills, research and innovation, and in the nation's transport and communications infrastructure.

2. The Core Cities group was formed in 1994 from the largest regional cities in England: Birmingham, Manchester, Liverpool, Newcastle, Nottingham, Leeds, Bristol and Sheffield.

3. Patrick Le Galès, Université de Paris, Speech to Core Cities Summit, April 2002.

4. See Parkinson *et al.*, 2004 for a discussion of this process.

5. See National Partnership Accord Toolkit at *www.cesi.org.uk*.

6. See Budget Speech and accompanying papers, 17 March 2004: *www.hm-treasury. gov.uk*.

7. Gordon Brown, Speech to the Urban Summit, 1 November 2002.

8. Local Area Agreements are a set of targets and performance indicators agreed between local authorities and central government. Achievement of targets releases discretionary funds for local authorities to invest in their areas.

9. Speech by John Hutton MP, DWP City Strategies Conference, May 2006.

10. The local tax levied on households according to the value of the property.

11. Lord Leitch has held various positions in UK companies and is Chairman of the National Employment Panel. He was previously a Chief Executive of Zurich Financial Services (United Kingdom, Ireland, Southern Africa and Asia Pacific) and Chairman of the Association of British Insurers.

12. DIUS press release, 17 July 2007.

Bibliography

Amin, A., D. Massey, and N. Thrift (2003), "Decentring the Nation: A Radical Approach to Regional Inequality", Catalyst Paper 8, Catalyst, London.

Barclays Bank (2002), "61 City Study", *www.newsroom.barclays.co.uk/news/data/712.html*.

Begg, I. (ed.) (2002), *Urban Competitiveness: Policies for Dynamic Cities*, Policy Press, Bristol.

Comedia (2001), "Releasing the Cultural Potential of our Core Cities", Comedia, Gloucester.

Denny, C. (2004), "Labour to Tackle Inner-city Culture of Worklessness", *Guardian*, 1 April.

DfES (Department for Education and Skills) (2007), "Raising Expectations: Staying in Education and Training Post-16", March 2007. See *www.dfes.gov.uk*.

DTI (Department for Trade and Industry) (1998), "Our Competitive Future: Building the Knowledge-Driven Economy", CM4176, DTI White Paper, London.

DTI (2003), "Innovation Report: Competing in the Global Economy: the Innovation Challenge", DTI, London.

DTI/Regional Studies Association (2003), "Regional Growth Rates, Delivery Plans and Targets", Seminar, DTI Conference Centre, London, 23 June.

DWP (Department of Work and Pensions) (2006), "Delivering on Child Poverty – What Would It Take", November.

DWP (2007), "Reducing Dependency, Increasing Prosperity: Options for the Future of Welfare to Work", March.

DWP and HM Treasury (2003), "Full Employment in Every Region".

Fujita, M., P. Krugman and A. Venables (1999), *The Spatial Economy: Cities, Regions and International Trade*, MIT Press, Cambridge, Mass.

Healey, J. and E. Balls (eds.) (2002), *The Age of Regions*, The Smith Institute, London.

Healey, J. and Natascha Engel (2003), "Learning to Organise", TUC and the Work Foundation.

HM Treasury (2004), "Meeting the Productivity Challenge", Treasury Budget Report.

HM Treasury and ODPM (Office of the Deputy Prime Minister) (2003), "Productivity in the UK : The Local Dimension".

Huggins, R. (2002), "The State of Urban Britain", Robert Huggins Associates, Cardiff.

Krugman, P. (1991), *Geography and Trade,* MIT Press, Cambridge, Mass.

Leitch Review of Skills (2005), "Interim Report: Skills in the UK: The Long Term Challenge", London.

Leitch Review of Skills (2006), "Final Report: Prosperity for All in the Global Economy – World Class Skills", *www.hm-treasury.gov.uk/leitch*.

London School of Economics and Political Science (2003), "London's Place in the UK Economy 2003", City Corporation of London, London.

Lundvall, B.-A., (ed.) (1992), *National Systems of Innovation: Towards a Theory of Innovation and Interactive Learning*, Frances Pinter, London.

Marshall, A. (1920), *Principles of Economics*, Macmillan London.

Martin, R. and P. Sunley (2003), "Deconstructing Clusters: Chaotic Concept or Policy Panacea?", Journal of Economic Geography, 3, pp. 5-35.

Mercer (2003), "Overall Rankings", Quality of Life Survey, London.

ODPM (Office of the Deputy Prime Minister) (2002a), "Cities, Regions and Competitiveness: Interim Report from a Working Group Representing Government Departments, London/Regional Development Agencies and the English Core Cities", ODPM, London.

ODPM (2002b), "Towns and Cities: Partners in Urban Renaissance", ODPM London.

ONS (Office for National Statistics) (2001a), "E-commerce: A Regional Analysis", *Economic Trends*, No. 574, September.

ONS (2001b), "Economic Trends", No. 576, November.

OECD (1999), *OECD Science, Technology and Industry Scoreboard: Benchmarking Knowledge-based Economies*, OECD, Paris.

OECD (2000), *A New Economy? – The Changing Role of Innovation and Information Technology in Growth*, OECD, Paris.

OECD (2003), *City and Regional Investment*, OECD, Paris, p. 170.

Parkinson, M., M. Hutchins, J.M. Simmie, G. Clark and H. Verdonk (2004), "Urban Renaissance Characteristics of EU Non-capital Cities", ODPM, London.

Porter, M. (1990), *The Competitive Advantage of Nations*, Macmillan, London.

Porter, M. (2002), "Regional Foundations of Competitiveness and Implications for Government Policy", Department of Trade and Industry Workshop, 16 April.

Porter, M. (2003), "The Economic Performance of Regions", Regional Studies, 37, pp. 549-578.

Porter, M. and C.H.M. Ketels (2003), "UK Competitiveness: Moving to the Next Stage", DTI Economics Paper No. 3, DTI, London.

Robson, B. and I. Deas (2000), "Slim Pickings for the Cities of the North", Centre for Urban Policy Studies, Manchester.

Rykwert, Joseph (2004), *The Seduction of Place: The History and Future of the City*, Oxford University Press, p. 20.

Simmie, J.M., (ed.) (2001), *Innovative Cities*, Spon, London.

Simmie, J.M. (2002d) "Innovation and Competitive Cities in Europe", in Begg, I. (ed.) *Competitive Cities*, Bristol, Policy Press, pp. 161-189, with James Sennett and Peter Wood.

Simmie, J.M. *et al.* (2004), "Realising the Economic Potential of London and the Core Cities", OBU, Oxford.

ANNEX 6.A1

Glossary of UK Institutions

This glossary provides a brief description of the key institutions and agencies in the UK involved in the delivery of skills.

England

Adult Learning Inspectorate (ALI) – formed in 2001, formerly the Training Standards Inspectorate, inspects the quality of all adult learning provision, including further education. Colleges, Work Based Learning (including apprenticeships), Jobcentre Plus programmes. Works with OfSTED on joint inspections.

Business Link – network of business and enterprise support partnerships newly overseen by RDAs. In existence since the 1990s. Forty-four local partnerships coterminous with LSC except London, where this is one service across four local London LSCs. Provides brokerage for NETP.

Centres of Vocational Excellence (CoVEs) – launched as quality-enhancing specialism programme in Success for All 2001. Mainly sited in colleges but also with private providers, employers and collaborative partnerships between colleges.

Connexions Service – operates as 47 local partnerships providing support and guidance to young people aged 14-19.

Higher Education Funding Council for England (HEFCE) – funding council for universities (not covering research funding).

Investors in People – launched in 1990 as a vehicle for accrediting good HR practice.

Jobcentre Plus – formed from merger of Employment Service and Benefits Agency to deliver all work-related benefits and welfare-to-work programmes. Also funds learning providers to deliver some skills programmes.

Learning and Skills Council (LSC) – launched in 2000, consists of National Council and 47 local LSCs. Resources gradually being shifted to regional tier. Controls vast majority of skills funding (over GBP 9 billion).

Learning and Skills Development Agency – to be relaunched as Quality Improvement Agency and Learning and Skills Network in 2006 (see below). Formed in 2001.

Local Education Authorities (LEAs) – Local Authority education services – mainly responsible for schools (including sixth forms) but also for local Adult Education services.

Office for Fair Access in Education (OFFA) – office for monitoring and regulating admissions processes and policies to UK higher education (HE) institutions.

Office for Science and Technology (OST) – a DTI body responsible for university research funding and a range of additional support and investment programmes. Manages and funds all of the United Kingdom's research councils.

OFSTED – inspection body for all education provision to age 19. Overlaps and collaborates with ALI.

Quality Assurance Agency for Higher Education (QAA) – safeguards and helps to improve the academic standards and quality of higher education in the United Kingdom.

Qualifications and Curriculum Authority (QCA) – body charged with regulating exams and curricula in England.

Quality Improvement Agency for Lifelong Learning, as set out in the 14-19 White Paper. It will be invited to propose a quality improvement strategy to address key government priorities and enable colleges and training providers to improve and respond to change. Continuing to improve quality of teaching and learning will be a priority. The agency will be fully operational by April 2006.

Regional Development Agencies (RDAs) – nine RDAs in England are responsible for economic development of regions. RDAs house Regional Skills Partnerships and are also responsible for Business Link network (and therefore NETP brokerage). NB London Development Agency reports to London Mayor.

Sector Skills Councils (SSCs) – 25 Sectoral bodies forming Skills for Business Network with SSDA (see below). Represents over 85% of UK workforce. Operate across whole of the United Kingdom.

Sector Skills Development Agency (SSDA) – supports and licenses Sector Skills Council across whole of United Kingdom.

Skills Academies – launched in 2005 as employer-sponsored skills institutions with LSC and private sector money. Expected to total 25 (one per sector) and be connected to CoVE network.

UK Skills – independent body with responsibility for promoting skills agenda. Oversees National Training Awards and Skills Olympics. Potentially merging with Investors in People.

Union Learning Academy – intended to bring together various union learning initiatives including further education training centres for Union Learning Representatives and Trade Union centres for UK Online/learndirect centres.

University for Industry (UFI) (learndirect) – advice and delivery organisation concentrating on information, advice and guidance (IAG) services, skills for life and ICT programmes. Operates learndirect and UK Online centres.

Scotland

Scottish Qualifications Authority (SQA) – responsible for supervising and developing Scottish qualifications and curricula.

Communities Scotland – a Scottish executive agency. Aims to work with others to ensure decent housing and strong communities across Scotland – similar to ODPM in England with some area- and community-based skills initiatives.

HMIE – Scottish education and training inspectorate.

Scottish University for Industry (SUFI) – similar to UFI in England, offering advice and information to individuals and businesses. However, does not offer any courses or programmes directly.

Learning and Teaching Scotland (LTS) – is an agency of the Scottish executive designed to support excellence in all teaching and learning activities.

Careers Scotland – all-age careers and guidance service, supervised by Scottish Enterprise and Highlands and Islands Enterprise.

Learning Connections – provides policy advice to ministers on all matters relating to community learning and development (CLD). Community engagement team works with communities to help them take decisions and develop solutions for the regeneration of their local areas.

Scottish Enterprise – main enterprise agency for Scotland. Operates jointly with Highlands and Islands Enterprise. The Enterprise Networks: Scottish Enterprise and Highlands and Islands Enterprise incorporate the all-age careers service, Careers Scotland; Futureskills Scotland; business support services and local enterprise companies.

Wales

Wales Employment Advisory Council (WEAP) – Advises on Employment and Welfare to Work Programmes (equivalent to NEP in England).

Business Eye – Free, impartial information service for Wales created to find the answers to business questions – equivalent to Business Link in England.

Business Partnership Council – The Wales equivalent to Skills Alliance in England.

Community Consortia for Education and Training (CCETs) – Their primary role is to achieve more efficient delivery of education and training and to promote collaboration between schools, further education and training providers and others so as to meet the needs of individuals and employers more effectively and coherently. CCETs will be the National Councils' essential link with the local learning market.

DYSG – Supports FE and work based learning in Wales, equivalent to Learning and Skills Development Agency in England.

Education and Learning Wales (ELWA) – Key government agency in Wales providing funding and strategic direction to other agencies and providers.

ESTYN – Welsh education and training inspectorate.

Higher Education Funding Council for Wales (HEFCW) – *the funding body for higher education in Wales.*

Networks for Excellence – Equivalent to CoVEs in England.

Team Wales Approach – Inward investment partnership of key agencies in Wales.

Welsh Development Agency – Main enterprise agency for Wales, made up of four sub-regional areas.

Northern Ireland

Council for the Curriculum, Examinations and Assessment (CCEA) – A non-departmental public body reporting to the *Department of Education* in Northern Ireland. Equivalent to QCA in England. QCA retains responsibility for some qualifications in Northern Ireland, such as NVQs.

Department for Education and Learning Northern Ireland (DELNI) – Main department overseeing (and funding) key initiatives, institutions and agencies in Northern Ireland.

Education and Library Boards (ELBs) – Five ELBs in Northern Ireland. Equivalent to Local Education Authorities.

Enterprise Ulster – Careers guidance and training agency for Northern Ireland. Offers advice and training for unemployed in conjunction with Jobcentre Plus.

Invest NI – Main inward investment partnership for Northern Ireland.

Northern Ireland Skills Taskforce – Formed in 1999 to advise the Training and Employment Agency (since incorporated into the Department for Employment and Learning) and Department of Education on action to address current and future skill needs in the NI economy and related labour market research. Members include employer and trade union representatives.

ISBN 978-92-64-04327-5
More than Just Jobs:
Workforce Development in a Skills-Based Economy
© OECD 2008

PART II

Chapter 7

Australia: Local Employment Strategies that Address Diversity

by

Cristina Martinez-Fernandez

Designing employment strategies is a complex issue in Australia, a vast continent with different labour market policy scenarios. One of the scenarios is found in the seven capital cities. These cities grow into extended metropolitan regions, where hubs of skills and knowledge-intensive activities coexist with suburbs of social disadvantage. Other scenarios are found outside these capital cities: in regional centres and remote communities. On the one hand are the booming, prosperous towns where there is a fierce demand for skilled workers, and on the other are the shrinking towns and declining regions, where simply retaining people is a major task for local agencies. These different scenarios indicate the challenges of applying centralised labour market policy instruments to areas with very different market and lifestyle conditions. They also show the important role of local knowledge relevant to local needs, and essential to the design of local employment strategies.

The Australian context

The performance of the Australian economy has been one of high economic growth for a long period – from the mid-1980s through to 2006 – with a short interval of recession in 1990-91. Among the factors that contributed to this economic prosperity are: low inflation; the opening of national economies into a global economy; increased productivity driven by technological development; the emergence of the knowledge-based economy; and economic policies associated with trade liberalisation, deregulation and micro-economic reform (Larcombe, 2007).

This high economic growth has led to impressive economic outcomes for Australia, with official unemployment rates declining from 11% in the early 1970s to the current rate of 4.5%. Incomes per capita have increased by 50% over the past 15 years due to high productivity and trade with Asian neighbours, especially China. The resources sector in Australia is experiencing very strong demand from the extraordinary growth of China and its importation of Australian minerals and energy commodities. Analysts, however, are warning that the Chinese economy is overheating and the global economy is entering a period of uncertainty – and therefore, Australia's economic bonanza might not last (Larcombe, 2007).

One of the consequences of strong economic growth with full employment is the emergence of skills shortages. It does needs to be taken into account, however, that in Australia a person is defined as "employed" if s/he works more than one hour per week. Many adults are thus underemployed or in employment conditions under the poverty line. In a good number of cases, these underemployed have limited skills and little to offer to help improve their employability. Skill shortages appear in a vast number of occupations. Unemployment rates for managers, professionals, associate professionals and advance clerical workers have historically low levels in the last decade, 1-2%. The unemployment rates for tradespersons and related workers are also declining, and significant skills shortages are emerging in these areas. There is thus a situation of rapid growth in both high-paid, knowledge-intensive jobs and casual, low-paid, low-skilled jobs, with many qualified people being employed in these lower-skilled jobs. This is especially the situation for many migrants and refugees entering the country.

Several programmes address the skills needed for the future of the country. Significant among these are the Skilled Migration programme;

Skilling Australia's Workforce; the Australian Apprenticeship Scheme; and the Skills for the Future Package. Attracting skilled migrants is an important policy for Australia's future. The Department of Immigration and Citizenship has established the Skills Matching Database (SMD) (Department of Immigration and Citizenship) to help match skilled people who have applied to migrate to Australia with skilled vacancies or skill shortages in Australia. This database is used by employers for employer-sponsored migration categories, as well as by state and territory governments. Industry sectors where the Employer Sponsored Migration is frequently used are building and construction, abattoirs and mining.

Skilling Australia's Workforce creates the basis for a partnership between the commonwealth, state, and territory governments[1] to work together to support new national training arrangements on a consensus approach (Australian Government, 2006). The agreement provides close to AUD 5 billion over the 2005-08 quadrennium, with the potential to create up to 128 000 additional training places Australia-wide.

Australian Apprenticeships is a scheme directed at attracting people to trades. It combines training and employment, and leads to a nationally recognised qualification. The apprenticeships are available to anyone of working age and do not require any entry qualification. In March 2006, there were 403 600 Australian apprentices in training (National Centre for Vocational Education Research). Since 1 July 2006, the Australian Apprenticeship Incentives Programme has provided financial incentives to employers who hire and train an apprentice. On 12 October 2006, the government released in the Skills for the Future package, worth AUD 837 million over five years, as a set of initiatives focusing on the need for continuous upgrading of skills within the workforce. Among these initiatives is the Australian Skills Voucher Programme for apprentices and the less qualified; those eligible can purchase training courses using these vouchers.

As can be seen from the above discussion, national priorities are strongly oriented towards solving the acute skills shortages in many trades, which represent a disappearing core of talent for innovation, especially in manufacturing regions. Trades are rapidly vanishing in Australia, as occupations related to the knowledge economy successfully attract the young. Tradespersons are responsible for many activities linked to firm innovation, as they provide skills related to the core competencies of manufacturing and engineering businesses. Apprenticeship programmes have been the traditional way to attract new talent into this sector, and skills programmes therefore seek to increase the number of apprentices. However, the absolute number of apprentices is not a good measure for understanding responses to labour market demand in the short term. Instead, the key measure is the training rate – the ratio of apprentices to tradespersons, and the average age of on-the-job tradespersons. These measures indicate the extent of the trade occupations reproducing themselves through the domestic training system. The Australian case is an interesting one because, due to the privatisation of government services, there has been a major decline in the training rate over the last decade – 16% in aggregate terms, but a decline of as much as 25% in some trades. If we add this to the fact that the average age in some of the trades is in the 50s, it shows the matter to be one of serious concern, as the training system is not able to reproduce these skills (Toner, 2003).

The reasons behind this situation are complex, and encompass both national and international factors that translate into an effect on the local labour market. In the case of Australia, prior to the major corporatisations and privatisations of the 80s and 90s, government-owned enterprises in major infrastructure services were large employers of tradespersons, not just in service provision but also in employing trainees. As a result of the privatisations, the focus was no longer on training, and a reduction of 80-90% in the intake of apprentices followed over the next ten years, although there has recently been an increase in public sector intake. Another influencing factor in the last 10-15 years has been the pattern of corporate restructuring to outsource maintenance services to labour hire companies, which basically employ no apprentices. In addition, the focus on corporate downsizing and outsourcing has led to a significant reduction in firm size in manufacturing, construction and mining technology services industries. These small firms have fewer training programmes and lower investment per employee than larger firms (Toner, 2003, 2005).

The implications of a training system that is not able to reproduce these skills are of concern at the local level, as well as for the industry as a whole. Economic implications are evident when companies are unable to find tradespersons locally or nationally, and so have to hire from overseas markets. However, there are other critical implications in terms of innovation, which are more difficult to see in the short term. Many of the trades experiencing skill shortages, such as metal, engineering, electrical and construction, represent an important source of innovative activity for the manufacturing, transport and mining industries that cannot be supplied by scientists or traditional research. Technological innovation needs the input of people on the job, because they provide feedback in the use of machinery or processes, which then goes back to universities, research laboratories and firm management. Thus, in reality, innovation activity is to a great extent fuelled from the floor of the workplace (Toner, 2003). Shortages of these key trade skills reduce the innovation capacity of a place and of the industry in general, as there is a collateral reduction of professionals' input in knowledge-intensive service activities (KISA) (Martinez-Fernandez and Miles, 2006; OECD, 2006).

The discussion above shows the elements impacting labour policy in Australia, national programmes addressing skills needs, and some of the consequences at the local level. However, national policies and programmes are designed for the country as a whole, and the flexibility to adapt and adjust to different environments is therefore limited. There is a need to translate and customise national labour policy to the local level. New planning processes beyond land management also need to be developed to achieve employment growth. Local institutions are best placed for developing processes of Strategic Employment Planning, where available talent and demand for skills can be analysed to design interventions in a particular employment space. It is within that context that this chapter seeks to contribute – by arguing that labour policy needs to be customised to different socioeconomic scenarios, which require different employment strategies.

Scenarios for Strategic Employment Planning (SEP)

Australia currently has a population of 20.6 million. Of this population, 76.9% are Australian-born and 23.1% are foreign-born. Up to 1.7% of the population are Indigenous. The fertility rate is low (1.76) – which, combined with an increase in deaths from an ageing population, will result in the fertility rate falling below zero in the mid-2030s. Up to 23% of the population are migrants, with the highest numbers coming from the United Kingdom, New Zealand and Italy. Australia is one of the world's most urbanised countries: 85% of the population live in urban areas and are concentrated in the seven capital cities, and 15% live in rural areas. Up to 70% of Australian land is arid and semi-arid; consequently, the population is concentrated in the coastal cities (Martinez-Fernandez and Wu, 2007). This demographic diversity results in at least three different scenarios for employment growth.

One scenario is found in the seven capital cities. These cities grow into extended metropolitan regions where hubs of skills and knowledge-intensive activities coexist with suburbs of social disadvantage. The other scenarios are found outside the capital cities: in regional centres and in remote communities. On the one hand are the booming, prosperous towns where there is a fierce demand for skilled workers, and on the other are the shrinking towns and declining regions where simply retaining people is a major task for local agencies. These different scenarios indicate the challenges of applying centralised labour market policy instruments to areas with very different market and lifestyle conditions. They also show the important role of local knowledge relevant to local needs, and essential to the design of local employment strategies. This section discusses the three scenarios, and the local initiatives that created customised national policies and programmes.

Scenario 1: Booming cities – Mackay

Mackay is a city of 84 856 inhabitants, located on the central coast of the state of Queensland in Australia – 1 948 km north of Sydney and 974 km north of Brisbane. Mackay has the distinction of being the largest sugar-producing region in Australia, with the largest bulk sugar facility in the world (737 000-tonne capacity). In addition, the Mackay region has the largest coal-loading terminal in the southern hemisphere (Hay Point), with a capacity of over 50 million tonnes per annum. The resources boom in Australia has seen Mackay's minerals and mining industry explode; there are over 20 coal mines now operating in the region. Mackay's unprecedented growth and subsequent wealth creation since 2004 has put significant pressure on company development; skill shortages in particular are a constant threat to industry growth.

Mackay's extraordinary growth draws attention to the mismatch of talent in the area, as well as the lack of skilled people. Skilled workers from the sugar industry needed retraining for the mining boom; there was a shortage of school-leavers wishing to enter a trade; and the available large Maltese and Indigenous populations are largely a pool of untapped talent. In particular, the last ten years show a growing population in the Mackay-Whitsunday region, which is expected to continue at a higher rate than the Australian average through to the year 2026. This growth is more acute in Mackay's city centre and some of the neighbouring local government areas, while other districts decline or experience small population gains. There is also movement of the younger population away from the shrinking towns and towards the growing areas in the region.

Employment-wise, Mackay has experienced a 6% increase since 1996, and a consistent decline in its unemployment rate since 2001. The demand for knowledge workers is higher than across Australia as a whole, especially within the computer professionals' category. The demand for other occupations (less knowledge-intensive but equally important for industry development and firm innovation) such as tradespersons, transport workers and labourers is also higher than at the national level. There is evidence of industry restructuring from an agriculture-related base towards coal mining, rail transport and mining technology services. The top employing industries are in the categories of services to the working population, such as education, retail and business services. The upskilling of Mackay's population has been larger than the national average in most areas, but particularly at the bachelor-or-higher degree level and in the specialised trades. Up to 84.3% of all apprentices in the region are registered in Mackay's city centre and are in diverse industries ranging from manufacturing to business services, retail and hospitality.

This economic bonanza is not unique to Mackay: The state of Queensland is experiencing an economic boom, with rapid business growth and a general shortage of skills in many areas. The low unemployment rate, which is under the national average, the strongest labour market competition in the last 30 years, and major structural shifts across industries and markets fuelled the design of skills strategies and reforms to the training and vocational system statewide in Queensland. The self-denominated "Smart State" undertook the most significant reform to Queensland's skilling and training in more than 40 years, with the release of the billion dollar Queensland Skills Plan in March 2006, which was designed to address the emerging skills shortages (Queensland Government, 2006).

The Skills Plan articulates specific mechanisms to respond to the loss of skills, the need to upskill the workforce, and the integration of hard-to-reach groups. The plan integrates education policies and reforms from the national and state level to respond to present and future challenges of the labour market. It is a top-down approach targeting broad skills infrastructure gaps affecting industry competition at the state level. An analysis of the Skills Plan shows four broad elements for the design of skills strategies: 1) the training system, through the vocational education sector (VET) and the technical and further education colleges (TAFE); 2) the industry and employers; 3) the employees and talent pool; and 4) a strong specific focus on trades as a key occupation that interrelates with the other elements.

Actions in the Skills Plan assess training needs, skilling and labour market development at the local level through partnerships with industry groups. These actions include:

- *Skills alliances* (sector-specific) – autonomous organisations made up of major industry stakeholders, unions and employers that provide strategic advice about industry skills needs by monitoring the needs of the industry and fostering open communications with the stakeholders on skilling issues. Among the services these alliances provide are: identifying the causes and effects of skill shortages; planning for future skill needs; promoting their industries to schools and regions; and encouraging each industry to take control of its skilling future.

- *Industry-government partnerships* – that capitalise on existing industry networks, and address the industries' skilling and workforce development needs through a whole-of-government approach.

- *Direct engagement* – that involves consulting with industry representative organisations to obtain expert advice on workforce development and skilling requirements for industries. Formal agreements are put in place in certain industries to keep on consulting.

- *Centres of Excellence* – whose mission is to identify skills requirements at the local level, so that training priorities, products and methods of delivery are tailored to local employers. A strong focus on development partnerships is supported by AUD 1 932 million over four years; specific actions are targeted, such as holding annual industry forums to discuss skills issues.

One of the difficulties of labour policy design is the need for flexibility to quickly adapt to local conditions. As the Skills Plan was being produced, the private sector in Mackay was having difficulty filling vacancies at many levels; this was especially the case at the trades level in some of the main employment industries, such as manufacturing, agriculture, forestry and fishing, mining, transport and storage, and construction. The shortages were across the board, and included what are consistently noted as "skills in demand" in the state of Queensland (DEWR, 2006): electrical and electronic trades, and metal and engineering trades (ABS, 2001).

A group of companies in Mackay's manufacturing and engineering sectors joined together to form a cluster-type organisation in 1996; their objective was to solve the dual problems of skills shortages within their companies and the lack of necessary skills associated with the national apprentice training system, which was not responding fast enough to the growth of the manufacturing industry. The companies involved in this organisation – called the Mackay Industry Network (MAIN)[2] – analysed the strategic needs required to remain competitive in Mackay under the mining boom, and how they could maintain their level of employment despite stiff competition. They decided on three major areas of focus: 1) networking information, 2 skills and 3) exports. The identification of skills shortages as one of the key areas of work led to the establishment of the CARE programme – the most successful activity of the network.

CARE serves as an intermediary agent, connecting industry with education agents. The programme manages the bookings for all their apprentices, and also focuses on the sorts of gaps prospective employers might have in the near future. Its role is not to train – other organisations such as the technical colleges do that – but to organise the logistics of training courses and job introductions that the technical college or other organisations deliver. The programme also provides the apprentices with basic, important information that companies are usually too busy to provide, explaining the expectations of the job from inside the workplace. This information is part of the introduction programmes MAIN delivers, subcontracted by the Mackay Technical and Further Education College. The programme has been able to introduce hard-to-reach people – the long-term unemployed, people with Indigenous backgrounds, women – into the workforce, although this is not its main focus. The reality is that the engineering sector in general would be able to employ only a small percentage of these groups. In particular, it would be very difficult to employ people with physical disabilities due to the nature of the jobs in the sector.

The case of the MAIN network highlights the importance of providing the private sector with mechanisms for participation in the design of solutions to their labour market imperatives. MAIN started to address the skills shortage in trades some time in advance of the Queensland Skills Plan, although the analysis MAIN companies performed on the impact of the mining boom on business was much less sophisticated than that conducted by the Queensland government. However, as these companies based their strategic analysis and planning around the direct local market impacts on their day-to-day work, they were able to move quickly and design a solution that targeted trades as the core skills needed by their businesses. Because the network includes state and local organisations that are also involved in the Queensland Skills Plan, it benefits from the analysis and strategies proposed in the Plan. It is also aware of the opportunities for extended partnerships with local agencies such as Skilling Solutions Queensland, which could provide a more tailored service for apprenticeship programmes for small and medium-sized enterprises (SMEs). Nevertheless, MAIN CARE is likely to continue operating mainly for the manufacturing sector in Mackay, as most of the companies are small and the benefits of the cluster model are evident. Enhancing local partnerships for a common local skills strategy would further strengthen the competitiveness of companies in MAIN, as well as the broader industry and community in Mackay.

However, some challenges associated with hyper-growth economies need to be noted. One of the difficult adjustments of Mackay's population has been the rising cost of housing. As the economic boom and the city attract more highly skilled and higher-paid professionals, the availability of housing has been dramatically reduced, leaving a growing demand. The result has been that disadvantaged groups are forced to move from their houses as they cannot cope with new rental prices. The instability of housing affordability only adds to the disadvantages already experienced by these populations in accessing sustainable employment, as they are moved further away from the centres of employment. This situation is very different from what is experienced in places where the economy is not that buoyant. It also suggests a different, rapid, urban gentrification that is normally only experienced in the big urban centres where the housing stock is greater and more diverse. Neither the Skills Plan nor the local strategies emerging in Mackay deal with the housing situation or the extent to which these disadvantaged groups can benefit from the current economic boom. Nor do they address the uncertainty over whether the skills these groups are acquiring are sustainable and transportable.

Scenario 2: Shrinking Cities – Broken Hill

Shrinking Cities are a global phenomenon also found in Australia; they are associated with processes of urbanisation-suburbanisation, climate change, and industrialisation. As the four major coastal cities (Perth, Melbourne, Sydney and Brisbane) continue to dominate the Australian urban system, another process at work is the consolidation of the major regional towns, which grow at the expense of smaller towns in their region. Some 245 local government areas (LGA) lost population numbers in the 2001 census, and this process is expected to continue (ABS, 2006). It is partly driven by changes in the agriculture economy, the out-migration of population (especially the young and educated) – now exacerbated by the drought – and the need for consolidation to gain economies of scale (Martinez-Fernandez and Wu, 2007). Another shrinkage process is occurring in industrial centres, where decline is characterised by the long-term population and/or economic decline of small and medium-sized cities servicing a mining site, a system of mining sites, mining settlements or a manufacturing industry. Many of these towns experience periods of both growth and shrinkage depending on international mineral and manufacturing markets.

Losing population, talent and skills can have a critical effect on shrinking cities[3] struggling to retain their population and businesses. Designing skills strategies for these cities requires approaches different from those for cities that are growing and where skills shortages therefore relate to strong industrial demand. The case of Broken Hill exemplifies ways in which these particular types of cities can renew their competencies in order to attract and retain their population, and involve firms in continuous learning.

Broken Hill is the largest regional centre in the western part of the state of New South Wales; it is 1 100 kilometres west of Sydney and 500 kilometres northwest of Adelaide. Broken Hill is Australia's longest-settled mining city, called variously over time the "Oasis of the West", "Silver City" and the "Capital of the Outback". Mining has been the main industry since the foundation of the town in 1883; the famous BHP Company (Broken Hill Proprietary) was the main mining operator until 1939. At its peak in 1952, the mining industry employed 6 500 people, with more than 30 000 people living in the city. Since then, Broken Hill has steadily declined to an estimated 20 223 people in 2006 and projections are for a further drop to 15 350 by the year 2031, with an annual average growth rate of –1.1.[4] Employment in the mining industry has declined from 51.26% in 1954 to 7.57% in 2001, and there are now fewer than 500 miners living in the town. The unemployment rate was 8.3% in 2006, well above the 4.6% national average.

Broken Hill's decline had a critical impact on skills supply and retention of the population. The challenges of remoteness, water shortages, annual rainfall of less than 250 mm and summer temperatures of 40 degrees Celsius put further stress on the city's development. Approaches adopted by growing regions such as upskilling the workforce, increasing the number of training places and sponsoring overseas workers to meet local demand might not be suitable for a city that is shrinking. These types of cities need to work much harder at offering lifestyle choices and a dynamic business environment. For example, Broken Hill City Council is developing a total rebranding of the city as a postmodern cultural centre, and a place of creativity, with the objective of attracting and retaining creative, skilled people. As a result of these efforts Broken Hill and its environs have now entered the nominations for inclusion on the Australian National Heritage List. If successful, the listing will include 179 sq km, including buildings and the landscape. It would be the first entire city entering the National Heritage List (Williams, 2007).

However, the challenges of providing a dynamic business environment in a remote community in the Australian outback requires a much more sophisticated approach than what urban design strategies can offer. Although the state of New South Wales has a State Plan, a Vocational Education and Training Plan, and a series of agencies located in Broken Hill, the application of these plans to upskilling remote business production spaces had only limited success until 2004, when an innovative programme was launched. A key agency for desert regions, Desert Knowledge Australia – funded by the Northern Territory, but with programmes linking all desert regions – partnered with Telstra[5] and the Australian government in 2004 to create the Desert Knowledge Linking Business Networks (DKLBN) project under the Small Business Enterprise Culture Programme. The project was also supported by the Desert Knowledge Cooperative Research Centre (DKCRC), which started at about the same time, and by key participating agencies from Broken Hill such as the Outback Area Consultative Committee and the Broken Hill Chamber of Commerce.

The project started as a pilot programme for the training and mentoring of businesses in desert regions. It works to develop networks between firms in Broken Hill, Alice Springs, Mt Isa, Kalgoorlie/Boulder, and the Upper Spencer Gulf (Whyalla, Port Pirie and Port Augusta). The network has linked 329 businesses and 15 organisations from these five remote desert regions. The focus has been on four industries: mining services (40% of companies); bush products and local foods (10% of companies); tourism (35% of companies); and sustainable building (15% of companies). The majority of the firms involved in the project were very small – between 1 and 20 people – and most were micro companies of 1-2 people with small annual turnover.

The project delivered a total of 902 sessions from 2005 to 2006. Skills development sessions numbered 377, with 31 small businesses using the service. Participants in these sessions were owners and managers who were trained on local/regional business skills and networking. Sessions addressed the following range of skills: human resources; business planning; industry-specific skills; marketing; information technology; and business clustering. Mentoring sessions numbered 525, with 329 small business owners/managers using the service. The mentoring services provided focused on business management and core industry capacity building in areas such as ICTs, regulation and finances, and technological innovation (Desert Knowledge CRC, 2006). As desert regions are located so far from each other, it was important to train and mentor "skills and network development facilitators" in each region. These were staff from the participating public institutions who would take the lead as DKLBN facilitators in their regions. In some instances, if a government department could not allocate a staff member to this role, the Chamber of Commerce or a business organisation would step in. All skills and network development facilitators have continued in their regional roles since the pilot project finished late in 2006. Video link and conference meetings are still being held across the desert regions, organised by Desert Knowledge Australia in co-operation with the skills and network development facilitators.

This project addressed an important constraint for desert businesses in Australia – their isolation from other businesses in different industries, from businesses within the same industry, from customers, from markets, and from publicly funded knowledge infrastructure such as R&D and training. As a result of this isolation, desert businesses tend to be self-contained and non-specialised, and service only local markets. As a consequence, these businesses are in a disadvantaged position compared to those in the coastal cities; they do not benefit from productivity improvements, do not serve profitable distant markets, and are less likely to tap into international networks. The objective of the mentoring and skills development services of the DKLBN was to built capabilities that enabled those involved to develop critical mass within regions and across borders. The project is unique in Australia because it covers large geographical distances, different time zones and different state/territory jurisdictions. Moreover, it involves local partnerships from different levels of government and a combination of local intra-industry networking, cross-border intra-industry networking, local cross-industry networking, and cross-border cross-industry networking. The investment in "networking skills" was therefore considered as a core capability to upskill employees.

An important lesson that has been learned is how the use of different technologies for communication can be effective in building trust and facilitating collaboration. One of the reasons why this has worked so well is that the long distance between cluster members does not allow for face-to-face meetings as in other cluster models. Therefore, participating business have had to become familiar with – and proficient in using – new media. They have been able to develop collaborations with limited face-to-face contact. This experience also indicates that distance might limit lifelong learning and the training of employees in these remote areas, as participation in meetings and knowledge-intensive service activities outside their towns is very costly.

The model explored in this project is especially significant for shrinking cities, where attracting and retaining population is difficult, entrepreneurship is low, and out-migration tends to be concentrated on the young and skilled. The case of Broken Hill shows that to maintain the vitality of the city, local agencies have to work hard at positioning the city as something special that stands up on the strength of its own cultural heritage. However, this is not enough to overcome the tyranny of distance in a world where the marketplace is global. The linked business network project targeted the core of the problem by providing much-needed business networking skills, to enable companies to tap into both national coastal markets and international markets. The fact that they are forced to use ICTs as their main method of communication added an important skill to their business networking, as well as providing critical training that was then used to explore new markets miles away from the desert. Participating businesses have been exposed to a knowledge-intensive service activity, with tangible benefits, in a very short time.

The result of this project for Broken Hill is that businesses and employees are more capable of being connected to national and international networks, and in a more sophisticated way than was possible before this project. Cross-industry and cross-border networks also facilitate renewal of a broad range of skills that support economic success, and provide access to both the information and knowledge needed to survive in an accelerated-change marketplace. The challenge now is in sustaining the innovation momentum, and turning the skills acquired into commercialisation outcomes to sustain and grow their businesses.

Scenario 3: Global Cities

Sydney is Australia's global city, with a current population of 4.5 million people and an additional 1.1 million people to be accommodated and 500 000 jobs to be created by 2031. Sydney has a reputation as the most multicultural hub in Australia, with up to 31% of its inhabitants born overseas. It is also the city of contrasts, with a high cost of living in key employment areas and marginalised communities of greater disadvantage in certain locations across the metropolitan region. For a long time the planning of Sydney occurred at multiple levels and by multiple agencies; then in 2005 the new "Metropolitan Strategy 2031" was prepared by the NSW government. The strategy departs from the image of Sydney as a city growing around the Central Business District; it instead shows Sydney as the "City of Cities", with Parramatta as the second CBD, Penrith in the North-West region, and Liverpool in the South-West region.

The Metropolitan Strategy 2031 (the Strategy) is a broad framework outlining a vision for Sydney over the next 25 years. The area of the strategy is the Sydney region, with strong links and relationships to surrounding regions such as the Sydney to Canberra corridor. The strategy covers over 10 000 square kilometres and incorporates 43 local government areas (LGAs). It sets out directions for government decisions such as timing and location of investment in transport and other infrastructure. It consists of seven interconnected sub-strategies:

1. Economy and employment.

2. Centres and corridors.

3. Housing.

4. Transport.

5. Environment and resources.

6. Parks and public places.

7. Implementation and governance.

The strategy was inspired by the need to have better urban development management in order to maintain Sydney's global competitiveness and unique liveability. The strategy seeks to increase employment opportunities by setting out employment planning capacity targets, especially within sub-regions and strategic centres. The employment capacity targets are compatible with and associated with sub-regional housing capacity targets. These targets are a guide to councils, state agencies and the private sector to ensure that there are sufficient and appropriately zoned commercial sites and employment lands to meet private sector demand (NSW Government, 2005).

Two of the sub-strategies are especially relevant for the discussion here: the "Economy and Employment" sub-strategy; and the "Centres and Corridors" sub-strategy. The Economy and Employment strategy has three main aims:

● Provide sustainable commercial sites and "employment lands" in strategic areas.

● Increase innovation and skills development.

● Improve opportunities and access to jobs for disadvantaged communities.

There are several innovative factors embedded in this sub-strategy. One is the concept of employment lands related to industrial areas, manufacturing, distribution, and non-centre urban services. They include Business Technology Parks with a mixture of research, manufacturing, distribution and office activities. Key initiatives are: mapping and updating of employment lands in Sydney, with a budget of AUD 1 million; the release of greenfield land, particularly in the Western Sydney Employment Hub, to allow 36 000 new manufacturing and distribution jobs; the regeneration of brownfield sites to support employment; and the improvement of planning strategies and delivery of employment lands across different government departments.

Innovation is supported by strengthening industry clusters in key locations, using infrastructure as "magnets" for investment and employment, and embedding learning activities at the local level. The sub-strategy has also taken into account the important contribution that disadvantaged communities can make at the local level and proposes to embed skills into major redevelopment and renewal projects. In particular, local environmental planning zones should include a mix of housing types across Sydney, to ensure diversity in the supply of local labour. Supporting entrepreneurship among these communities is also contemplated through the provision of appropriate affordable premises in high economic growth areas and imparting best practice advice.

The Centres and Corridors sub-strategy recognises the spatial dimension of innovation activity and the importance of "place" for employment targets. It aims to establish a typology of centres, along with employment targets for each, and to improve the liveability of these centres by clustering business and knowledge-intensive activities together and concentrating activities near public transport. The sub-strategy also recognises the role of "corridors" as areas for entrepreneurship and locations for local employment development.

The case of Western Sydney

The Metropolitan Strategy focuses particularly on Western Sydney as that city's strongest growth area, where greater attention needs to be paid to strategic urban management. Greater Western Sydney (GWS) is the fastest-growing economy in Australia, with a population of 1.85 million people who represent 43% of the Sydney population. The economic output for the region is AUD 71 billion (2004-05), which makes it the third-largest economy in Australia behind Sydney (as a whole) and Melbourne. It is home to approximately 241 976 enterprises, 20% of which include the country's top 500 exporters. The major industry sectors are manufacturing, construction, property and business services, finance and insurance, and wholesale trade. The GWS region contributed a sizeable 41.3% towards the gross regional product (GRP) of the Sydney economy and 29.8% to the state of New South Wales. Of the large percentage of GRP contributed by GWS, 20.5% was from manufacturing, which is higher than the industry average for Sydney and NSW. Property and business services and finance and insurance industries follow closely behind. However, the distribution of industry throughout the region is not homogeneous. South-West and Central Sydney contain many of the manufacturing, transport and storage industries. North-West Sydney is ahead in property and business services and retail trade.

It is estimated that the number of jobs in Western Sydney will grow from 663 000 in 2001 to 900 000 jobs in 2031, mostly within industry clusters of transport and logistics and manufacturing (NSW Government, 2005). Design of local employment and skills strategies needs to be informed by the sectors where these jobs would probably be created, and by the type of jobs that these industries are already producing. The Metropolitan Strategy predicts that employment would continue to grow around transport and logistics, and manufacturing. However, even at the level of the Western Sydney region, there is a large diversity of industry if smaller sub-regions are analysed. In relation to industry clusters, South-West Sydney – and specifically the area surrounding the LGA of Liverpool – is one the most significant manufacturing areas in Sydney's metropolitan region. Six local government areas in Western Sydney; Liverpool, Campbelltown, Camden, Fairfield, Bankstown and Penrith, account for 26.5% of Sydney's total manufacturing employment.[6] The highest concentration of activity is found in the "manufacturing triangle" of Bankstown, Fairfield and Liverpool, notably in the sectors of metals, furniture, plastics and chemicals (Martinez-Fernandez *et al.*, 2007).

In relation to the types of jobs in the area, again the whole region is far from homogeneous if three sub-regions are considered: North-West, including the LGA of Hawkesbury and Baulkam Hills; Central-West, including the LGAs of Blue Mountains, Penrith and Blacktown; and South-West Sydney, including the LGAs of Wollondilly, Liverpool, Camden, and Campbelltown. North-West Sydney has the highest number of knowledge workers (managers and administrators, professionals and associate professionals) and the lowest number of apprentices and trainees (workers in trades), and is the sub-region that has the most demography of knowledge occupations similar to the Metropolitan Sydney average. Business and information-related employment is ahead in this area due to the location of strong business parks in the North-West. The Central-West region has the highest number of apprentices and trainees, and is third in relation to the concentration of managers and professionals. The total number of trainees in September 2007 was 8 683, well above the 3 405 in the North-West or the 6 565 in the South-West. The South-West sub-region is slightly ahead of the Central-West in its number of managers and professionals, but significantly below the North-West. The area, however, is ahead in engineering-based occupations, which are especially found in manufacturing industries (the strength of this region).

The demography of industry and occupations among these sub-regions is sufficiently varied to indicate that attention needs to be paid to specific local factors so as to design strategies that target the characteristics and needs of each. It also suggests that local policies can influence the focus of industry and institutions in training the workforce and on upskilling the population. For example, Central-West Sydney consistently has had the highest number of apprentices among the three sub-regions since 2003. An analysis of policies designed by the local councils suggests that two of the councils in the North-West (Penrith and Blacktown) actually have the most innovative economic and employment development strategies. The role of industry development and infrastructure investment in these areas notwithstanding, it also needs to be acknowledged that a strong government framework for development and employment growth can have a positive influence on the capacity of the sub-region for learning and upskilling. This intertwining of local council's strategic plans with labour policy and the design of skills strategies therefore becomes extremely important for the rollover of the Metropolitan Strategy; it is difficult to foresee a successful implementation if this does not occur.

This case shows the potential for local labour policy to influence economic development – but social cohesion and innovative activity is not without its barriers, and the complexity of the task cannot be accomplished without the participation of multiple stakeholders from government layers, industry, and knowledge-providers.

Lessons for local employment policy and governance

The three scenarios discussed in this chapter exemplify the different skills imperative for cities and regions in Australia and the need for local labour policy instruments. The following lessons can be drawn.

There is a need to "customise" labour policies where skills and employment strategies are embedded in local conditions. Local governments are increasingly realising the need to shift attention away from managing land resources and attracting investment that creates *jobs*, and instead directing it towards Strategic Employment Planning (SEP), which acknowledges the complexity of creating employment. This form of planning is concerned with the *types* of jobs created, *where* they are created and *for whom* they are created. SEP is also concerned with promoting innovation activities, and with the development of available local pools of human capital.

An important process in SEP is facilitating industry clusters to take the lead in addressing skill shortages at the local level, which can result in creating skill-hubs for the current and future needs of the industry. This discussion has demonstrated the power of industry networks in both growing and shrinking cities. Investing in local employment strategies requires connecting talent with employers in ways that may be more sophisticated than simply offering recruitment or information services. Companies need support to initiate collaboration structures, where "thinking spaces" focused on skills and business development can take place. It is too hard for companies, especially those in declining areas, to obtain capital to create the organisational structure such clusters need. This is where governments and local agencies can help through supporting clusters and networks to enable creation of skills-hubs. The investment is usually small, and the solutions companies come up with together are usually very well tailored to the local operating context. This local focus is difficult for agencies at the state or national level, and although overarching skills and employment plans are necessary, they also require the companies at the other end of the employment equation to fast-track solutions for their business.

Pools of local talent from hard-to-reach groups are still difficult to integrate, and more work is needed to ensure the industry sector (including government) is committed to offering work options to these groups. Industry does not necessarily have a good understanding of the different characteristics of disadvantaged groups, including the types of jobs adapted to their abilities, or the types of mechanisms needed to guarantee their success (*e.g.* peer-to-peer mentoring). Governments have an important role in educating industry from both private and public sectors on the skills available from these groups and the advantages of their employment. In rapidly growing areas, the housing and infrastructure environment needs to be carefully analysed and included in overarching plans, so as not to further alienate disadvantaged groups who are already finding it difficult to participate in the labour market. Loss of housing affordability is a significant collateral effect of hyper-growth economies, and a critical challenge for disadvantaged groups attempting to participate in the wealth creation of their city.

International mobility of workers from shrinking cities to growing cities is a rising trend calling for new roles and investments by local governments. More work is needed to understand the pressures occurring at both urban ends, the sustainability of the imported skills, and the significance of informal networks operating across international regions.

Skills strategies need to take a whole-of-region approach. The regions analysed here show the potential that exists to capitalise on the different collaboration schemes emerging from public and private organisations. Creating local employment alliances – where providers and users of knowledge and all stakeholders involved in skills development could come together to discuss their skills needs and initiatives, and to integrate their different knowledge into strategic plans that can later be implemented at their own organisation level – would bring enormous benefits to the scenarios exemplified here. The three scenarios also suggest that the approach needs to be customised: the same strategies would not work for growing regions, shrinking regions, and global cities.

The analysis of these scenarios suggests key reforms that can stimulate economic growth. One is the need to upskill the unemployed and the less qualified. Another is the need to tap into marginalised groups such as people with disabilities, Indigenous people, and refugees. Focusing on urban infrastructure to boost productivity growth through reducing commuting time, providing affordable housing, reducing traffic congestion and providing services for parents such as childcare is a further key reform. Overall, a greater integration of where people live and where people work, concentrated around regional centres in metropolitan cities, is needed.

New models of network governance need to be explored, with closer collaboration between government departments involving planning, infrastructure, economic development, skills, and training. The different tiers of government need to develop collaboration infrastructures with the local level, industry bodies and the local community. Network governance is a new territory for many institutions and requires innovative approaches and public-private partnerships with citizens and industry that can ultimately result in an increase of social cohesion.

Notes

1. Australia is a federal parliamentary democracy with six states and two territories: Australian Capital Territory, New South Wales, Northern Territory, Queensland, South Australia, Tasmania, Victoria, and Western Australia.

2. Information regarding this network was collected through in-depth interviews with MAIN staff and other organisations in Mackay, December 2006 to April 2007.

3. Cities experiencing a decline in population and/or economic terms for a sustained period of time although spurs of growth can occur.

4. ABS population projections, June 2006.

5. An Australian telecommunications company.

6. Unless otherwise noted, all statistical material is drawn from the ABS 2001 and 1996 Census of Population and Housing, Journey to Work Data Set.

Bibliography

ABS (Australian Bureau of Statistics) (1997, 2002), *1996 Census, 2001 Census.*

ABS (2006), *Regional Population Growth,* 3218.0 2004-05, ABS, Canberra.

Australian Government, Department of Education, Sciences and Training (DEST) (2006), *Skilling Australia: 2005-2008 Commonwealth-State Agreement for Skilling Australia's Workforce,* DEST, June.

DEWR (Department of Employment and Workplace Relations) (2006), *Skills in Demand Lists – States and Territories 2006,* DEWR Occupational and Skills Analysis Section, July 2006.

Department of Immigration and Citizenship, *Skills Matching Database* (SMD), *www.immi.gov.au/skills/,* accessed 06/04/07.

Desert Knowledge Cooperative Research Centre (CRC) (2006), *Desert Knowledge Australia Linked Business Network Project, Final Report*, Desert Knowledge Australia, Alice Springs.

Larcombe, G. (2007) "Planning for Metropolitan Employment Growth", presented to the *Metropolitan Planning Summit*, Melbourne, 15-16 May.

Martinez-Fernandez, M.C. and I. Miles (2006), "Inside the Software Firm: Co-production of Knowledge and KISA in the Innovation Process", *International Journal Services Technology and Management*, IJSTM Special Issue V7 (2), pp. 115-125.

Martinez-Fernandez, M.C., M. Rerceretnam and S. Sharpe (2007), "Manufacturing Innovation in the New Urban Economy: Responses to Globalisation", University of Western Sydney, Urban Research Centre and Liverpool City Council, Sydney.

Martinez-Fernandez, M.C. and C.-T. Wu (2007), "Stadtentwicklung in einer differenten irklichkeit: Schrumpfende Städte in Australien" (Urban Development in a Different Reality: Shrinking Cities in Australia), *Berliner Debatte Initial*, Schrumpfende Stadte International 1/2007, pp. 45-61.

National Centre for Vocational Education Research, News and Events, March Quarter Apprentice and Trainee Statistics Released *www.ncver.edu.au*, retrieved 10/06/2007.

NSW Government (2005), "City of Cities: A Plan for Sydney's Future – Metropolitan Strategy Supporting Information", NSW Government, Sydney.

OECD (2006), *The Role of Knowledge Intensive Service Activities (KISA) in Innovation*, OECD, Paris.

Queensland Government (2006), *Queensland Skills Plan: A White Paper*, Department of Employment and Training, Queensland Government.

Toner, P. (2003), "The Case of the Vanishing Apprentice", Broadcast in *The National Interest*, 21 September, ABC Radio National, Australia.

Toner, P. (2005), *Getting It Right: What Employers and Apprentices Have to Say About Apprenticeships*, Dusseldorp Skills Forum, Group Training Australia Ltd, Australian Industry Group, Dusseldorp Skills Forum 2005.

Williams, S. (2007), "Silver City Shines", *The Daily Telegraph*, September.

ISBN 978-92-64-04327-5
More than Just Jobs:
Workforce Development in a Skills-Based Economy
© OECD 2008

PART II

Chapter 8

Japan: Rural Areas' Need for Local Employment Strategies

by

Yoshio Higuchi

In Japan, fiscal measures for expanding public works have played an important role in creating jobs in rural areas. However, as financial conditions have deteriorated, there is less room for increasing regional employment through macroeconomic policies such as greater fiscal spending. Meanwhile, economic globalisation and changes in labour supply are widening divergences among regions. Regional communities therefore have all the more need to take the initiative in implementing employment strategies for creating jobs, developing employability and avoiding skills mismatch. This has implications for the distribution of fiscal resources as well for the technical and strategic capacities at local level.

Growing regional differences in employment

There are significant regional differences in labour supply and demand. As the economy recovers, the number of job offers in the Kanto and Tokai regions is rising considerably. The ratio of job offers to applicants is greater than 1, and it appears there is now a labour shortage in these regions. In contrast, job offers have not shown a significant rise in the Hokkaido, Tohoku or Shikoku regions where the ratio of job offers to applicants is still far below 1. In some prefectures in rural areas, the job offers to applicants ratio has even gone down.*

Economic effects spread at different speeds in different regions. They manifest themselves quickly in Tokyo and other large cities, but become evident more slowly in rural areas. Undeniably, there is a possibility that the current regional differences in labour conditions merely reflect the differences in how the economic effects spread, and that as the economy enters a phase of real recovery labour market conditions may dramatically improve in rural areas. It is clear, however, that the spillover of economic recovery from large cities to rural areas is happening at a slower pace than in the past. Formerly, employment in rural areas began to increase after a time-lag of about a year. This time, however, it has not shown notable improvement even though more than three years have passed since job demand in Tokyo began increasing.

The labour market in Japan has been deteriorating since the 1990s. It showed an especially sharp decline in 1997 when the financial crisis hit. Since then, regional differences in the unemployment rate and the number of workers have been widening. Figure 8.1 shows the rate change from 1997 to 2006. During this time, the unemployment rate for Japan as a whole rose by 2.0% from 3.4% in 1993 to 5.4% in 2002, and fell to 4.1% in 2006. In Metropolitan Tokyo, however, the rise was only 0.9%. In other prefectures constituting the greater Tokyo area, such as Kanagawa, Chiba and Saitama, the increase was much smaller than the national average. Aichi prefecture showed a decline of only 0.1%. In contrast, the unemployment rate increased sharply in Hokkaido and in prefectures in the Tohoku, Kansai and Kyushu regions, indicating further deterioration in employment in rural areas.

---

* An earlier version of this chapter has been published in Giguère, S., Y. Higuchi and JILPT (2005), *Local Governance for Promoting Employment*, JILPT (for the English version) and Nikkei (for the Japanese version), Tokyo. The editors would like to thank the Japan Institute for Labor Policy and Training for their permission to re-use and update this contribution.

Figure 8.1. **Percentage change in the unemployment rate (1997-2006)**

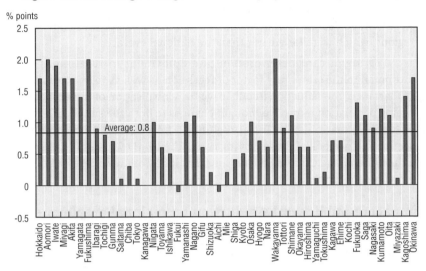

Source: Statistics Bureau, Ministry of Internal Affairs and Communications, Labour Force Survey.

The decline in employment in rural areas can also be confirmed by the number of workers. Figure 8.2 shows changes in the number of workers from 1997 to 2006. For all of Japan, this number declined by 4.16% during that period. In comparison, the number of workers hardly declined in the greater

Figure 8.2. **Percentage change in the number of workers (1997-2006)**

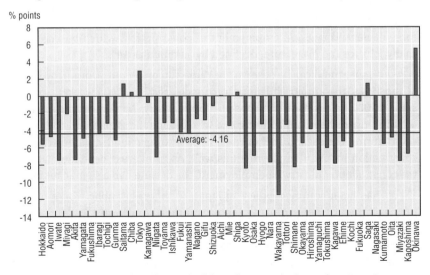

Source: Statistics Bureau, Ministry of Internal Affairs and Communications, Labour Force Survey.

Tokyo area – in fact, it increased slightly. The decline in Aichi and Shizuoka prefectures was also below the national average. On the other hand, there were marked decreases in prefectures within the Tohoku, Kansai and Shikoku regions, which were far greater than the national average.

The significant deterioration of employment in rural areas can be attributed to the temporary factor of recession as well as to structural factors. For instance, the reduction in public works, globalisation of the economy, and ageing population may have brought changes to both the supply and demand of labour, creating substantial regional differences in employment. The sections below look at these factors, consider how they have affected regional employment, and examine the reasons that local communities need their own employment strategies.

The impact of public works reduction on regional employment

Looking at labour market conditions by region in the early 1990s – immediately after the burst of the bubble economy – we find that unemployment rates in rural areas were lower than those of large cities where there were major cutbacks in jobs, and employment in rural areas was stable, with only minor job reduction. One of the reasons for the limited effect of recession in rural areas was that an increase in public works created jobs in construction and other related industries.

For example, employed labour force in all industries in Hokkaido prefecture in the first half of the 1990s grew by 5.6% in just five years (*Establishment and Enterprise Census*), with an increase of over 8% in the construction industry alone. Indeed, employment increased in spite of the collapse of the bubble economy. During the latter half of the 1990s, however, the employed labour force decreased by 5.9%; employment in construction, which had created so many jobs for the prefecture, declined by as much as 14%.

A similar trend can be observed in Yamagata prefecture. During the first half of the 1990s, the employed labour force increased by 17 000 workers, of which some 10 000 held jobs in the construction industry. Already, employment was diminishing in the manufacturing and wholesaling industries, and continued to do so during the second half of the 1990s, accompanied by a steep decline in construction industry employment as well. As rural areas depended largely on the construction industry for employment, the decline had a significant impact.

It has been common policy in Japan to increase public works to create jobs at times of deteriorating labour market conditions. Essentially, the objectives of public works projects are to maintain and preserve the country's land and improve people's lives by building dams and other public infrastructures, as well as to build up the nation's and its regional areas' industrial competitiveness by improving economic efficiency through the use of roads, bridges, and railroads. In addition to reinforcing supply, public works projects are carried out in Japan and many other countries to reduce regional divergences by creating jobs and expanding demand in each regional area. It can be said that this trend has been particularly marked in Japan.

Demand policy based on increasing public works spending is effective in supplementing temporary demand shortages brought about by recession. But that effectiveness is gradually diminished the more a recession is prolonged. At times, such policies can even be harmful. A long-term increase in fiscal spending will create enormous fiscal deficits and generate concern among the people about the possibility of future tax hikes and reduced fiscal spending to reduce the deficits. A chronic increase in public works spending may also make people habitually dependent on the government and impede gains in regional communities' competitiveness.

Some people liken the drawbacks of chronic expansion in public works spending to drug addiction: "It gives relief when things are tough, but as soon as its effect wears off, you want more. And as you continue to take it, you can no longer stand on your own feet." Public works may be useful as a temporary remedy, but they do not leave the body sound once their effect wears off. A complete cure calls for a change of lifestyles, daily exercise, and structural reform to improve one's constitution.

In addition to an increase in public works spending, the government in recent years is playing a greater role in creating jobs by increasing social security benefits, such as pensions and healthcare and nursing care benefits; these also help increase regional consumer demand. The sections below consider the government's role in creating jobs in regional areas by examining data on prefectures in Japan.

The large size of Japan's public works compared to other countries

The percentage of workers employed in the construction industry is higher in Japan than in other countries. Table 8.1 shows the percentages in ten countries.

One of the reasons Japan has the highest percentage is undoubtedly the effect of vast public works spending. Demand in the construction industry is made up of private investments in the building of factories and housing (private expenditures on gross fixed capital formation) and public investments in public works (gross fixed capital formation of government). Compared with other advanced countries, the percentage of public investments is particularly high in Japan. Figure 8.3 shows the changes in public works spending as a percentage of the gross domestic product in the United Kingdom, the United States, Germany, France and Japan. The figures for recent years clearly indicate that the percentage of public works spending is noticeably higher in Japan compared to the other four countries.

Table 8.1. **Percentage of workers in the construction industry**

	1980	1990	1999	2005
Japan	9.9	9.4	10.2	8.9
United States	6.3	6.5	6.7	7.1
Canada	5.8	6.2	5.3	6.3
United Kingdom	6.5	8.0	7.0	7.9
Germany	8.0	6.6	8.9	6.6
France	8.6	7.0	5.6	5.9
Italy	10.0	8.8	7.7	8.6
Sweden	6.8	7.2	5.5	5.9
South Korea	6.2	7.4	7.3	7.9
Australia	7.7	7.5	7.5	8.6

Source: OECD, *Labour Force Statistics.*

Figure 8.3. **Changes in advanced countries' public works spending as a percentage of GDP**

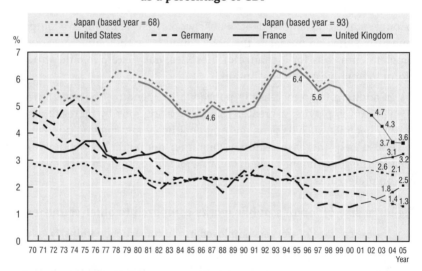

Note: Figures for Germany before 1990 are those of the former West Germany. Public works spending is indicated by gross domestic fixed capital formation of governments

Source: Japan: Economic Planning Agency of Japan, *Annual Report on National Accounts* (fiscal year). Other countries: OECD, *National Accounts*, 2005.

At the beginning of the 1970s, Japan did not stand out compared to other countries in this regard. The United Kingdom and Germany were above 4%, and France was higher than 3.5%. Only the United States – even with federal, state and county governments combined – had a low percentage. The percentage of public works spending in the United Kingdom and Germany, however, began to decline in the latter half of the 1970s. During the 1980s, Japan's high figures became particularly noticeable.

The decline in the percentage of public works spending in Europe can be attributed to a growing awareness of the drawbacks and its fading effect on economic recovery, mentioned above. In Japan, the percentage was temporarily reduced in the latter half of the 1980s as the shortage of demand in the private sector was resolved and the bubble economy was overheating. Even then Japan continued to have a higher percentage compared with other advanced countries, as it was believed that social infrastructures were still lacking. In the early 1990s, after the bubble burst, the percentage was raised even higher. In 1995, as calls for fiscal consolidation grew stronger, the percentage was pushed down.

Figure 8.4 shows the changes in non-farm/non-forestry and construction payrolls when the payrolls in 1985 are 100. Comparing this figure with Figure 8.3, which shows the changes in the percentage of public works spending in Japan, we find that construction payrolls correspond remarkably with the trends in public works spending. Excepting the end of the 1980s, when construction payrolls grew due to increases in private capital investment and housing investment during the period of the bubble economy, the trends in construction payrolls followed the trends in public works spending with a time-lag of about two years.

For instance, during the first half of the 1980s, the percentage of public works spending trended downwards and construction payrolls also decreased. After the latter increased at the end of the 1980s, the bubble burst in the early

Figure 8.4. **Changes in construction and non-farm/non-forestry payrolls (1985 = 100)**

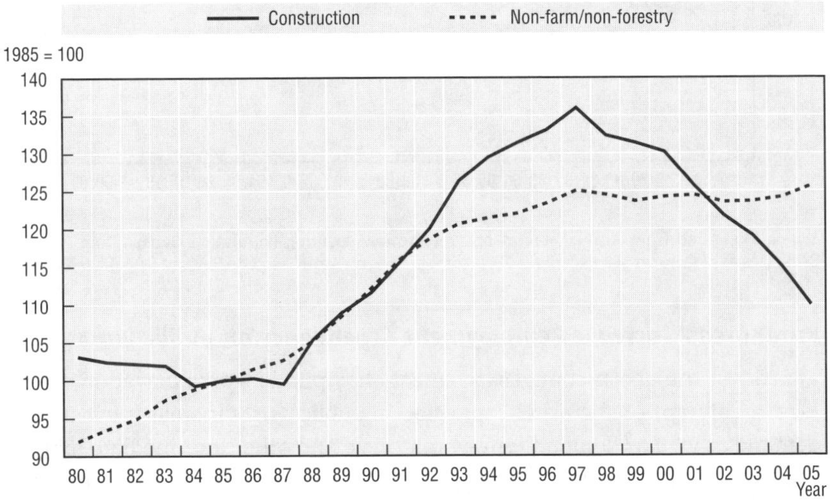

Source: Statistics Bureau, Ministry of Internal Affairs and Communications, Labour Force Survey.

1990s, and the government increased the public works budget as part of a stimulus package. Consequently, construction payrolls continued to grow even though the growth of non-farm/non-forestry payrolls decelerated considerably during the same period. And when public works spending was suppressed after 1996 for fiscal consolidation, construction payrolls also began to decline following their peak in 1997.

A comparison of per capita public works spending in urban area (Tokyo, Nagoya and Osaka) and in rural areas shows that spending has been consistently higher in rural areas for the purpose of diminishing regional divergences (Figure 8.5). Until around 1995 the two were mostly in parallel, and the differences between the two remained fairly even. After a general spending cut was introduced in 1996, however, public works spending was reduced in metropolitan areas, while spending in rural areas was capped and remained flat. As a result, the differences between the two widened. And after 2000, public investment finally decreased.

Figure 8.5. **Per capita public sector investment (thousands JPY)**

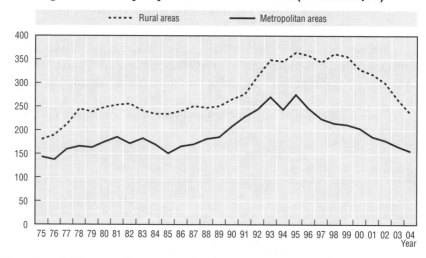

Source: Compiled from Annual Report on Prefectural Accounts, Population Census, and Population Estimates as of October 1st, except for 2000, for which figures are based on Revised SNA (based year = 93).

Rural areas' increased employment dependency on public works

Given the above changes, what role has public works played in creating jobs in different prefectures? Expansion in public works increases construction demand as well as demand for raw materials and other intermediate materials used in the construction industry. It increases the number of workers in the industry and, by raising employment incomes, it leads to greater consumer spending in particular regions. This in turn creates more job opportunities for retailers and manufacturers. Considering these spillovers, what percentage of workers in each prefecture is created by central and local governments' public works spending? Correlating various statistics – including an inter-industry relations table (non-competitive inter-industry relations table shows outflows of demand to other prefectures and exports), wage statistics and consumer statistics – an estimate was made of the employment dependency on public works (for more details see Higuchi *et al.*, 2001).

The estimate is shown in Table 8.2. Among all workers, the percentage of those who found jobs created directly or indirectly by public works, on average in 47 prefectures, was 8.5% in 1990 and 11.0% in 1999. In other words, dependency on public works rose by about 2.5 percentage points in ten years. A comparison between metropolitan and rural areas shows that employment dependency in large cities remained at low levels: 6.6% in 1990 and 8.2% in 1999, a small rise of 1.6 percentage points. On the other hand, dependency in rural areas is high: it was already 10.3% in 1990 and rose a further 3.5 percentage points to 13.8% in 1999.

Let us examine the figures by prefecture. In 1999, Okinawa prefecture had the highest percentage of jobs created directly or indirectly by public works: 23.3%. After Okinawa prefecture, Kochi, Shimane and Hokkaido prefectures had the next highest dependency on public works. In each of these prefectures, more than 20% of all workers, including farmers who are self-employed, held jobs generated by public works. Moreover, the dependency is rising in these prefectures compared with ten years ago: in Okinawa it rose 5.2 percentage points, in Kochi by 7.2 percentage points, in Shimane by 6.4 percentage points, and in Hokkaido by 4.1 percentage points. Reflecting the expansion of public works spending in rural areas as shown in Table 8.2, dependency on public works in these prefectures grew much more than the national average of 2.5 percentage points. As a result, the number of workers employed in jobs created by public works was about three times that of such workers in Tokyo's city centre and Kanagawa and Shizuoka prefectures.

Rise in government debt

In the past, employment in rural areas was more or less guaranteed through public works. In particular, the decrease in private demand after the burst of the bubble economy was offset by jobs generated by these works. If we look at construction in terms of both private investment (residential and non-residential) and government investment, private investment – which in fiscal 1990 was JPY 55.7 trillion – declined to JPY 49.2 trillion in fiscal 1996. During the same period, the government's construction investment rose from JPY 25.7 trillion to JPY 34.6 trillion, more than offsetting the decline. As a result, the overall construction investment increased by JPY 1.4 trillion.

Table 8.2. **Workers employed in jobs created by public works as percentage of all workers in each prefecture**

	1985 (%)	1990 (%)	1995 (%)	1999 (%)	99-90 (% point)
Hokkaido	17.5	16.8	20.6	20.9	4.1
Aomori	14.7	11.2	15.2	15.6	4.4
Iwate	10.9	10.3	13.6	14.0	3.6
Miyagi	10.0	9.5	12.3	12.7	3.2
Akita	12.6	13.5	18.2	18.0	4.4
Yamagata	10.0	10.2	14.1	14.4	4.1
Fukushima	8.9	8.0	10.8	11.5	3.5
Niigata	11.6	10.9	14.8	15.2	4.3
Ibaraki	6.9	7.6	10.7	10.9	3.3
Tochigi	–	5.7	8.2	8.4	2.7
Gunma	–	5.9	8.6	8.8	2.9
Saitama	6.3	6.3	8.5	8.7	2.4
Chiba	8.4	7.8	9.9	8.3	0.5
Tokyo	5.7	5.6	7.6	7.2	1.5
Kanagawa	7.6	5.9	8.1	7.2	1.3
Yamanashi	8.8	7.4	12.2	11.5	4.2
Nagano	9.0	7.8	11.1	8.7	1.0
Shizuoka	6.2	5.4	7.4	7.2	1.8
Toyama	9.2	8.4	12.8	13.9	5.5
Ishikawa	9.7	8.0	13.0	13.9	5.9
Gifu	7.9	7.5	10.2	10.7	3.2
Aichi	6.2	6.2	8.2	7.8	1.7
Mie	7.6	7.4	9.7	9.6	2.2
Fukui	10.8	11.8	11.7	12.1	0.3
Shiga	–	5.9	7.5	7.2	1.3
Kyoto	7.4	8.1	10.9	9.9	1.8
Osaka	6.2	7.1	9.9	8.5	1.4
Hyogo	7.7	7.9	11.8	9.2	1.2
Nara	10.4	9.7	11.2	10.3	0.7
Wakayama	8.8	8.5	13.4	16.3	7.8
Tottori	–	11.3	15.7	17.0	5.6
Shimane	15.9	14.8	17.4	21.2	6.4
Okayama	10.3	9.0	14.0	13.8	4.8
Hiroshima	8.6	9.1	11.9	12.2	3.1
Yamaguchi	10.4	11.4	13.7	15.3	3.9
Tokushima	12.1	12.5	16.4	17.1	4.7
Kagawa	11.9	8.2	10.2	10.6	2.5
Ehime	9.8	10.8	13.8	14.1	3.4
Kochi	14.2	15.0	19.4	22.2	7.2
Fukuoka	11.0	9.1	11.4	12.2	3.0
Saga	11.8	12.5	16.0	15.5	3.0
Nagasaki	12.5	17.4	16.8	16.4	–1.0
Kumamoto	12.0	12.2	16.1	15.0	2.8

Table 8.2. **Workers employed in jobs created by public works
as percentage of all workers in each prefecture** (cont.)

	1985 (%)	1990 (%)	1995 (%)	1999 (%)	99-90 (% point)
Oita	11.8	11.4	15.3	14.2	2.8
Miyazaki	13.4	13.0	18.3	18.8	5.8
Kagoshima	13.3	13.1	17.7	18.1	5.0
Okinawa	20.9	18.1	22.8	23.3	5.2
Nationwide	8.9	8.5	11.3	11.0	2.5
Metropolitan areas	6.7	6.6	9.0	8.2	1.6
Greater Tokyo	6.5	6.1	8.2	7.6	1.5
Greater Nagoya	6.8	6.6	8.8	8.6	2.0
Greater Osaka	7.0	7.6	10.6	9.0	1.4
Rural areas	11.3	10.3	13.6	13.8	3.5

Source: Higuchi et al., 2001.

The government, however, cannot continue to offset declines in investment and job numbers. As of the end of fiscal 2006, it had accumulated a debt of JPY 767 trillion, which amounts to JPY 6.09 million for each Japanese citizen. Since fiscal 1998, the government has been reducing construction investment: in fiscal 2006 the figure was JPY 18.2 trillion – a decline of 47% in ten years.

Social infrastructures that do not improve the economic efficiency of regional areas

Another reason for the reduction in public works spending is that an increase in spending does not result in improved economic efficiency in regional areas. An increase in public works spending leads to development of social infrastructures related to both the general public (water and sewer systems, public housing, parks) and industry (roads, harbours, airports). Development of industry-related infrastructures in particular is expected to improve the economic efficiency of particular regions and reinforce firms' competitiveness. For instance, if a highway is built to ease traffic congestion, the time it takes to travel to a destination can be shortened. As a result, a person would be able to work with greater productivity over the same duration of time. How much does an increase in public works spending contribute to enhancing economic efficiency of prefectures? And how has it changed from the past?

The economic efficiency of each prefecture can be estimated by subtracting inputs – such as labour, capital and raw materials – from outputs, which are the same as total production. In economics, this is called "total factor productivity". In the past, labour productivity was often used as an indicator of production efficiency. But because labour productivity rises even when actual economic efficiency is not improved, when investment in capital is increased and when the capital equipment ratio per worker is raised, labour productivity was recently replaced as an indicator of economic efficiency by total factor productivity; in this case an increase in capital is also subtracted. Therefore, the annual total factor productivity was estimated for each prefecture, along with the percentage by which total factor productivity rises given an increase in social infrastructures of JPY 1 million (for details see Higuchi et al., 2001).

Figure 8.6 shows the percentage of improvement made to economic efficiency by increasing social infrastructure investment by JPY 1 million in real terms in each prefecture in 1975. Clearly this additional investment improves economic efficiency more in metropolitan areas than in rural areas.

Figure 8.7 shows the improvement in economic efficiency in 1998. The graduations of the vertical axis are the same as in Figure 8.6 (1975). A comparison of the two clearly indicates that the improvement in economic efficiency is significantly smaller in 1998 than in 1975 – in most prefectures, half the level. This decline can also be observed when estimates are taken by extracting data only on industry-related social infrastructures.

Partly, these changes are explained by the fact that in recent times, most social infrastructures have already been introduced and so new public works projects are less likely to have the same effect in improving regional supply efficiency.

Figure 8.6. **TFP growth through an increase in infrastructure investments (¥ 1 million per capita, real) by prefecture (1975)**

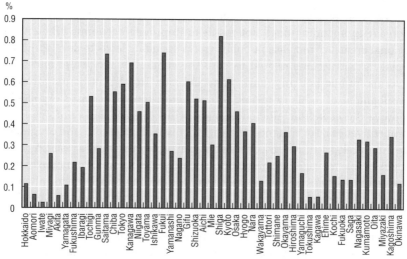

Figure 8.7. **TFP growth through an increase in infrastructure investments (¥ 1 million per capita, real) by prefecture (1998)**

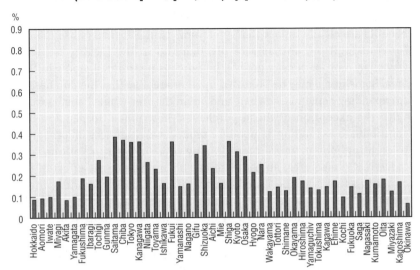

When the decline is considered together with greater dependency on public works for employment, another implication emerges: the objectives of public works have changed substantially. In the past, the primary objective of public works was improvement of economic efficiency in each region. In other words, it was to use the roads they built. In recent years, however, the objective is shifting from improving economic efficiency, as in the past, to creating jobs. In other words, it is now building the roads that is the objective.

If the social infrastructures that are being built through public works projects can benefit future generations, there would at least be a plausible rationale for the future generations to pay for the costs by financing government debt. If, however, the infrastructures are not beneficial to them, there is no rational reason for them to pay the costs. In that case, it can only be said that using public works to create jobs and reduce unemployment can no longer be continued.

Percentage of workers employed in jobs created by pension benefits in prefectures

There are many employment opportunities that the government provides apart from public works. At times in the past when the government used to determine rice prices, there was a back spread where producers' prices were higher than consumer prices, and the government could transfer incomes to rural areas through its rice price policies. This provided farmers with opportunities to earn incomes and reduced regional divergences. Today, some say that instead of rice prices, social security benefits lessen regional differences.

In areas where there is a large population of senior citizens, pension benefits are clearly higher than premiums paid. Pensioners use the benefits for consumption, and as a result, demand in the locality is increased. Obviously, not all pensioners will be purchasing in retail stores in the local area. Some items may be produced in other areas so that the purchase will go to expanding demand elsewhere and not in the area where benefits were paid. With the exception of those purchases, how much do pension benefits contribute to expanding demand for products and services in local areas and to creating jobs in those areas? Using inter-industry relations tables of individual prefectures, an estimate has been made of the effect of pension benefits as well as the repercussion effect of unemployment insurance benefits. This was done by calculating the percentage among all workers of those employed in jobs created by the rise in consumption from payment of public pension and unemployment insurance benefits.

The results are shown in Table 8.3. The national average in 1999 was 2.9% of all workers. In other words, 1.9 million jobs were created by pension benefits and unemployment benefits. By prefecture, Yamaguchi had the highest percentage with 4.9%, followed by Kochi, Shimane and Kumamoto prefectures. In contrast, the percentage in Tokyo's city centre is low at 1.6%. The differences in these percentages are not as wide as in the percentage of recipients in each prefecture's population. This is because the number of contributors to employees' pensions – which provide more benefits than national pensions – is relatively small in rural areas as there are more self-employed workers than employees. It is also because contributors to employees' pensions in rural areas receive fewer benefits per person, as premiums are linked to salaries. Nevertheless, pension and employment insurance benefits generate large numbers of jobs, and their effectiveness in doing so rose over ten years by more than 1 percentage point. Even though ageing of the population will advance further in the future, if pension benefits are reduced, that would deal a serious blow to the regional economy.

Percentage of civil servants among workers in prefectures

Another area in which the government is playing an important role in generating jobs in regional areas is the civil service. As of 2000 there are some 800 000 national civil servants and 3.2 million local civil servants, who together make up 6.2% of all workers. An international comparison shows that France has 104 civil servants for every 1 000 people in its population, the United Kingdom 83 civil servants, the United States 80, Germany 68, and Japan 40. Apparently the number of civil servants in Japan is comparatively small, but since the percentage

Table 8.3. **Workers employed in jobs created by the rise in consumption from payment of public pension and employment insurance (as percentage of all workers in each prefecture)**

	1985 (%)	1990 (%)	1995 (%)	1999 (%)	99-90 (% point)
Hokkaido	2.9	2.9	3.1	4.0	1.1
Aomori	2.7	2.1	2.1	2.6	0.5
Iwate	1.9	2.0	2.3	3.0	1.1
Miyagi	1.6	1.6	2.0	2.8	1.1
Akita	2.5	2.7	3.1	3.9	1.2
Yamagata	2.1	2.1	2.5	3.1	1.0
Fukushima	2.1	1.8	1.9	2.5	0.6
Niigata	2.6	2.6	2.9	3.7	1.1
Ibaraki	1.2	1.4	1.7	2.2	0.9
Tochigi	–	1.3	1.6	2.0	0.7
Gunma	–	1.5	1.8	2.3	0.8
Saitama	1.4	1.4	2.0	2.8	1.4
Chiba	1.6	1.5	1.8	2.5	1.0
Tokyo	1.0	0.9	1.3	1.6	0.7
Kanagawa	1.5	1.4	2.1	2.8	1.4
Yamanashi	1.6	1.5	1.8	2.3	0.8
Nagano	1.8	1.7	1.9	2.5	0.8
Shizuoka	1.7	1.6	1.9	2.5	0.9
Toyama	2.3	2.3	3.1	3.9	1.6
Ishikawa	2.2	2.0	2.6	3.3	1.3
Gifu	1.9	1.8	2.3	2.9	1.1
Aichi	1.5	1.6	2.0	2.5	1.0
Mie	1.8	1.7	2.1	2.6	0.9
Fukui	2.1	2.0	2.8	3.5	1.5
Shiga	–	1.5	1.9	2.4	0.9
Kyoto	2.0	2.3	2.4	3.1	0.8
Osaka	1.5	1.8	2.3	2.9	1.1
Hyogo	2.1	2.1	2.7	3.3	1.2
Nara	2.2	2.3	2.8	3.7	1.4
Wakayama	2.3	2.3	2.9	3.5	1.3
Tottori	–	2.5	3.1	4.0	1.4
Shimane	2.6	3.0	3.4	4.2	1.2
Okayama	2.2	2.5	3.2	4.1	1.6
Hiroshima	2.3	2.4	2.9	3.7	1.3
Yamaguchi	2.8	3.6	3.9	4.9	1.3
Tokushima	2.4	2.7	3.0	3.7	1.0
Kagawa	2.3	2.2	2.3	2.9	0.8
Ehime	2.6	2.8	3.5	4.2	1.4
Kochi	2.9	3.2	3.8	4.6	1.4
Fukuoka	2.8	2.8	2.8	3.5	0.7
Saga	2.4	2.6	2.8	3.5	0.8
Nagasaki	2.8	2.9	3.2	3.8	0.9

Table 8.3. **Workers employed in jobs created by the rise in consumption**
from payment of public pension and employment insurance
(as percentage of all workers in each prefecture) *(cont.)*

	1985 (%)	1990 (%)	1995 (%)	1999 (%)	99-90 (% point)
Kumamoto	2.7	2.8	3.4	4.2	1.5
Oita	2.2	2.4	2.8	3.5	1.1
Miyazaki	2.6	2.8	3.1	3.9	1.1
Kagoshima	2.7	2.8	3.2	3.9	1.1
Okinawa	1.9	2.0	2.4	3.0	1.1
Nationwide	1.9	1.9	2.3	2.9	1.0
Metropolitan areas	1.4	1.5	1.9	2.5	1.0
Greater Tokyo	1.2	1.1	1.6	2.2	1.0
Greater Nagoya	1.6	1.6	2.1	2.6	1.0
Greater Osaka	1.8	2.0	2.4	3.1	1.1
Rural areas	2.3	2.3	2.6	3.3	1.0

Source: Higuchi *et al.*, 2001.

of work in that domain commissioned farmed out to the private sector and the number of people considered as quasi-civil servants in public agencies differ from country to country, that cannot be concluded based on the above figures alone.

What then are the numbers of civil servants and the scope of job opportunities created for civil servants who receive their salaries and use them for consumption in each prefecture? What percentage of all workers in each prefecture hold jobs generated by civil service employment? Estimates are shown in Table 8.4.

In 1999, 8.7% of all workers in Japan were civil servants or employed in jobs created by the civil service through a repercussion effect. By prefecture, Hokkaido had the largest percentage with 12.6%, followed by Shimane, Okinawa, Aomori and Kochi prefectures, which had more than 12 percentage points each. The number of civil servants continued to grow until 1994 but was subsequently cut back, reflecting financial difficulties. As a result, employment dependency on civil service employment, including its repercussion effect, has hardly changed in the last ten years.

Rising employment dependency on the government in rural areas

As employment opportunities created by the government, the discussion has covered public works, social security and the civil service and its repercussion effect. On aggregate, what percentage of all workers in each prefecture is generated by the government? Table 8.5 combines the results of the previous three tables.

The percentage of workers employed in jobs created by the government among all workers, which was 18.9% (national average) in 1990, rose to 22.5%

Table 8.4. **Workers employed in jobs created by the civil service (as percentage of all workers in each prefecture)**

	1985 (%)	1990 (%)	1995 (%)	1999 (%)	99-90 (% point)
Hokkaido	13.1	12.8	12.4	12.6	−0.2
Aomori	12.2	12.3	12.1	12.0	−0.3
Iwate	9.9	10.3	10.2	10.4	0.2
Miyagi	10.3	9.9	9.8	9.9	−0.1
Akita	10.5	10.3	10.3	10.7	0.4
Yamagata	9.4	9.5	10.0	10.1	0.5
Fukushima	8.4	8.3	8.3	8.7	0.3
Niigata	8.8	8.8	8.8	9.1	0.3
Ibaraki	8.8	8.6	8.6	8.6	0.1
Tochigi	−	7.3	7.2	7.2	−0.1
Gunma	−	7.8	8.0	7.9	0.2
Saitama	8.3	7.7	7.8	7.8	0.1
Chiba	10.0	9.2	9.1	8.9	−0.3
Tokyo	7.3	6.7	6.8	6.7	0.1
Kanagawa	8.7	8.0	7.9	7.7	−0.3
Yamanashi	9.2	9.1	9.2	9.3	0.2
Nagano	7.9	8.0	8.2	8.3	0.3
Shizuoka	7.0	6.9	6.9	7.0	0.1
Toyama	8.6	8.4	8.2	8.4	0.1
Ishikawa	9.3	9.0	9.1	9.5	0.5
Gifu	8.1	7.9	8.4	8.6	0.7
Aichi	7.1	6.9	6.7	6.8	−0.1
Mie	8.9	8.8	8.8	9.0	0.2
Fukui	8.7	8.7	9.1	9.4	0.6
Shiga	−	9.4	9.3	9.1	−0.3
Kyoto	9.1	8.8	8.8	9.1	0.3
Osaka	7.0	6.6	6.6	6.8	0.2
Hyogo	9.4	9.1	9.1	9.2	0.1
Nara	11.7	11.9	11.5	11.5	−0.4
Wakayama	10.1	10.0	10.1	10.8	0.8
Tottori	−	10.3	10.7	11.2	0.9
Shimane	10.6	10.9	11.4	12.1	1.2
Okayama	8.6	8.4	8.6	8.9	0.5
Hiroshima	9.3	9.1	9.3	9.6	0.4
Yamaguchi	10.0	10.0	10.1	10.6	0.6
Tokushima	10.6	11.2	11.4	11.9	0.7
Kagawa	9.9	9.9	9.8	10.1	0.2
Ehime	8.8	8.8	9.2	9.5	0.7
Kochi	11.7	11.5	11.6	12.0	0.6
Fukuoka	9.6	8.7	8.5	8.4	−0.3
Saga	10.3	10.5	10.5	10.5	0.0
Nagasaki	11.5	11.2	11.5	11.7	0.4
Kumamoto	10.1	10.1	10.0	10.2	0.1

Table 8.4. **Workers employed in jobs created by the civil service (as percentage of all workers in each prefecture)** (cont.)

	1985 (%)	1990 (%)	1995 (%)	1999 (%)	99-90 (% point)
Oita	10.6	10.4	10.4	10.5	0.1
Miyazaki	10.2	10.0	9.8	10.0	0.1
Kagoshima	11.0	11.2	11.1	11.2	0.1
Okinawa	13.5	13.4	13.3	12.1	−1.4
Nationwide	8.9	8.6	8.6	8.7	0.1
Metropolitan areas	8.0	7.5	7.6	7.6	0.1
Greater Tokyo	8.1	7.4	7.5	7.4	0.0
Greater Nagoya	7.6	7.4	7.4	7.5	0.1
Greater Osaka	8.2	7.9	7.8	8.0	0.2
Rural areas	9.9	9.6	9.6	9.7	0.1

Source: Higuchi et al., 2001.

in 1999. Moreover, the percentage is particularly high in a number of prefectures. For instance, in Kochi, dependency on the government for employment opportunities grew 9.2 percentage points during this period to mark a record 38.9% in 1999. This meant that close to 40% of all workers, including farmers and the self-employed, were engaged in jobs generated by government spending. Kochi prefecture was followed by Okinawa with 38.4% and Shimane and Hokkaido both with 37.5%. As many as 12 prefectures out of 47 had more than 30 percentage points.

What would happen if fiscal spending were to be cut because of financial pressures? Suppose fiscal spending is reduced 10% across the board on all items in all prefectures. As a result, Kochi prefecture would lose 3.89% of all jobs in the prefecture. As the unemployment rate was 4.7% in 2002, if all people who lost their jobs become unemployed, the unemployment rate would almost double to 8.6%. In Hokkaido prefecture, the unemployment rate would rise from 6.1% to 9.9%. In Okinawa prefecture, it would grow from 8.3% to 12.1%.

Considering that the central and local governments have accumulated debt that amounts to JPY 5.38 million for each Japanese citizen, it goes without saying that fiscal consolidation is imperative. In this fiscal spending cut scenario, what would happen to employment in rural areas? As it is no longer possible to depend on the government for employment, we will need a new mechanism for creating jobs in regional areas.

The impact of economic globalisation on regional employment

During the latter half of the 1980s, globalisation's emphasis shifted from movement of goods across national borders through imports and exports to movement of capital across national borders through foreign direct investment. This led to substantial changes in the international division of

Table 8.5. **Workers employed in jobs created by the civil service, public works, public pensions and employment insurance benefits (as percentage of all workers in each prefecture)**

	1985 (%)	1990 (%)	1995 (%)	1999 (%)	99-90 (% point)
Hokkaido	33.5	32.6	36.1	37.5	4.9
Aomori	29.6	25.6	29.5	30.3	4.6
Iwate	22.8	22.6	26.1	27.4	4.8
Miyagi	21.8	21.1	24.2	25.3	4.2
Akita	25.6	26.5	31.6	32.6	6.0
Yamagata	21.4	21.8	26.5	27.5	5.7
Fukushima	19.3	18.1	21.0	22.6	4.5
Niigata	23.1	22.3	26.4	28.0	5.7
Ibaraki	17.0	17.5	21.0	21.7	4.2
Tochigi	–	14.3	16.9	17.6	3.3
Gunma	–	15.1	18.4	19.0	3.9
Saitama	16.0	15.4	18.3	19.3	3.9
Chiba	20.0	18.5	20.7	19.7	1.2
Tokyo	14.0	13.2	15.7	15.6	2.4
Kanagawa	17.8	15.3	18.2	17.7	2.4
Yamanashi	19.7	18.0	23.3	23.1	5.1
Nagano	18.6	17.5	21.3	19.5	2.0
Shizuoka	14.9	13.9	16.2	16.6	2.7
Toyama	20.1	19.0	24.1	26.2	7.1
Ishikawa	21.2	19.0	24.7	26.7	7.7
Gifu	17.9	17.2	20.9	22.2	5.0
Aichi	14.8	14.6	16.9	17.2	2.6
Mie	18.3	18.0	20.6	21.3	3.3
Fukui	21.6	22.5	23.6	25.0	2.5
Shiga	–	16.8	18.6	18.7	1.9
Kyoto	18.6	19.2	22.1	22.1	2.9
Osaka	14.8	15.5	18.7	18.2	2.7
Hyogo	19.3	19.2	23.7	21.7	2.5
Nara	24.3	23.9	25.6	25.5	1.6
Wakayama	21.1	20.7	26.4	30.7	9.9
Tottori	–	24.1	29.6	32.1	8.0
Shimane	29.1	28.7	32.3	37.5	8.8
Okayama	21.2	19.9	25.8	26.8	6.9
Hiroshima	20.2	20.6	24.1	25.4	4.8
Yamaguchi	23.2	24.9	27.6	30.8	5.9
Tokushima	25.1	26.3	30.8	32.8	6.4
Kagawa	24.1	20.2	22.4	23.7	3.5
Ehime	21.2	22.3	26.5	27.9	5.5
Kochi	28.8	29.7	34.8	38.9	9.2
Fukuoka	23.3	20.6	22.8	24.0	3.4
Saga	24.5	25.6	29.3	29.5	3.9
Nagasaki	26.9	31.6	31.5	31.9	0.3

Table 8.5. **Workers employed in jobs created by the civil service, public works, public pensions and employment insurance benefits (as percentage of all workers in each prefecture)** *(cont.)*

	1985 (%)	1990 (%)	1995 (%)	1999 (%)	99-90 (% point)
Kumamoto	24.8	25.1	29.5	29.4	4.4
Oita	24.6	24.2	28.5	28.2	4.1
Miyazaki	26.2	25.8	31.2	32.8	7.0
Kagoshima	26.9	27.1	32.0	33.3	6.2
Okinawa	36.3	33.4	38.4	38.4	5.0
Nationwide	19.8	18.9	22.1	22.5	3.6
Metropolitan areas	16.2	15.6	18.5	18.3	2.7
Greater Tokyo	15.8	14.6	17.3	17.2	2.5
Greater Nagoya	16.0	15.6	18.2	18.7	3.1
Greater Osaka	17.0	17.4	20.9	20.1	2.7
Rural areas	23.4	22.2	25.8	26.8	4.6

Note: Errors in the value of changes from 1990 to 1999 are the result of rounding.
Source: Higuchi *et al.*, 2001.

labour. It meant a shift from a pattern of producing goods domestically by employing workers inside one's own country and exporting the goods overseas, to a pattern of building production sites overseas, producing goods by employing local workers there, and selling the goods in the local country or exporting them to third countries or at times back to one's own country.

There are two types of foreign direct investment. One is direct investment abroad in which Japanese firms set up production and sales sites overseas. The other is inward direct investment in which foreign firms set up production and sales sites in Japan. Direct investment abroad may have a negative impact on domestic employment, while inward direct investment may create jobs in the domestic labour market. In fact, there was growing concern about the hollowing out in the United States as that country's firms were moving their plants to Mexico and South America in the latter half of the 1980s. But because Japanese firms and other foreign firms set up operations in the United States and hired American workers, unemployment did not become a serious issue. In recent years, an increasing number of Japanese firms are closing domestic plants in order to relocate their production bases overseas. Meanwhile, inward investment by foreign firms is also on the rise. In view of the US example, can reduction in Japan's domestic employment resulting from Japanese firms' transfer of production sites overseas be offset by employment by foreign firms?

As shown in Tables 8.6 and 8.7, the amount of investment and employment through Japanese firms' investment abroad and foreign firms' investment in Japan is growing along with globalisation. There was, however, a wide gap between the two levels. Until very recently, foreign firms'

Table 8.6. **Changes in Japan's foreign direct and inward direct investment (investments reported or notified)**

	Foreign direct investment (USD million)	Inward direct investment (USD million)
Fiscal 1980	4 693	328
1981	8 931	389
1982	7 703	1 057
1983	8,145	1 115
1984	10 155	418
1985	12 217	930
1986	22 320	940
1987	33 364	2 214
1988	47 022	3 243
1989	67 540	2 860
1990	56 911	2 778
1991	41 584	4 339
1992	34 138	4 084
1993	36 025	3 078
1994	41 051	4 155
1995	52 748	3 934
1996	49 715	7 082
1997	54 776	5 608
1998	40 283	10 230
1999	66 080	21 057
2000	50 276	28 992
2001	33 239	17 913
2002	35 895	17 466
2003	35 189	18 253
2004	35 324	37 223

Note: Because investment figures were published in yen after 1995, the figures were converted to dollars based on the exchange rates at the half-year point.
Source: Kinzai Institute for Financial Affairs, Inc., Annual Report of the International Finance Bureau, Ministry of Finance. All figures for 1995 and subsequent years are estimates of JETRO.

investment in Japan, in comparison with Japanese firms' investment abroad, had been small. The gap had been particularly pronounced even compared with other advanced countries. Table 8.6 shows that inward direct investment in 1995 was only a fourteenth of outward direct investment. Meanwhile, Table 8.7 shows that the number of workers employed by foreign firms in Japan was only one-tenth that of workers employed by Japanese firms abroad – i.e., by comparison, overwhelmingly small.

Since 1998, however, there has been a sharp increase in foreign firms' investment in Japan due to various factors, such as deregulation in Japan and a fall in the prices of domestic assets. As a result, the gap between outward direct investment and inward direct investment narrowed to a ratio of 1.9 to 1 by fiscal 2004. Relatively speaking, the number of workers employed by foreign

Table 8.7. **Changes in the number of persons employed by Japanese firms overseas and by foreign firms in Japan**

Number of employees

	Japanese firms abroad	Foreign firms in Japan
Fiscal 1982	–	114
1983	–	140
1987	–	129
1988	1 326	169
1989	1 157	172
1990	1 550	182
1991	1 621	203
1992	1 404	192
1993	1 947	172
1994	2 194	227
1995	2 328	225
1996	2 745	230
1997	2 835	243
1998	2 749	264
1999	3 100	316
2000	3 450	331
2001	3 180	329
2002	3 410	294
2003	3 770	435
2004	4 140	431

Source: Ministry of Economy, Trade and Industry, Basic Survey of Overseas Business Activities and Survey of Trends in Business Activities of Foreign Affiliates.

firms in Japan has also been growing since 1999. There are now significant expectations on the part of foreign firms with regard to job creation in Japan.

Creation of jobs by foreign firms by region

There are, however, significant regional differences in the number of jobs created by foreign firms in different prefectures. For instance, 69% of foreign firms' head offices in Japan are located in Tokyo's city centre, 9.1% in Osaka prefecture, and another 8.9% in Kanagawa prefecture – together, 87% of all foreign firms' head offices. Statistics on all establishments of foreign firms also show that 36% of jobs created by foreign firms are concentrated in Tokyo, followed by 13% in Kanagawa prefecture and 9% in Osaka prefecture (1996). Foreign firms' employment as percentage of all employees in each prefecture is 2.4% in Tokyo's city centre, 2.6% in Kanagawa, and 2.7% in Hiroshima. Foreign firms play an important role in creating jobs in these prefectures, but in others the percentage is very small (Fukao and Amano, 2004).

One of the reasons foreign firms' employment is concentrated in large metropolises is the urban orientation of many of the industries involved, such as finance and IT. Japanese firms that entered the United States were mainly manufacturers of automobiles and electrical machinery; most of them were therefore located in provincial areas, and jobs created by them were not concentrated in cities.

The impact of external direct investment on domestic employment by region

What effect does Japanese firms' direct investment abroad have on domestic employment in Japan? Does firms' foreign investment reduce domestic employment? An analysis of data on a number of firms indicates that those that relocated their production plants to other parts of Asia have actually reduced domestic employment temporarily. The effect, however, is not long term. On the contrary, compared with firms that do not have production sites overseas, those that do tended to succeed in improving productivity and profitability, and subsequently in expanding domestic employment (Higuchi and Matsuura, 2003). Therefore, it cannot be concluded that firms' overseas investment will reduce overall domestic employment. The issue, rather, is one of regional differences in effect: clearly, firms moving overseas are decreasing employment in rural areas while increasing employment in large cities.

Firms decide to make direct investment abroad with a view to setting up an international division of labour within their firms. Domestically, these firms are now trying to strengthen their research and sales divisions in order to switch to producing high value-added products inside Japan. As a result, firms are employing more employees in their head offices and building prototype plants in large cities but closing down (or reducing output from) mass production plants built in rural areas during the period of rapid economic growth, or at a time of labour shortage during the period of the bubble economy (Horaguchi, 1997, 1998). Those plants had employed a large number of high school graduates; the reduction in their employment is making job-search more difficult for fresh high school graduates in rural areas than for college graduates in urban areas.

Judging from foreign firms' employment creation and the effect of Japanese firms' direct investment abroad on domestic employment, it can be said that so far, economic globalisation has tended to decrease employment in rural area. As firms can today choose the location of their production sites across national borders, local economies will need to offer advantageous conditions in order to attract firms. Considering the high wages in Japan, however, it would be difficult to offer better pecuniary conditions than found overseas. Local economies should promote industry-government-university collaboration, attract high-calibre individuals and prepare the infrastructures for information networks, so that they can show the rest of the world that they can offer attractive conditions to firms that relocate to their regions.

The impact of declining birth rate and ageing population on regional employment

If employment in rural areas were to decline and more jobs were to be created in large cities, regional employment mismatches could be eased through the population shift from rural areas to cities. In fact, large numbers of youths from rural areas came to large cities in groups during the period of rapid economic growth to find employment, which helped to reduce regional differences. The same thing happened during the years of the bubble economy. But that kind of population shift is not observed today. The population is ageing, and cross-regional movement has decreased. Moreover, the decline in the birth rate has increased the number of single-child families, which also raises the percentage of youths who remain in their hometowns and so reduces cross-regional movement.

The Basic Resident Register shows that recently, the percentage of people who move across municipal borders in a year has consistently hit new lows. The percentage in 1956 was 5.43%. It rose to 8.02% in 1970 but began declining after that: in 2002, it was 4.72%. The decline is particularly large among young people; the *Population Census* shows that the percentage of people who moved to different prefectures dropped sharply among young people in their 20s compared with ten years ago (Figure 8.7). In the past, large numbers of young people moved to large cities to be employed or to study, but that trend has not been observed recently. On the contrary, young people today have a greater tendency to stay in their hometowns. It is very likely that one of the reasons for this is an increase in single-child families in society. As families have fewer children, parents have stronger desire to keep their children near them. Also, an increasing number of children wish to live close to their parents in order to receive financial assistance, resulting in a higher percentage of youths who stay in their hometowns. In contrast to the decline in cross-prefectural movement, movement within single municipalities is increasing, and a large percentage of young people are living close to their parents (Figure 8.8).

According to the National Institute of Population and Social Security Research's *Population Projection by Municipality*, the population in more than half of all municipalities will, by 2030, decrease by more than 20% compared to the level in 2000. At the same time, senior citizens 65 years old or older as a percentage of the entire population of a municipality will be higher than 40% in more than 30% of all municipalities. These projections indicate that it would be difficult to resolve regional employment mismatches through population shifts.

Figure 8.8. **Percentage of persons who lived in a different prefecture five years ago (men)**

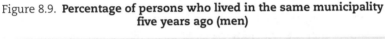

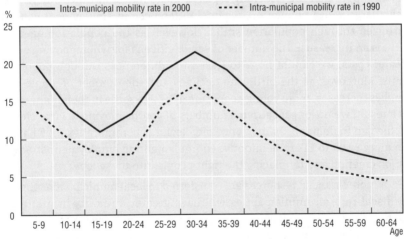

Source: Population Census.

Figure 8.9. **Percentage of persons who lived in the same municipality five years ago (men)**

Source: Population Census.

A shift in perspective will show that as more youths stay in their hometowns, local municipalities will be able to use their strengths for local development. It can be said that the stage is set for local communities to take the initiative and implement employment strategies involving young people.

Local municipalities need to adopt endogenous measures for job creation

In Japan, fiscal measures for expanding public works have played an important role in creating jobs in rural areas. However, as financial conditions deteriorate, there is now less room to increase employment through such macroeconomic policies, and it is difficult to increase regional employment through greater fiscal spending. Economic globalisation also has an effect on widening regional differences. Until the first half of the 1980s, economic globalisation meant the flow of goods across national borders in the form of imports and exports. From the latter half of the 1980s, however, direct investment rapidly expanded, and the flow of capital across national borders began to increase. These changes altered globalisation's effect on employment. Growth in exports contributed substantially to increasing domestic employment and particularly to employment in rural areas where many plants were located. Japanese firms' direct investment abroad, however, resulted in a cutback of mass production plants in rural areas and has made employment for high school graduates more difficult. On the other hand, the increasing penetration of foreign firms in Japan has created jobs in cities but has not led to increasing employment in rural areas.

In addition to these changes in labour demand, there are changes in labour supply that are widening regional inequalities. In times where there was a large youth population, regional differences in employment could be narrowed through population shifts. However, as the population ages and there is an increase in the number of senior citizens for whom moving entails greater costs, we cannot hope to lessen the differences through population shifts. Moreover, as the birth rate declines and the number of single-child families increases, more young people are opting to settle in their hometowns. As a result, we no longer see large numbers of youths moving to large cities to fill the gap in demand, as they once did. Regional communities thus have all the more need to take the initiative in implementing employment strategies for job creation and for placing the right people into those jobs.

If more financial resources are transferred to local municipalities through the fiscal reform, municipalities will have greater authority in matters of finance. To make best use of this authority, they will need a staff that can devise and implement policies. Training such a staff will not be easy and will take time and require strategy, but it must be done in order to prepare people to take on a leadership role.

Unlike employment measures, an employment strategy is a plan that brings together a large number of measures executed to achieve a specific goal. Implementing a number of measures means verifying in advance that they do not conflict. In the second half of the 1980s, the Equal Employment

Opportunity Law was implemented in Japan to facilitate women's entry into the labour market. At the same time, however, the "special exemption for spouse" was introduced to the income tax and "class III insured person" (housewife) to the pensions system, which provided favourable treatment for full-time housewives and women with less than a certain level of income. This simultaneous implementation of conflicting practices effectively suppressed women's participation in the labour force. To be effective, individual measures must be consistent. In implementing a "strategy", it must be clearly indicated what the goals are, who will take the initiative, what measures will be adopted, and the time horizon.

For many years, countries in Europe struggled with high unemployment rates and tried many different measures to combat unemployment. In their search for an effective countermeasure, they came to realise the importance of employment strategies implemented as a community-wide effort. On issues such as reduction in public works spending, Japan is in some respects facing problems similar to the ones European countries faced in the past. As one can no longer expect much from exogenous measures for job creation, there will be a greater need for local governments, firms, labour unions and citizens to unite and execute employment strategies that take advantage of the strengths in each locality. The experience of other countries should serve as valuable reference when implementing similar measures in Japan.

Bibliography

Fukao, Kyoji and Tomofumi Amano (2004), *Tainichi Chokusetsu Toshi to Nihon Keizai* (Direct Investment in Japan and the Japanese Economy), Nihon Keizai Shimbun, Inc., Tokyo.

Higuchi, Yoshio (2001), *Koyo to Shitsugyo no Keizaigaku* (Economics of Employment and Unemployment), Nihon Keizai Shimbun, Inc.

Higuchi, Yoshio, Takanobu Nakajima, Masaki Nakahigashi and Ken Hino (2001), "Todofuken no Keizai Kasseika ni okeru Seifu no Yakuwari" (The Government's Role in Stimulating the Economy in Prefectures), Policy Research Institute, Ministry of Finance.

Higuchi, Yoshio and Toshiyuki Matsuura (2003), "Kigyo Panel Data niyoru Koyo Koka Bunseki: Jigyo Soshiki no Henko to Kaigai Chokusetsu Toshi ga Sonogo no Koyo ni Ataeru Eikyo" (Employment Effect Analysis Using Data on A Panel of Firms: The Effect of Changes in Business Organisation and Direct Foreign Investment on Employment), Discussion Paper 03-J-019, Research Institute of Economy, Trade and Industry.

Horaguchi, Haruo (1997, 1998), "Nihon no Sangyo Kudoka" (The Hollowing-Out of Industry in Japan), *Keiei Shirin*, Vol. 34, Nos. 3 and 4, Hosei University Keiei Gakkai.

ISBN 978-92-64-04327-5
More than Just Jobs:
Workforce Development in a Skills-Based Economy
© OECD 2008

PART II

Chapter 9

Korea: Proposal for a New Type of Partnership

by

Hyo-Soo Lee

Macroeconomic policy challenges that range from economic growth and unemployment to inflation and social polarisation issues call for a dynamic and healthy labour market. Job-skill mismatch in the changing economic environment can be minimised by building an economic and social system that provides equal opportunity to nurture "knowledge workers" and improve job skills, and by creating a Learning and Job Information Centre (LJIC) to reduce asymmetric information flow in both the labour market and the education sectors. Regional Economic and Social Advancement Partnerships (RESAP) should be designed to develop human resources in a knowledge economy.

Introduction

The importance of human resource development is gaining ever wider acceptance from both scholars and the general public as transition to "knowledge economy" becomes more and more evident (OECD, 2000). Thomas A. Kochan (2005, p. 6) stresses that human capital is becoming the most valuable resource and strategic asset for any nation or company that wishes to compete in a global marketplace while offering high standards of living.

A. Marshall wrote earlier (1920) that "the most valuable investment anyone can make is investing on human resource". Taking Marshall's lead, labour economists such as J. Mincer (1958), G.S. Becker (1962) and T.W. Schultz (1960) all contributed to develop the human capital theory in the late 1950s and undertook scientific analysis in areas such as training and education as a form of investment in human resources as well as return on investment. P.B. Doeringer and M.J. Piore (1971), on the other hand, have emphasised the importance of accumulating firm-specific skills through in-house education and training (on-the-job training) in their internal labour market theory. L. and Z. Nadler (1989) define "human resource development" as an organised learning experience provided by the employer for a determined period of time for the purpose of improving work progress and individual growth. Most scholars discuss human resource development in terms of its educational and training aspects aimed at improving the job skills of employees.

We need a new paradigm about human resource development in a knowledge economy. We should focus not only on education and training but also on the development of *knowledge workforce* and *vocational ability* in a knowledge economy. A knowledge worker can be defined as someone who has the ability to create new knowledge and information by collecting, analysing and processing the knowledge and information available. New knowledge and information can be generated by integrating and fusing various kinds of experiences, ideas and explicit and tacit knowledge. Although not everyone might be a knowledge worker, everyone has the potential to become one through "humanware", regardless of education levels and occupations. According to the Production, Distribution, and Rule-making (PDR) System Theory (Lee, 1996, 2001), a knowledge workforce could be developed by humanware that transforms human resources into creative resources by activating the positive mechanism between the mind-set and one's abilities.[1]

Vocational ability does not merely refer to knowledge and job skills; it also encompasses other abilities such as the ability to function in a group, co-operativeness, communication skills, vocational ethics, a healthy job attitude, a sense of adventure and leadership. This is an ability that is required of those in the manufacturing, clerical, technical, professional and self-employed sectors regardless of whether they work in the knowledge-based economy or industrial society.

Vocational ability determines not only personal job competitiveness and quality of life, but also the competitiveness of the organisation he or she works for. In order to secure a decent job, one must be armed with the vocational ability that job demands. Anyone who loses their competitiveness in this society of ongoing change is all the more likely to become unemployed. Universities, companies, regional economies and nations can maintain their competitive advantage only with a workforce with a high degree of vocational ability and knowledge.

That vocational ability will differ from person to person and from job to job. The ability that a given job requires constantly changes amid the changing economic environment and technological advances. As such, the importance of human resource development cannot be overemphasised. Naturally, that importance is highlighted as economies integrate into the global market and move to the knowledge economy. As can be readily observed, the acceleration of competition and technological changes are causing the destruction of traditional jobs and the creation of new ones. The combination of that creation/ destruction and changing vocational requirements in effect forces everyone to constantly develop their vocational ability and learn new knowledge.

We need an infrastructure for developing the "knowledge workforce", "vocational ability" and "regional knowledge competitiveness". Regional knowledge competitiveness is defined as a regional social capital to produce, diffuse and utilise new knowledge and high-value information in a given area. With high regional knowledge competitiveness, a region has a competitive advantage for both persons and companies to acquire knowledge and information; the cost of doing so is low because of positive externalities and the high interaction effect, and because of fluent tacit knowledge in the area.

The changing economic environment and a paradigm shift in economic policies

Korea is in the midst of a transition from an industrial to a knowledge economy, and is moving on to a global market and an ageing society. Economic policies and competition strategies therefore also need to change in a fundamental way to keep up with the changing environments. Table 9.1 summarises a new paradigm in economic policies that reflect such needs.

Table 9.1. **Paradigm shift in economic policies**

	New paradigm	Old paradigm
Economic environment	• Knowledge information society • Global market: competition and speed • Ageing society	• Industrial society • National market • Young generation society
Economic policies and competition Strategies	• Focus on labour market policy • Decentralisation • Competitive advantage strategy: knowledge competitiveness, speed • Flexible production system (networking and partnership) • Quality competition strategies	• Focus on macroeconomic policy • Centralisation • Comparative advantage strategy: factor cost competitiveness • Mass production system (economy of scale and division of labour of process) • Price competition strategies
Labour market and social policy	• Dynamic and healthy labour market • Job creation policy • Partnership between school and work • Workfare policy • Learning and Job Information Centre (LJIC) • High-road strategies	• Rigid-flexible labour market • Unemployment policy • Supplier-centric policy • Welfare policy on social security fund • Employment Security Centre • Low-road strategies
Human resource development policy	• Fostering of knowledge workers • Driving concept: Everyone in their productive age • Developing overall vocational ability • Regional initiatives and partnership (partnership between regional and central gov'ts) • Universities, colleges and training institutions	• Nurturing of technical manpower • Driving concept: Employees and unemployed • Equivalent to skill training • Central gov't initiatives (top-down system, orders, regulations) • Vocational training institutions
Expected results	• High-skill equilibrium economy	• Low-skill equilibrium economy

Source: Author.

First, the rising information society is causing fundamental changes in the very DNA of industry and principles of competition. Knowledge and IT convergence industries are rapidly growing while companies failing to adapt to these changes are quickly losing their competitive edge. The economic order itself – from production and distribution to logistics and consumption – is changing.

Second, in the industrialised society it was possible to protect and foster infant industries as markets were separated by tariff and non-tariff barriers. But as the IT revolution is under way and the WTO is increasingly liberating trade, individual national markets are quickly consolidating into one global market. As fierce competition builds, speed and flexibility as well as low prices and high quality are regarded as fundamental.

Third, the rapid transition to the ageing society gives rise to fundamental changes in the supply and demand structure of the economy. If a new approach to meet these changes is not taken, the productivity and growth engines are bound to suffer and national economies will lose steam due to overwhelming social security expenses.

From macroeconomic policies to DHLM-oriented policies

In the industrial society period, traditional macroeconomic polices were prime tools but labour market polices were very limited in their ability to tackle macroeconomic challenges such as economic growth, unemployment and inflation. On the other hand, microeconomic policies to create a "dynamic and healthy labour market" (DHLM) are extremely important to face up to the macroeconomic challenges of a globalising knowledge economy.

At this point we need to embrace a new proposition, namely that knowledge workers and regional knowledge competitiveness will contribute to job creation in the knowledge economy. As a matter of fact, not only will these two factors contribute to constant innovation and improvement in productivity, but they will also help maintain the competitive advantage to incubate new businesses and attract foreign businesses. Constant innovation and competitive advantage will create jobs, promote economic growth, and alleviate inflationary pressures. This mechanism is the right way to tackle macroeconomic challenges in the global knowledge economy.

If these two factors are insufficient in a high-wage society like Korea, the nation will have a difficult time with knowledge-based industries that do not grow well and with labour-intensive industries moving to low-wage countries. In this situation, macroeconomic policies will not be very effective in preventing accelerated job destruction.

Vocational ability development for the aged will help create jobs for them, and so help forge a workfare rather than welfare society. Workfare polices are crucial in an ageing society, because they help minimise welfare costs and reduce the amount of fiscal budget earmarked for non-productive areas. This will in turn result in alleviating fiscal crunch and vitalising the economy.

Therefore, government should redistribute its resources to develop its knowledge workforce, vocational ability and regional knowledge competitiveness as a new strategy for national competitiveness. At the same time, it should adopt a dynamic and healthy labour market (DHLM) policy to minimise both job mismatches and skill mismatches.

Shift from central government to regional governance initiatives

In Korea, employment and human resource development have been led by central government initiatives, while local governments and their institutions simply implement them under the guidance of the central government.

As is well known, constant innovation and speed-enabling flexibility will act as critical strategies for enhancing national competitiveness in the global knowledge economy. However, the centralised top-down system is no longer adequate to secure regional innovation and flexibility (OECD, 2004).

Flexibility can be achieved when there is a culture of creation, participation and co-operation, and when the structure leading an idea to policy development, implementation and feedback is simple and clear. Therefore, the centralised top-down method must be replaced by regional governance initiatives. This means that regional governance initiates human resource development and local employment policies in partnership with each department of the central government.

Change of strategy in corporate competition

In the new economic climate, a new principle of competition has emerged. With the advance of a global market, all markets are being required to be equipped with flexibility and speed (Tolentino, 2002). Therefore, companies that maintain the traditional mass production system will inevitably lose their competitive edge. That system worked for the most competitive production seen in the 20th century. But the system suffers from lack of flexibility due to its pyramid structure and bureaucratic control methods. Furthermore, because it was based on the principles of division of work and specialisation, jobs were excessively isolated from each other and ideas too removed from their implementation. Under such a system, it was difficult to bring out innovation based on the values of creation, participation and co-operation.

A low-flexibility production system makes it difficult to swiftly respond to changes. Quick response to change in the global market is a basic survival strategy, and only those who lead change can create higher value. Therefore, companies must build a flexible production system, nurture a knowledge workforce based on labour-management and industry-academia partnerships, and create and make full use of a humanware system, vocational ability development, and innovation cluster.

RESAP model: Strategic choices for the knowledge economy

A new paradigm

This chapter proposes the Regional Economic and Social Advancement Partnership (RESAP) model as a strategic choice for the global knowledge economy. RESAP contains three very important strategic components: national competition strategies led by regional governance initiatives; economic and social advances pursued simultaneously; and partnerships to carry out these tasks.

Regional governance initiatives are demanded in the new economic environment, because the growth engine of a nation will be revved up by a knowledge workforce and innovation cluster that can effectively work on a regional level. Economic advancement should be accompanied by social cohesion. The RESAP should be built and operated by a partnership among the innovation leaders in the governance system.

The new paradigm's primary task is to build a Regional Human Resource Development (RHRD) cluster that promotes the development of a knowledge workforce and vocational competency at every stage of the life cycle. Vocational ability development systems for both innovation clusters and the marginalised need to be established based on such an RHRD cluster.

Once an innovation cluster that has international competitive advantage in knowledge and human resources is set in motion, jobs will naturally be created as regional businesses expand in size – helped by their competitiveness – and new companies are created and attracted. The establishment of a human resource development system for the marginalised will also contribute to alleviating social polarisation and strengthen social cohesion, as it will enable the marginalised to improve their quality of life through workfare.

Meanwhile, it is critical to have in place an information hub that can integrate both learning information – the supply side of the labour market – and job information, its demand side. To achieve this objective, the existing employment security centre needs to be expanded and reorganised into the Learning and Job Information Centre (LJIC). The purpose of LJIC is to deal effectively with all aspects of the labour market, from offering vocational ability tests (VAT) to learning and job information all under the same roof. End-users of the labour market can also make full use of this one-stop service system by being able to hire high-quality workers as needed and at a reasonable recruiting cost.

The LJIC will make it possible to reduce market failures such as job mismatch and skill mismatch caused by severely asymmetric information. LJIC will also maximise the integration and efficiency of the RHRD cluster and vocational ability development systems, and ultimately contribute to creating a dynamic and healthy labour market (DHLM).

Figure 9.1 summarises the vision and strategies for the knowledge-based economy.

Mission of RESAP: Building DHLM

The core mission of RESAP is to achieve competitive advantage and social inclusion at the same time by creating a dynamic and healthy labour market (DHLM). The term "healthy labour market" has been used by London's Framework for Regional Employment and Skills Action (London Skills Commission, 2002); it is defined differently in this chapter. Here, DHLM refers to a labour market that quickly responds to changes in, *e.g.*, technology, industry and competition structures. More specifically, the DHLM is characterised by a labour market with a narrowed quantity gap (job

Figure 9.1. **RESAP model: Vision and strategies for the knowledge economy**

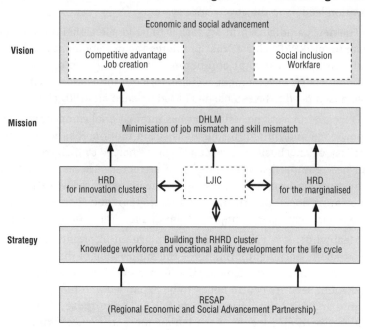

mismatch), a narrowed quality gap (skill mismatch), equality of access and opportunity, and the capacity to offer better jobs to workers. The characteristics of the DHLM are elucidated, from both the demand side and the supply side, in Table 9.2.

Table 9.2. **Characteristics of a dynamic and healthy labour market (DHLM)**

Demand side characteristics
• Regional economies create decent jobs by expanding growth and knowledge based industries.
• Regions foster a culture that values entrepreneurship and creativity.
• Regions provide an investment friendly environment.
• Regional companies make efforts to attain global competitiveness.
• An environment of equal opportunity is nurtured enabling persons to display their potential.

Supply side characteristics
• Individuals, companies and regional societies highly value vocational ability development.
• Regions run diverse vocational ability development institutions that are flexible, reliable and of high quality for students, workers and the unemployed.
• Regions have universities that can foster and provide a high quality knowledge workforce.
• The trainability, adaptability and employability of workers entering the labour market are very high.
• There is an abundance of knowledge workers who can quickly respond to changes.

The concept of the DHLM is fundamentally different from that of a flexible labour market (FLM). FLM places excessive emphasis on competition among businesses, and so corporate restructuring becomes a norm in the global market. However, the FLM policies ultimately exacerbated polarisation of the labour market and job insecurity by placing its focus on employment flexibility. Of course, employment flexibility can contribute to corporate competitiveness by labour cost reductions in the short term, but it weakens incentives for investing in education and training in the long run. That in turn makes it difficult to build and accumulate firm-specific skills and knowledge workers. As a result, low-skill equilibrium causes the growth engine of a nation to slow down.

By comparison, DHLM provides everyone with the opportunity to develop their vocational abilities based on a comprehensive, systematic human resource development system (HRDS) and extensive information network (LJIC). As it provides and nurtures a knowledge workforce, DHLM brings forward high-skill equilibrium as business achieves incremental innovation and competitive advantage. It also evaluates the job skills of the marginalised and provides them with job opportunities. Such opportunities minimise the polarisation of the labour market and greatly contribute to social cohesion.

In order to build a DHLM, the following two conditions must be satisfied. First, more people need to become knowledge workers and their respective vocational abilities must be improved accordingly. Second, an infrastructure must be built to overcome the serious problem of asymmetry of information in the labour and education markets.

Governance of the RESAP initiatives

In order to realise RESAP, the Regional Economic and Social Advancement Board (RESAB) must be launched as its driving body. The governance system under which the DHLM is built is based on the principle of regional governance initiatives. RESAB should be built in provinces and in city and/or county areas.

The RESAB of a province should be composed of variety of representatives such as governor, the chairperson of a university/junior college consortium, the president of the chamber of commerce, the president of the employer federation, the superintendent of education, the director of the labour office, a union leader, the director of the SME office and experts on the labour market.

The RESAB should also be supported by affiliated organisations such as the Knowledge Competitiveness Council (KCC), which will be in charge of building the RHRD cluster and the vocational ability development system for the life cycle, to enable lifelong learning on a regional basis. The Innovation

Table 9.3. **Functions of the RESAP organisation**

RESAP	Functions
RESAB	Deliberation of the agendas and policies submitted by the KCC, ICC and LCC. Horizontal partnership among the participants. Vertical partnership with relevant departments of the central government.
RDA and Forum	An administrative office of the RESAB including KCC, ICC and LCC. JHR (Job and Human Resource) Forum.
KCC	RHRD Cluster: Vertical and horizontal partnership for universities, junior colleges, training centre, high, middle and elemental schools. Local universities and knowledge competitiveness. Cultivating knowledge workforce and talent.
ICC	Design and administration of regional innovation cluster. Design and administration of sector council. Vocational ability development programme design for innovation cluster.
LCC	Design and promotion of learning city and lifelong learning programme. Vocational ability development programme design for the aged, women and the disabled. Formation of social capital.
LJIC	Information hub of the local labour market: Provide information about learning and vocational ability development programme, and provide job information. A talent bank and a job bank. One-stop services for jobseekers and firms. Provide the RESAB with information to make polices.

Figure 9.2. **Governance of RESAP: Regional initiatives**

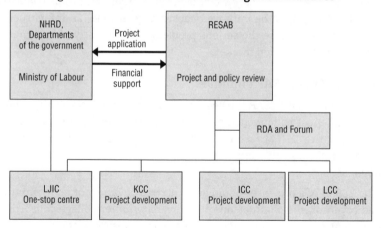

Cluster Council (ICC) would develop and manage the sector council and the vocational ability development system per industry cluster based on the RHRD cluster in order to secure a growth engine for regional economies. The Learning Communities Council (LCC) would be in charge of developing and managing the vocational ability development system for the marginalised, in order to minimise social polarisation in regional society and to contribute to social cohesion.

The KCC, ICC and LCC would all develop their respective projects and policies while exploring methods on securing funds for policy implementation, and report to the RESAB. The RESAB would then make relevant requests to the central government for projects in need of government support. Then the central government would decide whether to support the project based on a thorough examination of its innovativeness and possibility of success.

The RESAB would also be supported by the Regional Development Agency (RDA) and the Job and Human Resource (JHR) Forum. The JHR Forum would be a place to exchange ideas and success cases, learn from each other, and form partnerships and social capital.

Cities and/or counties could launch their own RESAB and operate one-stop service centres of the LJIC and LCC. They could also operate an Innovation Cluster Committee (ICC) if necessary. Although cities would control their own RESAB, they may request that government and provinces help support projects through funding.

HRD per life cycle and strategies for knowledge workforce

In this age, a person cannot expect to work in one job for their entire working life. Even the same job requires different vocational ability due to changes in economic climate and technological advances. This chapter has made it clear that to meet the new needs in the changing environment, everyone must develop their vocational ability continuously. This is the reason why we need a vocational ability development system for the entire life cycle, or a lifelong learning system (World Bank 2003; Hodgson, 2000).

While the vocational ability in demand obviously differs according to job types, even those working in the same field can have different vocational abilities. Therefore the method and time needed to develop vocational ability also vary from case to case. Some vocational abilities take little time to develop; others take longer.

This is why human resource development system should be divided into the life cycle phases shown in Figure 9.3. The first phase is the basic workforce development stage, where basic abilities required universally are developed. The second is the general training stage, where skills, technology and knowledge are developed. Third is the vocational ability upgrading stage, which enables workers to respond actively to the changing business climate and its implications in terms of new technology. The last stage is the new starting stage, where vocational ability is developed after retirement.

Figure 9.3 presents the basic process of human resources development per life cycle. First, build a co-operative network connecting schools and split the vertical roles of human resources development among high schools, colleges and universities. Second, set the direction of a co-operative network

Figure 9.3. **Four stages of human resource development for the life cycle**

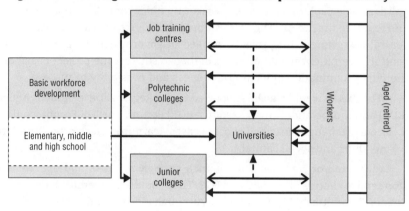

and horizontal role-splitting to develop job skills of the technical workforce among job training institutions, junior colleges and polytechnic colleges.

Third, develop the course of an industry-academia co-operative system to expedite a school-to-work movement. Fourth, build an industry-academia cooperative system (work-to-school) to upgrade the job skills of workers. Fifth, build a role-splitting system for training institutions to develop the job skills of the retired.

RHRD cluster for knowledge competitiveness and knowledge workforce

Nations are increasingly finding it difficult to directly support and incubate businesses or industries in the new global economic order symbolised by the WTO. Therefore they must devise a strategy to enhance the international competitive advantage of their industries and businesses by nurturing and providing a knowledge workforce through R&D or human resource development.

Recently the regional innovation cluster based on knowledge workforces has been recognised as a good way to develop regional economies. In order to effectively develop regional knowledge competitiveness, the RHRD cluster should be built on a regional basis. To this end, a vertical and horizontal partnership among schools needs to be built. There should also be a horizontal partnership between industry and academia.

The economic environment of the 21st century is seeing the creation of a number of jobs that demand vocational abilities in linguistics, mathematics and design, as well as team spirit and an ability to take on risks and challenges. The groundwork for these types of vocational abilities is best laid in high school or earlier. In order to develop a new curriculum and teaching methodology, an integrated system of co-operation must be built through RHRD cluster-linking local high schools and universities.

Junior colleges in the region need to group together to form a junior college consortium (JCC) and establish a system of competition and collaboration under the shared goal of generating new cohorts of technicians able to compete in a world market. Membership would not be mandatory for all colleges, but the JCC would only accept selected junior colleges that have passed rigorous evaluation and have been approved by like-minded junior colleges that share in the mission and goals of JCC. Members must possess not only the will but also a concrete strategy to foster knowledge workers. Junior colleges must play a complementary and co-operative role with universities in order to build an RHRD cluster.

In order for local industry to build global competitiveness, the local universities must foster and supply a pool of globally competitive talents. It is very difficult for individual local universities to achieve a global competitive edge purely through their own discrete efforts. That is why a system of competition and co-operation between local universities that maximises each school's internal strengths must be established to encourage the specialisation of each school and explore ways to jointly utilise faculty and facilities. The RHRD cluster enhances regional knowledge competitiveness.

Importance of the innovation cluster and its HRD

Clusters have been around a long time. But they only started receiving attention as a strategy for competitive advantage in the 1990s, following M.E. Porter's Diamond Model (1998). An innovation cluster is different from a conventional industry cluster. Since it is evident that the economic environment will continue to change and rivals will never stop seeking innovation, individuals, organisations or nations that do not innovate will lose their competitive edge. The innovation cluster is needed in order to spur innovation (Lundvall, 1992). It is here defined as our socioeconomic system's accumulative base for creative R&D capacity and the knowledge workforce, whose networking and partnerships will serve as a constant driving force for self-innovation. Innovation is born when diverse knowledge and information are fused together. The cluster will provide an enabling environment for that convergence. Consequently, innovation is the growth engine of the cluster, while the cluster allows innovation to flourish.

According to the author's GALIC Model (Lee, 2005), the innovation cluster is formed by all five elements working within one system – Governance, Actors' partnership, Localisation, Innovation milieu and Cluster convergence. Innovation clusters will be developed by different categories such as industries or regions. The innovation cluster's governance could be developed

Table 9.4. **The GALIC model for innovation clusters**

GALIC		Content and functions	Actors, basic principle
Governance (ICC)		Governing organisation which establishes and executes vision/strategy/policy.	Networking and partnership univ., local gov't, core firms, etc.
Actors' partnership (VIPS)	VP	Provide cluster vision, foster knowledge workforce, R&D provider (basic and source technology).	Univ., research institutes, other HR institutes.
	IP	Create innovation milieu, provide infrastructure to support VP and PP, provide management and legal services (SP), capital provider (CP).	Gov't, local gov't, financial institute, NGO, venture capital, Management Support Centre.
	PP	Producer of goods and services.	Firms, core/linked firms, forward/ backward linkage effect.
	SO	Establishment and integration of role and function of innovation actors.	Connect, networking and partnership.
Localisation		A local unit of cluster activity, the effective size of area actors cover so as to ensure easy geographical access to each other.	External effect, specialisation effect based on division of labour, distance effects, minimisation of transaction costs.
Innovation milieu		Culture of learning and exchange, culture of competition and co-operation, entrepreneur spirit, culture of innovation.	Spread of innovation and synergistic effect, RIS, NGO.
Cluster convergence		Convergence of industrial cluster, RHRD cluster and R&D clusters, convergence of technology.	Principles of division of labour and specialisation, network effect, forward/ backward linkage effect.

to formulate and carry out polices for the cluster. The cluster might not be newly developed but replaced by the ICC or system organiser (SO).

The innovation cluster will be worked in partnership with the actors such as vision providers (VP), infrastructure providers (IP), production providers (PP) and the system organiser (SO). The vision providers (VP) like universities present a vision for the cluster, foster knowledge workers and R&D, and develop basic or source technology. The role of an infrastructure provider (IP) is to produce, *e.g.*, an attractive residential environment, a labour market information hub and HRD-net. Infrastructure providers will be not only from government but also from the private sector, such as capital providers (CP) and business service providers (BSP). Capital providers might include grants, business angels, venture capital, public capital and various foundations, etc. Production providers (PP) such as companies produce goods and services, and create jobs. The system organiser (SO) must co-ordinate between VP, IP and PP so that they can work in partnership by integrating through networking. In the auto cluster in Toyota city, the dominant company like Toyota plays double roles as PP and SO. If an innovation cluster does not have such a dominant company, ICC or governance for the cluster must play the role and take on the functions of system organiser. In the innovation cluster, new companies must be created constantly. The system organiser needs to connect VP, IP and PP to create new companies, which is shown in Figure 9.4.[2]

Figure 9.4. **New company creation model**

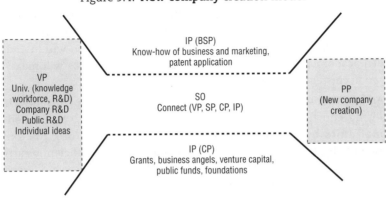

VP, IP, PP and SO must all maintain close co-operation and a close partnership. The VP must not only provide vision for the innovation cluster but also lead innovations by supplying knowledge and knowledge workers to the IP and PP. The IP must lay infrastructures that make the VP and PP perform at their best. The PP must fully utilise knowledge workers and infrastructure to produce high value-added goods and services.

Localisation indicates an agglomeration of functions such as R&D, human resource development and production within a certain area close by that acts as a unit of economic activity. Localisation is still needed to build an innovation cluster, although knowledge and information flow without the limitations of time and space due to the ICT revolution. Localisation is a necessary but not sufficient condition to make an innovation cluster because innovation comes from tacit knowledge that is delivered through repetitive face-to-face contact and mutual interactions.

Neither localisation alone nor actors' networking in itself will be sufficient to create and diffuse innovations. Good partnerships as well as innovations are actively generated in an innovative milieu; for the innovation cluster they are units of social capital that learn from each other, exchange ideas and nurture entrepreneurship in the culture of competition and co-operation. Diverse innovation forums or academy sessions should be organised on a regular and sustained basis in order to help create an innovation milieu.

The last point of the GALIC model focuses on cluster convergence, consisting of an HRD cluster capable of continuously developing knowledge workers and job skills; an R&D cluster that can create new knowledge and technologies; and an industrial cluster that can maximise the forward/backward linkage effects of industry and business, etc. It is of course possible for a certain industry, university, or R&D centre to simply group together into a cluster without building a cluster convergence. However, the cluster convergence strategy can produce synergistic effects; these are made possible by the forward and backward linkage effects of the industry cluster, the brainstorming effects of the R&D cluster and the effective HRD for a knowledge workforce via vertical and horizontal co-operation within and/or between academia and industrial circles. Cluster convergence will make an innovation cluster more successful.

An innovation cluster is a key strategy for national competitiveness in a globalising knowledge economy, and the clusters can only be formed in regional units owing to the localisation effect. Therefore, job skills development for the cluster would be more effectively and efficiently carried out on a regional basis or around the cluster. HRD for knowledge workforces in a company and/or an industry is key element for them to acquire competitive advantage.

HRD for the vulnerable and socially excluded

A social safety mechanism that protects a society's underprivileged is a prerequisite for a region or a nation to move forward to become an advanced economy. The definition of the vulnerable needs to be clarified, stressing the strategic importance of their vocational training. "The vulnerable" is here defined as persons in involuntarily unemployed due to diminished job skills, irregular contract workers, small-scale business owners, unpaid family workers, the handicapped, the elderly retired, and others who may hold jobs but endure a poor quality of life. Nowadays, anyone may find themselves in the vulnerable or disadvantaged category since job creation and job destruction have been occurring so frequently and job skill requirements change so rapidly. Traditional European social security systems are therefore no longer adequate for solving the issue of the disadvantaged. More than anything, job creation should be the first strategic choice in protecting the vulnerable, which signifies the importance of job skill development for these persons.

Under the jurisdiction of RESAB, the Learning Communities Council (LCC) will be needed at the county level as well as in the state level to develop polices for job creation and job skills development for the disadvantaged. The LCC must utilise information provided by the LJIC to assess the current status of the region's vulnerable. Another basic strategy in these efforts is to create a learning environment. Since the vulnerable typically exist outside of the general organised labour markets, they rarely have the opportunity to improve job skills or engage in learning programmes. Moreover, they often do not recognise the importance of job skill training. A "learning city" could be created as a place for seminars, citizen talks, or learning festivals for all social groups to promote awareness of the importance of learning in the local community and foster a good environment for learning.

Not only is the percentage of irregular workers extremely high, but job skill development for these people lies in a grey area. Companies are not willing to make investments in job training for these workers, who are usually on short-term contracts. If this situation continues, we may be trapped in national low-skill equilibrium. If companies fall into that trap, they will be hindered in their efforts to improve productivity and end up losing global competitiveness. The risk of job destruction may then outrun job creation and lead to high rates of structural unemployment. This is why a job skills development programme is needed for irregular workers.

Figure 9.5 shows us a conceptual framework of job skills development for irregular workers. The government support system for this development may be carried out either on a company basis or an individual worker basis. A company determines what job skills should be taught to irregular workers and sets a limit on the number of participants. After consultations with the LJIC, it then applies for government support. In turn, the government will take into account training costs and headcount before handing out a certain number of job skills development vouchers to workers through the company. The company will then draw up a contract with a job skills development provider. The government may offer extra support as an incentive when the programme for the irregular workers enjoys high utilisation rates.

The irregular workers who hold employment insurance should be allowed to apply for job skills development programmes on their own without going through the company. Irregular workers can take up a vocational ability development programme that they have chosen from among various skills development programmes in the RHRD cluster by using their vouchers. The training institutes can receive money in exchange for vouchers in the LJIC.

An unemployed person could find a new job or develop new job skills through skills/aptitude tests and consultation with the LJIC. If the vocational

Figure 9.5. **Conceptual framework of job skills development for irregular workers**

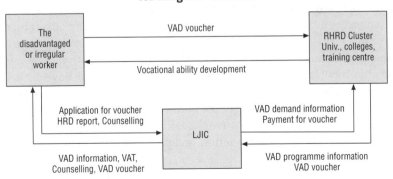

ability test (VAT) reveals they need new skills, they can get a vocational ability development (VAD) voucher over the employment counter in the LJIC.

Elements and functions of the LJIC

The functions and the working mechanisms of LJIC information hub are illustrated in Figure 9.6. LJIC performs a myriad of tasks. These include vocational ability tests (VAT), career counselling for career portfolio (CP), on-site consultation programmes, the learning mart (LM), talent banks (TB), job banks (JB), labour market information offices, business customer service centres (BCSC), employment insurance benefits, new job programmes (NJP) and job fairs, as well as providing information on employment incentives.

Figure 9.6. **Functions of LJIC**

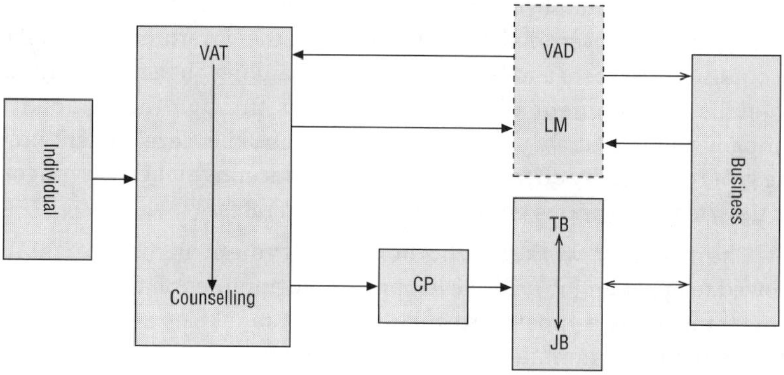

There are a number of phases that individuals would undergo when they walk into the LJIC. In phase 1, he or she can take a VAT. Based on the test results, they will be given a counselling session to determine whether they should receive education and training to develop a new job skill, or simply need to register in the talent bank (TB) to initiate a job-search (phase 2). They will also receive counselling on how to manage their career portfolio (CP) based on the available information in both the education and labour markets. In phase 3, they will be introduced to vocational ability development (VAD) programmes suiting their job aptitudes if it is deemed that they need to develop new vocational abilities. In phase 4, they will have finished a vocational ability development course and thus take another VAT. Subsequently, they will be registered in the TB. In phase 5, they will be able to look for jobs in the JB and be offered advice and instruction on how to write resumes and self-introduction letters and prepare for job interviews.

The Business Customer Service Centre (BCSC) provides all kinds of information and services related to job offers and workforce management. It also offers comprehensive consulting services on government tax incentives and wage compensation, as well as strategies to help SMEs retain their employees. Pre-screening of jobseekers for businesses is also provided to cut hiring costs in enterprises. Should a company planning to restructure register with the New Job Programme (NJP), the BCSC will operate special programmes to help soon-to-be-dismissed workers find new jobs.

Expected results of LJIC: Transition cost and transaction cost

First, the most important function and expected effect of LJIC is to maximise the production function of the economy by alleviating the problem of information asymmetry in both education and labour markets. Asymmetric information makes it difficult for the market to function properly, resulting in soaring transaction costs and inefficient allocation of resources. When information is shared by all, entry and exit to the market will happen smoothly and fairly. This in turn will contribute to a dynamic and healthy labour market.

Second, once the system of information sharing is securely in place, incompetent vocational ability development institutions will be driven out of the market while new, competitive and innovative systems will be created continually. When the information gap in the education market is narrowed and eventually eliminated, a fair competitive environment will be fostered; human resource development institutions such as universities, junior colleges and training institutes will become more specialised; and the competitiveness of vocational ability development will be enhanced in a consistent manner.

Third, integrating information in the education and labour markets will help minimise the transition costs that occur in the move from school to work. Asymmetric information leads to many cases of job and skill mismatches. This worsens the youth unemployment rate, prolongs their unemployment, and lowers the quality of employment as more people turn to irregular part-time jobs. Moreover, the transition from school to work becomes very costly. Fourth, LJIC helps reduce transaction costs by providing a one-stop service to those in both the supply and demand sides of the labour market.

Conclusion

The RESAP Model is here offered as a new paradigm for both economic competitiveness and social cohesion in a knowledge-based economy. The key components of RESAP are its regional governance initiatives, simultaneous pursuit of economic and social advancement, and partnership among the participants. As regional governance, the Regional Economic and Social Advancement Board (RESAB) may be organised at the county level as well as the state level.

Economic advancement can be delivered through enhanced competitiveness, and social advancement from the realisation of social inclusion. In order to attain economic competitiveness and social inclusion at the same time, a dynamic and healthy labour market (DHLM) must be created. In order to create a DHLM, a human resource development system capable of fostering knowledge workers and developing job skills must be instituted on a regional basis, which is the RESAB. Also, a Learning and Job Information Centre (LJIC) must be established to minimise the lack of information correlation in the education and labour markets.

The RESAB must include a KCC (Knowledge Competitiveness Council), to develop knowledge workforces and a lifelong learning system; an ICC (Innovation Cluster Council), for the development of job skills on a cluster-by-cluster basis in order to secure an engine for local economic growth; and an LCC (Learning Community Council), to develop job skills for the vulnerable and promote social inclusion.

Notes

1. The author (Lee, 1996) introduced the concept of "humanware" in his PDR System Theory, defining it as a ware that transforms a human resource into a creative resource. According to Lee, the fact that human resource can be so transformed is attributable to its intangible assets, such as mind-set and ability. These intangible assets are differentiated from other assets such as land or capital, due to their creative characteristic and high interactivity.

2. The basic idea of Figure 4 originated from CONNECT in San Diego.

Bibliography

Becker, G.S. (1962), "Investment in Human Capital: A Theoretical Analysis", *Journal of Political Economy*, Vol. 70, No. 5.

Coleman, J. (1988), "Social Capital in the Creation of Human Capital", *American Journal of Sociology*, p. 94.

Doeringer, P.B. and M.J. Piore (1971), *Internal Labour Markets and Manpower Analysis*, Heath and Company.

Giguère, S. (2007), "Governance and Strategies for Local Economic and Employment Development in OECD Countries", Job and Human Resource Forum, 3 October, Daegu, Korea.

Hodgson, A., (ed.) (2000), *Policies, Politics and the Future of Lifelong Learning*, Kogan Page, London.

Kochan, T.A. (2005), *Restoring the American Dream*, The MIT Press.

Lee, H.S. (1996), "The Interaction of Production, Distribution, and Rule-Making Systems in Industrial Relations", *Relations Industrielles/Industrial Relations*, 51-2, pp. 302-332.

Lee, H.S. (1997), *The Economics of Mutual Gains*, Korea Labour Education Institute (in Korean).

Lee, H.S. (2001), "Paternalistic Human Resource Practices: Their Emergence and Characteristics", *Journal of Economic Issues*, Vol. XXXV, No. 4, pp. 841-869.

Lee, H.S. (2005), "Regional Human Resources Development Strategies for Innovation, Competitiveness and Social Inclusion", Conference on Local Employment Development organised by the Korea Labor Institute, the Ministry of Labor and OECD LEED, October.

Lundvall, B. (1992), *National Systems of Innovation: Towards a Theory of Innovation and Interactive Learning*, Printer Publishers, London.

London Skills Commission (2002), *London's Framework for Regional Employment and Skills Action*, *www.london.gov.uk/assembly/past_ctees/econmtgs/2002/*.

Marshall, A. (1920), *Principles of Economics*, 8th Edition, ELBS (1974).

Mincer, J. (1958), "Investment in Human Capital and Personal Income Distribution", *Journal of Political Economy*, Vol. 66, August.

Nadler, L. and Z. Nadler (1989), *Developing Human Resources*, 3rd Edition, Jossey-Bass Publishers, San Francisco.

OECD (2000), *Human and Social Capital and Sustained Growth and Development: Reconsidering New Economies and Societies – The Role of Human and Social Capital*, OECD, Paris.

OECD (2004), *New Forms of Governance for Economic Development*, Paris: OECD, Paris.

Porter, M.E. (1998), *The Competitive Advantage of Nations* (with a new Foreword), The Free Press, New York.

Schultz, T.W. (1960), "Capital Formation by Education", *Journal of Political Economy*, Vol. 68, December.

Tolentino, A. (2002), "Productivity and Competitiveness Strategies", *www.ilo.org/public/english/employment/mandev/public*.

World Bank (2003), *Lifelong Learning in the Global Knowledge Economy: Challenges for Developing Countries*, World Bank, Washington DC.

ISBN 978-92-64-04327-5
More than Just Jobs:
Workforce Development in a Skills-Based Economy
© OECD 2008

About the Authors

Petra Bouché studied Education and Sociology in Dresden and Berlin. Her work has focused on the transformation of science and technology systems in Eastern Europe and, more recently, on implementation issues in labour market policy at the state and local level. She is currently collaborating with Hugh Mosley on the ongoing evaluation of the Hartz IV reforms in Germany undertaken by the Social Research Centre (WZB) in Berlin.

Randall Eberts is Executive Director of the W.E. Upjohn Institute for Employment Research, an independent non-profit research organisation that conducts and supports research on policy-relevant employment and regional economic issues. His current research examines the role of local partnerships in workforce and economic development. Mr. Eberts also works closely with the federal and state governments to develop management tools that use statistical analysis to help improve the performance of workforce programmes. He received his Ph.D. in economics from Northwestern University.

Sylvain Giguère is Deputy Head of Local Economic and Employment Development (LEED) at the OECD. As part of his responsibilities he leads a multi-disciplinary work programme on employment and governance which seeks to improve policies and practices on labour markets, skills, migration and economic development in the context of globalisation and policy interdependence. Sylvain co-ordinates LEED's programme of work, oversees the LEED Directing Committee sessions, and heads the OECD Forum on Partnerships and Local Governance. He studied economics at UQAM and Queens' University in Canada and holds a PhD (econ.) from Université Paris I (Sorbonne).

Xavier Greffe is Professor and Director of Doctoral Studies in Economics at the Université de Paris I (Panthéon-Sorbonne). He is an expert for the European Commission and the OECD on issues related to decentralisation, local development, the social economy and the economic impact of culture. He held various high-level positions in the French administration, chaired a European association for local development (LEDA Partenariat) and is currently the co-ordinator of the OECD LEED Scientific Advisory Group on Local Governance, based in Trento, Italy.

Yoshio Higuchi is Professor of Labor Economics at Keio University in Japan. His research interests include the employment policy and employment practices in Japanese firms from the viewpoint of human capital theory. Professor Higuchi is a member of Science Council of Japan. He is currently also Executive Director of National Life Finance Corporation. Professor Higuchi received his B.A., M.A. and Ph.D. in Business and Commerce from Keio University in 1976, 1977, and 1991.

Hyo-Soo Lee is Professor of Economics and Labour Relations at Yeungnam University. He was President of the Korea Industrial Relations Association from 2006-07 and President of the Korean Labour Economics Association from 2004-06. He currently serves as Commissioner of the Presidential Committee on Government Innovation and Decentralisation, Korea. He is President of the Job and Human Resource Forum, and chairperson of the Regional Human Resource Development Association, Daegu-Gyongbuk province. He obtained a Ph.D. degree in economics from the Seoul National University in 1984 and has been a visiting scholar at UC Berkeley, Harvard University and MIT.

Cristina Martinez-Fernandez is Senior Research Fellow at the University of Western Sydney's Urban Research Centre, which is specialised in the study of cities. Previously, she was a Senior Research Fellow in AEGIS – an UWS research centre specialised in industry innovation and policy analysis. Cristina is an expert on local economic development and strategic planning. She leads the research programme of Urban and Regional Dynamics at the Urban Research Centre, which include the analysis of industry, skills and innovation processes of growth and shrinkage, and policies and strategies related to urban life.

Hugh Mosley is Senior Research Fellow in the Labour Market and Employment Research Unit at the Social Research Centre (WZB) in Berlin where he has worked since 1986. His recent work has been on implementation issues, especially on public employment service reforms, and on policy evaluation. Hugh has published extensively in specialised journals and advises the European Commission and the OECD on labour market policy. His current work focuses on the evaluation of the Hartz labour market reforms in Germany for the German Ministry of Labour.

Dave Simmonds OBE is the co-founder and Chief Executive of the Centre for Economic and Social Inclusion. Dave has been involved in social exclusion, labour market and regeneration policy for the last 22 years, both in policy formulation and practical implementation. He has advised government and social partners on welfare reform and the delivery of support to unemployed people. He previously worked as Director of Policy for the UK National Council for Voluntary Organisations.

Andy Westwood is currently a Special Advisor to the UK Government's Secretary of State for Innovation, Universities and Skills. Previously he worked in HM Treasury on a review of the United Kingdom's skills targets and delivery. Andy was a Director of the Centre for Economic and Social Inclusion and previously Head of Policy at the Work Foundation. He has published extensively on skills and employment policy and has been an advisor to a wide range of independent and government bodies.

OECD PUBLICATIONS, 2, rue André-Pascal, 75775 PARIS CEDEX 16
PRINTED IN FRANCE
(84 2008 02 1 P) ISBN 978-92-64-04327-5 – 56067 2008